D1766212

3 8014 07047 8133

FIGHTING BRIGADIER

THE LIFE & CAMPAIGNS OF BRIGADIER JAMES HILL DSO** MC

'Why do I refer to myself as a fighting brigade commander as there are obviously many others?

The reason is: the number of men in a parachute brigade was very limited. Our organisation was simple and my Brigade Headquarters had an 80-strong defence platoon; in total, therefore, we numbered some 180 fighting men. It was always my plan in defence to place my headquarters in such a position that its officers and men could actively participate in any defensive action. This made a significant contribution when the line was thin or stretched.

Moreover, I always considered that any commander up to brigade level in a parachute formation should always lead from the front – always with the proviso, however, that he can maintain control of his battle.'

James Hill

FIGHTING BRIGADIER

THE LIFE & CAMPAIGNS OF BRIGADIER JAMES HILL DSO** MC

BY
PETER HARCLERODE

Pen & Sword
MILITARY

Other Titles by Peter Harclerode

"Go To It!" The Illustrated History of The 6th Airborne Division
Unholy Babylon – The Secret History of Saddam's War
(as Gregory Alexander with Adel Darwish)
PARA! Fifty Years of The Parachute Regiment
Arnhem – A Tragedy of Errors
The Lost Masters – The Looting of Europe's Treasurehouses
(with Brendan Pittaway)
Equinox: Warfare
Secret Soldiers – Special Forces in The War Against Terrorism
*Fighting Dirty – The Inside Story of Covert Operations From Ho Chi Minh
to Osama bin Laden*
Gurkha – The Illustrated History (with David Reynolds)
Wings of War – Airborne Warfare 1918–1945

First published in Great Britain in 2010 by
Pen & Sword Military
An imprint of
Pen & Sword Books Ltd
47 Church Street
Barnsley
South Yorkshire
S70 2AS

Copyright © Peter Harclerode 2010

ISBN 978 1 84884 214 4

The right of Peter Harclerode to be identified as Author of this work has been asserted by him
in accordance with the Copyright, Designs and Patents Act 1988.

A CIP catalogue record for this book is available from the British Library.

All rights reserved. No part of this book may be reproduced or transmitted in any form or by
any means, electronic or mechanical including photocopying, recording or by any information
storage and retrieval system, without permission from the Publisher in writing.

Typeset by Acredula
Printed and bound in England
By CPI

Pen & Sword Books Ltd incorporates the imprints of Pen & Sword Aviation,
Pen & Sword Family History, Pen & Sword Maritime, Pen & Sword Military, Wharncliffe
Local History, Pen & Sword Select, Pen & Sword Military Classics, Leo Cooper, Remember
When, Seaforth Publishing and Frontline Publishing.

For a complete list of Pen & Sword titles please contact
PEN & SWORD BOOKS LIMITED
47 Church Street, Barnsley, South Yorkshire, S70 2AS, England
E-mail: enquiries@pen-and-sword.co.uk
Website: www.pen-and-sword.co.uk

Contents

Foreword

By Lieutenant General Sir Michael Gray KCB OBE DL
Former Colonel Commandant The Parachute Regiment.
Current Joint President of The Airborne Assault Normandy Trust

When you read this truly remarkable narrative about one man's campaigns, you may be forgiven for thinking that the oft-used 1940s expression 'He had a good war' was apposite. I am sure that Brigadier James Hill would not have agreed with you. Total war is exacting: hundreds of his men were killed and maimed in action while he himself was severely wounded and close to death on two occasions, and 'winged' by a grenade on a third. He might have agreed, however, that because he survived, luck was on his side, but I suspect that he made quite a lot of that luck for himself. He also believed most fervently that the Almighty kept a watchful eye on him.

James was involved at the forefront of history for six years of almost continuous fighting at senior rank. As a leader he was able to have a direct, personal influence on events and in particular on the development of Airborne tactics and training.

When you have read this book you may also be forgiven for imagining that here was a 'rough tough warrior' who enjoyed the 'cut and thrust' of combat. You would be wrong. Certainly he excelled in battle, as did the men he trained and led, but James was in fact one of life's true gentlemen, who was thoughtfully modest and quietly but precisely spoken. He was also a fitness fanatic and his battle discipline was fierce and exacting, because he wanted his officers and young men to survive both in mind and body. He dearly 'loved' his soldiers (his words) and he knew that he had to harden their hearts if they were to cope with the traumas they would experience almost every day. All who served with him trusted his judgement, especially in battle, because they knew he would be there with them. Thereafter, as the years passed, he continued to be held in awe and deep respect by all of the men in his brigade and by others besides.

James was an exceptional Airborne leader who became a legend in his own lifetime. In modern times there can be few brigade commanders who, for example, have fought their brigades continuously for five weeks on offensive mobile operations across 275 miles of hostile territory. After crossing the River Rhine into Germany, 6th Airborne Division, as a leading element of the Allied armies, sped northwards to Wismar, on the Baltic, to meet up with the advancing Russians; for political reasons speed was necessary to block their westward advance. James Hill's 3rd Parachute Brigade was the leading formation for most of this long journey, with James himself well forward on the back of a motorcycle with his signaller!

As the war drew to a close, James was despatched to take command of 1st Parachute Brigade, a formation comprising those remnants of 1st Airborne Division that had survived the Arnhem debacle. It was sent to secure Denmark and prevent it falling prey to Russian occupation. On his arrival, James was appointed as Military Governor of Copenhagen. His tenure of command there was short, however, and in June 1945 he returned to Britain where, during the following month, he supervised the disbanding of the brigade.

James then retired to civilian life, at the age of only 35. Shortly after he left the Army, however, he was summoned by the then Colonel Commandant of The Parachute Regiment, Field Marshal the Lord Montgomery, who invited him to raise a Territorial Army Airborne formation in London. As a result, the 4th Parachute Brigade TA started life in 1947 and James was appointed to command it. Subsequently, it became 44th Independent Parachute Brigade Group (TA).

James's many subsequent commitments to The Parachute Regiment and his life as an accomplished international businessman are well documented in this book. He seldom missed a regimental or Old Comrades' gathering either with Airborne Forces, or indeed with his parent regiment, The Royal Fusiliers. In particular, he had a personal warmth for his much-loved veterans of 1st Canadian Parachute Battalion and they for him. As well as going to enormous lengths to record his wartime memories and pass on his military wisdom to Airborne Forces' gatherings and to the Army Staff College, he also participated in numerous battlefield tours 'on the ground' in Normandy and across the Rhine.

James was always, however, a very private person and a devout Christian. Furthermore, he was a fanatical 'twitcher'; indeed he was one of the world's leading ornithologists. In 1986 he met his 'soulmate', Joan, who changed his life. He married and became a loving and devoted husband. Inseparable, they often sought tranquillity in 'retreat', while Joan always accompanied him on the many regimental events and reunions he attended. She herself 'followed the flag' with enthusiasm and enjoyment, albeit in later years, as James became increasingly frail, she protected him from veteran excesses.

Brigadier James Hill set an example to us all. He was an extraordinary man who was a huge inspiration to Airborne soldiers. He was also an unobtrusive puppeteer in the life of The Parachute Regiment. Such was his continuing influence that he was consulted as to how the Regiment might celebrate the millennium year. He conceived the idea that it should hold cathedral services at St Paul's in London and York Minster, and two others in Glasgow and Belfast. His suggestion was that we should 'rededicate ourselves to God, Queen, Country and Humanity'. This highlighted his belief in the Almighty that had kept him staunch in war and in peace. He was indeed 'a man for all seasons'.

January 2010

Preface

This is an account of the life and campaigns of a very remarkable man who, in the words of a former senior officer of Airborne Forces, was 'the founding father of The Parachute Regiment'. The emphasis is on the campaigns rather than his life because James Hill was a man of great modesty, inclined towards reticence about himself, while never hesitating to extol the exploits of those splendid men of 1st Parachute Battalion and 3rd Parachute Brigade whom he commanded and led with such great courage and distinction.

Some may question why I have included accounts of the exploits of the other elements of 6th Airborne Division rather than concentrating on those of 3rd Parachute Brigade. I have done so after consulting certain Airborne 'elders' who were of the opinion that to exclude them would inevitably mean that the accounts of the campaign in Normandy, the operations in the Ardennes and Holland, the crossing of the Rhine and the advance to the Baltic would be incomplete. I am confident that James Hill would have concurred because 6th Airborne Division was a unique and closely knit band of brothers, as I discovered twenty years ago when researching and writing *"Go To It!"*, my history of the Division with which he, along with a large number of other veterans was kind enough to assist me.

When asked to produce this biography, I was fortunate in being able to resort to material already in my possession, but inevitably I needed to carry out additional research. In this I was assisted by the following, to whom I am indebted for their unstinting help and support: Lieutenant General Sir Michael Gray KCB OBE, a former Colonel Commandant of The Parachute Regiment and Joint President of the Airborne Assault Normandy Trust; my old friend Major Jack Watson MC, Joint President of the Airborne Assault Normandy Trust, who served with 13th Parachute Battalion; Major Tony Hibbert MBE MC who served in 1st Parachute Battalion with James Hill, later distinguishing himself at Arnhem as Brigade Major of 1st Parachute Brigade; Major Miles Whitelock, who was James Hill's adjutant in 1st Parachute Battalion; Mr Doug Charlton, who also served under him in 1st Parachute Battalion during operations in North Africa before transferring to the Special Air Service; the late Mr Alan Jefferson, a former officer of 9th Parachute Battalion and author of the authoritative book *Assault on The Guns of Merville*; Mr Jan de Vries, President of the 1st Canadian Parachute Battalion Association; and last but by no means least Mr Jon Baker, Colonel David Malllam OBE and Holly Johanneson of the Airborne Assault Museum at Duxford, who spent hours digging up additional material from the archives for me.

Finally, I would like to express my sincere thanks to Mrs Joan Hill, James Hill's wife of twenty years and now his widow, for very kindly providing me with photographs and further information about her late husband, and to her secretary, Mrs Sue Peterkin.

Peter Harclerode
Suffolk, September 2010

List of Maps

Prologue

As Number One in his stick, Brigadier James Hill DSO MC, the 33-year-old commander of 3rd Parachute Brigade, was seated next to the open door of the C-47 Dakota transport carrying him and the men of his headquarters through the summer night sky, one small element of a huge airborne armada. On the darkened ground hundreds of feet below, the air was filled with the deep drone of engines as the steady stream of aircraft flew over the sleeping English countryside. Only those who happened to be abroad at that hour of night saw their silhouettes passing overhead as they headed east towards Nazi-occupied France.

The dim light inside the C-47 was sufficient for Hill to observe the other members of his stick. Some were conversing with those seated on either side of them, while others remained silent, lost in thought as they pondered apprehensively on what lay ahead of them in the coming battle. He glanced down at one of the items he held on his lap: a football bearing an image of the face of Adolf Hitler in luminous paint that had been produced to amuse the men of the Canadian battalion. Everyone knew that he intended to throw it out of the door along with the three bricks also nestling in his lap, inscribed by some of his men with ribald messages of varying degrees of vulgarity, before the green light went on and he and his stick jumped into the darkness.

As the aircraft flew on through the dark sky, he reflected on the last four momentous years of his life: he had left France in 1940 as a young staff captain and now, four years later, was returning at the head of a brigade of paratroops.

Time passed and all too soon the armada had crossed the glinting restless waves of the Channel, the coast of France appearing ahead as a dark mass.

'Stand up!' The despatcher's voice could be clearly heard, despite the roar of the engines.

'Check equipment!' The members of the stick carefully checked each other's parachutes and static lines.

'Tell off for equipment check!'

'Number twenty okay!'

'Nineteen okay!'

'Eighteen okay!'

The shouts grew progressively clearer to Hill as the members of his stick reported themselves ready for action.

'Number One okay! Stick okay!' As he called out, he kept a firm grip on his football and bricks. He stood near the door, his equipment container a dead weight against his leading leg. Minutes passed and then the red light above the door suddenly glowed.

'Red on! Stand to the door!'

At the despatcher's command, Hill moved forward and looked down, seeing below the white line of surf stretching away into the distance. Lobbing the football and bricks out into the night, he braced himself.

'Green on! Go!'

The words had hardly left the despatcher's lips when James Hill was gone, leaping out into the aircraft's slipstream with his stick close on his heels.

Chapter 1

Stanley James Ledger Hill was born on 14 March 1911, the son of Major General Walter Pitts Hendy Hill who, himself born in 1877, was the eldest son of a family of twelve children. The custom in those days was that eldest sons inherited the estate and the family business, while their younger male siblings entered the Church or the armed forces, or were despatched to seek their fortunes in the far-flung colonies of the Empire. The Hill family was no exception, except that none of its younger sons opted for the Church.

Walter and his three younger brothers were all educated at Marlborough College. Their father was a firm believer in country pursuits, however, and during the holidays engaged a tutor whose principal task was to teach them to ride, hunt, shoot and fish. His duties were made that much easier because the upper reaches of the River Avon ran through the family estate of Bulford Manor, which included a very considerable sheep farm stretching from Bulford through Netheravon in the north, away to Tidworth in the east.

On leaving Marlborough, Walter Hill was sent to the Agricultural College at Cirencester while his brothers Willy and Douglas entered the Army, subsequently being commissioned into the 5th Royal Irish Lancers and 7th Queen's Own Hussars respectively. The fourth brother, Harold, meanwhile was despatched to the highlands of Kenya.

The advent of the Boer War and the expropriation of the family estate by an Act of Parliament in 1898, to incorporate it into what would become familiar to future generations of soldiers as the Salisbury Plain Training Area, however, put paid to Walter's aspirations to become a farmer and thus he too became a soldier, initially joining the Militia and subsequently the Regular Army in which he was commissioned into The Royal Fusiliers in 1900. He served with distinction in the Boer War, in which his brother Willy was killed at Ladysmith, and thereafter in the First World War; in 1916 he was awarded the DSO and the following year was promoted to the rank of lieutenant colonel.

Although only some three years old at the time, James Hill was always able to recall very clearly the outbreak of the First World War:

My father was serving as an instructor at the Royal Military College Sandhurst and I remember welcoming him outside the front door of our home Belgony, a house situated near the top of the hill in Camberley. Over 6 feet tall with a dark, clipped moustache and a slim upright figure, he wore a well-cut uniform and his Sam Browne belt shone magnificently. It was a lovely sunny day and, having ridden over from the College at lunchtime, he jumped off his horse with the words, 'We are now at war with Germany.' My childish mind registered that something important had occurred which much disturbed my parents. My father, who had been Adjutant of the 4th Battalion The Royal Fusiliers before being posted to Sandhurst, desperately wanted to rejoin his battalion which sailed for France in the van of the British Expeditionary Force (BEF). No posting of instructors from Sandhurst was permitted, however, until one year later at the end of the summer term of 1915, due to the importance attached to the training of young officers for the BEF.

This breathing space enabled my parents to arrange for my mother, my sister Bridget, who had been born a year earlier, and me, now aged 4, to move to Lincolnshire. There, together with our nanny, Nurse Kiel, we were ensconced with my mother's parents, George and Gertrude Sandars, who lived at Scampton House, situated some 7 miles to the north of Lincoln where my grandfather farmed some 2,000 acres. His two sons, my uncles, both served in The Royal Fusiliers. The elder of the two, Sam, commanded the 8th Battalion in France where he won the DSO and MC before being wounded in action in 1918 and losing his right leg. My grandmother, Gertrude, served in the Red Cross and would do so again during the Second World War, being awarded the OBE at the age of 80 for her services in both wars.

The war years were happy ones for James and his sister. Their grandparents' home was a large red-brick Georgian house covered by creeper and a slate roof, surrounded by parkland and approached by a drive lined with flowering chestnuts. To the right-hand side of the front gate stood the village church and to the left three pairs of semi-detached red-brick farm cottages occupied by farm-hands whose wives worked as members of the staff of seven in Scampton House. At the rear of the house were the stables and garage to which was attached a small cottage in which lived the chauffeur, whose importance was enhanced by the fact that he was in charge of only the second car to be licensed in all of Lincolnshire.

It was a close-knit community that appeared a happy one to James and his sister, but as the war years dragged on the staff of Scampton House became depleted. Gertrude Sandars, who appeared to her small grandson to be a replica of Queen Mary in both stature and demeanour, ruled her household by example and single-mindedness; for five days a week, summer and winter, she bicycled 7 miles into Lincoln and back to work for the Red Cross at the Great Northern Hospital.

Meanwhile George Sandars, assisted by forty-four men, continued to run his two farms. He attached much importance to retaining his workforce year in and year out, and thus both farms were maintained in immaculate condition as his grandson later recalled:

> Mechanisation at the outbreak of war was in its infancy. The maintenance of the buildings and machinery was carried out in the winter, together with the hand-clipping of all the hedgerows and cleaning of the ditches. As the land surrounding the home farm was mostly clay, most hedges had a ditch to ensure good drainage. The men who carried out the hedging and ditching were divided into teams of four and were responsible for the same hedges year after year. As a result the hedgerow trees – elm, oak and ash – were cosseted and encouraged, and woe betide the man with a slipshod blade who cut back a 'good young 'un'. In some fields the blackthorn or hawthorn hedges were encouraged as protection for sheep and cattle and after seven years or so, by the time they had grown long and straggly, were termed 'bullfinches' by the hunting fraternity because the small birds of that name thrived on their berries. It took a good horse with a stout heart and a courageous rider to jump through them and clear the ditch on the far side.

All this, with the changing seasons and the arrival of steam engines to drive the threshing machines – along with the great shire horses, the pedigree herd of Lincoln Red cattle (their grandfather's pride and joy), the stock yard and granaries – provided a hinterland full of curiosity and great adventure for young James and his sister.

One day in 1915, however, this picture changed suddenly when George Sandars walked down the drive of Scampton House, through the village and up a ridge some 200 feet high which ran from Lincoln Cathedral northwards for some 20 miles. Situated on the top of this ridge was one of his two farms, comprising lighter land that was ideal for raising sheep and growing grain. To his dismay, however, instead of encountering his shepherd he discovered an army of workmen who had, unbeknownst to him, taken over the farm buildings that morning with orders to construct an airfield – to be called Scampton Aerodrome – which was to be the home of the Royal Canadian Flying Corps. As James Hill would later comment:

> There was only one thing for a gentleman and farmer to do in such circumstances and that was to blow his top. My grandfather had a hot temper and proceeded to let off much steam, but all to no avail. It was not so much the expropriation by the government of a top-ranking food-producing farm that he had nurtured over the years that rankled, rather the fact that it had been carried out without notification, consultation or agreement! The highly successful combination of two farms, one with light land and the other with heavy, had been destroyed by the war and thus some hard thinking and rebalancing became a matter of some urgency for my grandfather. For my part, however, the arrival of the aeroplane left almost nothing to be desired.

Throughout his childhood, young James was brought up according to the ideals and standards in which his parents and grandparents believed firmly and maintained with a firm discipline, these embracing a loyalty to King and Country, the family unit and the British Empire. He and his sister were taught to respect their seniors who ranged from the great political officers of state, judges, admirals and generals to teachers, the village postmistress, the parson and the gamekeeper. All were to be held in much esteem and their integrity was not to be doubted.

In 1919, immediately after his eighth birthday, James was packed off to boarding school at Wellesley House, Broadstairs, on the coast of Kent, returning to Scampton House for the holidays. Five years later, in September 1924, he went on to his father's old school, Marlborough College in Wiltshire, where by his own admission he did not excel academically but shone in other areas of prowess, notably in athletics and in the Officers Training Corps (OTC) in which he rose to the rank of senior under officer. In later years, he described his time at Marlborough:

> It was a hard school with no physical mercy. To say I enjoyed my time there would not be true, but it did me no harm. It was not an Army school and my background was different to most of the other boys. Nevertheless, I survived. I was always expected to go into the Army and I thought that would be my lot. I was lucky because as youths or teenagers we were, in this country, very proud of our great empire which was the largest the world had ever seen. Moreover, we

had a king and queen whom we automatically loved and revered. These days, it seems to be the fashion to decry the establishment and status quo; in our day, however, very few of us would have queried politicians in power, regardless of party.

In 1929, he succeeded in entering the Royal Military College Sandhurst, passing out two years later second in the order of merit and winning the Sword of Honour and the Sword for Tactics. On 27 August 1931, he was commissioned into The Royal Fusiliers, of which his father was appointed Colonel of the Regiment two years later.

Second Lieutenant Hill was posted to the 2nd Battalion, which he joined as a platoon commander in a rifle company. He took to his duties like a duck to water and revelled in the comradeship and friendship that existed in the Regiment, and in the opportunities that were offered to him and his fellow young officers.

This early part of his military career, however, would prove to be somewhat brief. Hill was courting a young woman, Denys Gunter-Jones, whom he had known for six years; very much in love, they both naturally wished to marry. There was, however, an obstacle to their doing so as he later recounted:

> My father had issued an edict that no officer in the regiment would marry under the age of 28 as there were not enough officers to participate in games and other extra-curricular activities with our soldiers. I felt, however, that I could wait no longer and, of course, being the son of the Colonel of the Regiment, knew full well that he could not break his rule just for me. I therefore left the Army in 1936 and transferred to the Supplementary Reserve of Officers.

Hill and Denys were married the following year. In the meantime, he had joined J.R. Wood, the family business of coal distributors which owned a fleet of fourteen small vessels in which it shipped coal and other commodities from the north of England to the south, where it owned a number of wharves along the south coast. During the following two years, he applied himself assiduously to his new roles as businessman and husband. In 1939, however, the clouds of war gathered once more over Europe when an increasingly belligerent Nazi Germany invaded Poland on 1 September. Two days later Britain, together with France, Australia and New Zealand, declared war on Germany and shortly afterwards Hill was recalled to the Colours.

Chapter 2

Having rejoined the 2nd Battalion The Royal Fusiliers in September 1939, Hill was despatched to France in command of the Battalion's advance party. Prior to his departure, his mother sent for him and said, 'James, if you are going to survive this war, you have got to learn to harden your heart.' It was advice that he would remember and heed well throughout the following years.

Christmas 1939 found him commanding a platoon, as he later wrote in an account of his experiences in France in 1940:

On Christmas Day 1939, I found myself commanding an outpost platoon of the 2nd Battalion of The Royal Fusiliers in the ligne de contact of the Maginot Line south-east of Metz during the coldest winter for forty years. Motor transport was impracticable and we were thus forced to rely on horses and mules. The fort covering us was a superb piece of military engineering, but the soldiers manning it appeared to have been poured into gumboots and imbued with what can only be described as the 'Maginot Spirit'.

Two days earlier, a Fortnum & Mason hamper addressed to me had arrived by horse transport. My company commander had deemed it reckless to expose such a hamper to an outpost and had said that company headquarters should hold it until the great day. His kind offer caused me considerable anxiety! However, at about midday I was summoned to company headquarters, which were located in the stationmaster's house of a disused railway station. Before entering the house I stopped to wish a happy Christmas to the fusilier on anti-aircraft duty who was manning a Lewis gun that was mounted on a tripod just outside.

I was opening my hamper as the clock struck twelve midday when suddenly my high expectations and tranquillity disappeared. Our brigade commander, a fiery man whom we feared but much respected, arrived full of bonhomie to wish his troops in the front line a happy Christmas.

All would have been well had not the only German reconnaissance aircraft that we had seen chosen that moment to zoom low over the railway embankment, just missing the chimney pots of company headquarters. The arrival of this first real-life target proved too much for our ack-ack fusilier, who, in his excitement to maintain fire and keep the enemy in his sights, tripped over the tripod, bringing the gun to the ground to the immediate danger of all around, including the brigadier. As the enemy plane sped out of sight, our by now irate brigadier stormed into our headquarters, his bonhomie having completely vanished, and we were all given a severe dressing-down for the laxity of our anti-aircraft defences in the front line. All in all, any vestiges of Christmas atmosphere swiftly evaporated!

Fortunately, however, the day was not entirely lost. We had suffered no casualties from either the enemy or our own ack-ack defences. The enraged brigade commander soon recovered his composure and sense of humour – the hamper with its considerable delicacies lay open on the table and this enabled us, with some diffidence, to offer him hospitality, which he graciously accepted. He left shortly thereafter with a warm feeling in his heart which he no doubt attributed to a successful mission restoring anti-aircraft proficiency and martial ardour. We felt that the hamper with its ports, Stilton cheese and Bath Oliver biscuits had more than contributed to that happy effect.

At 'stand-to' on that bitterly cold evening I sensed that we had received an appropriate gift for which to thank the Almighty on this his greatest of days.

On withdrawal we were addressed by Neville Chamberlain, complete in black Homburg, pinstripe suit and umbrella. He was excellent, the soldiers were grateful to him to a man for his much-maligned visit to Hitler, returning with the piece of paper on which was written 'Peace in our time', for it showed Hitler and many of his henchmen to be the complete bastards which they proved to be – this was not lost on the private soldier.

Hill was not to remain with his platoon and battalion for long, however, as in January 1940 he was posted as Staff Captain 'A' at the headquarters and command post of the Commander-in-Chief of the British Expeditionary Force (BEF) in France, Field Marshal the Lord Gort VC. As he later recalled:

The start of the battle proper found me as Staff Captain 'A', accompanied by thirty-two military policemen, crossing the Belgian border on 10 May and being followed by the 12th Lancers at midday. My responsibility under a splendid boss, Lieutenant Colonel Bert Herbert, was the organisation and control of refugees from Brussels, to assist the advance of the British Expeditionary Force (BEF) to the River Dyle and then regrettably, a week later, the start of the enforced withdrawal to the River Dendre.

During the following weeks, Hill found himself responsible for the organisation of refugee control from the front to Brussels and thence to Renaix, in order to ensure that the withdrawal of the BEF was unhindered; at one stage the traffic was such that it was proceeding down the main refugee route at an average rate of 4,500 vehicles per hour from 0500 hours until nightfall.

On 12 May, I went via the main refugee route to Courtrai to ensure that stops had been effectively imposed along the French border to prevent refugees filtering out of their reception area. I visited the mayor who promised to offer every possible assistance, as did the commander of the local gendarmerie. I passed through Courtrai aerodrome after it had been subjected to an attack by thirty enemy bombers. The hangars were still blazing and no attempt was being made to extinguish the fire. Dead horses were littering the ground and there were at least twenty-five Belgian aircraft on the aerodrome, most of which had been riddled with machine-gun fire from low-flying attacks or were burnt-out. Although the aerodrome was pitted with bomb craters, and the houses, it was surprising that more damage had not been done.

On 13 May, I returned to the command post, and it was then confirmed that I should make my headquarters at Nederbrakel and continue to be responsible for the direct routes from the front to Renaix. I returned to work that evening, and on the 14th went to the embassy in Brussels which was then closing down. I also made a tour of the main refugee routes leading into and out of Brussels. I liaised with the 7th Cheshires, 6th Argyll & Sutherland Highlanders and the 5th Royal Northumberland Fusiliers who were the three battalions on traffic control on the main northern, central and southern routes. Nederbrakel was bombed on two occasions but little damage was done. We were also machine-gunned by low-flying aircraft twice without effect. On one occasion, I saw about twenty German parachutists descending last thing at night in the vicinity of Ellezelles, but we were unable to locate them.

The withdrawal started on the 17th when the BEF was ordered to occupy the line of the River Senne running from Brussels. This, of course, created an additional flood of refugee traffic, which by this time comprised primarily horses and carts, pedestrians and cyclists. Hill visited Brussels that evening and arranged for all refugee traffic out of the city to be stopped at 1800 hours. He also went to Alost, to check the guards on the bridges which had been bombed heavily, before going on to Audenarde that evening. To add to his problems, he was informed that a French light mechanized division would be crossing our routes from north to south. As this formation took eight hours to pass a given point, and the Belgian Army was continuing to go flat out in the opposite direction to the sound of the guns, the prospects for the evening were far from good. It took all night getting the French through, delays being caused by drivers falling asleep in their vehicles, and by a medium tank which somehow became stuck broadside on in the only street through Nederbrakel.

On the night of the 18th, the second stage of the withdrawal from Brussels to the River Dendre was carried out, as he later described:

> It was more than ever important now to keep the roads clear of refugees to enable the BEF to withdraw unhindered. That evening, together with the Commanding Officer of the 7th Cheshires, we went up to Ninove where there was an artillery duel in progress. On the morning of the 19th, we found ourselves in Nederbrakel with an 8-mile jam of traffic away to the west, and with a German reconnaissance aircraft continuing to fly up and down overhead things did not look too rosy. However, thanks to the assistance of my two provost sections, about thirty men in all, we were able to get the road clear.
>
> On 19 May, I was instructed to proceed to Ninove and withdraw between the infantry rearguard and the last mobile units of the rearguard that had been left out in front, in order to ensure that no obstructions were placed across the road to impede them at the last minute. At about midday, I went up to the rearguard positions and then to one of our refugee parks that was bombed by approximately twenty enemy aircraft. The scene in the refugee park was indescribable – horses bolting in all directions, women and children screaming. I discovered later that the Germans had made a concentrated attack on all the parks along the route.

Other tasks allotted to Hill included the organization of the movement of main dressing stations and ambulance columns, and the carrying of despatches from Lord Gort to Calais. As his adventures continued, he

11

witnessed first-hand the German blitzkrieg as it crossed the plain north-east of Calais: at one point he was caught in an enemy ambush but fortunately succeeded in making good his escape:

> I had decided to return to the command post while there was a sporting chance of getting through. I therefore set off towards St Omer, taking an easterly route. However, when I was about 5 miles from Calais, we swung round a right-angled turn only to find a farm cart placed across the road. Behind it was a German armoured car which opened fire but fortunately we were able to back round the corner and get away, the Boche having made the mistake of placing his roadblock 50 yards from the bend in the road.

At one point, Hill arrived at Dunkirk where he briefed a group of senior officers, including Major General Andrew McNaughton, commander of the 1st Canadian Infantry Division, on the situation in Calais where the Canadians were due to land that morning. McNaughton was about to depart in a destroyer and so Hill, who was keen to return to Calais, accepted an offer of a place aboard the vessel. He soon found himself out at sea but shortly afterwards the ship was attacked by a German bomber. Fortunately, however, a Spitfire appeared and succeeded in shooting down the enemy aircraft.

Such was his exhaustion that he fell asleep, only to find himself a few hours later entering Dover harbour. While he was slumbering, a signal had been received from the War Office informing Major General McNaughton that his division was not to land at Calais that morning and ordering him to return to Britain. Dismayed at his involuntary crossing of the Channel, Hill hastened to find some means of returning to Dunkirk and eventually succeeded in hitching a lift aboard a drifter laden with a cargo of high explosives and detonators for blowing bridges, and a load of medical stores. The vessel left Dover at 0300 hours and, following an uneventful crossing, reached Dunkirk which was being subjected to a heavy air raid. Two of the enemy bombers proceeded to attack the drifter but fortunately their bombs missed the vessel and its lethal cargo.

Once ashore, Hill succeeded in acquiring a staff car and driver before setting off for Lord Gort's command post at Premesques, travelling via Furnes, Ypres and Menin, where he learned there were Germans in the vicinity and, even more ominous, that the Belgian Army had surrendered. He lost no time in leaving Menin and returned via Ypres and Armentières from where he eventually succeeded in reaching BEF Headquarters. Not long afterwards, however, he found himself under fire once again:

On May 27, it was decided to move to the command post from Premesques to a village about 2 miles to the east of Cassel, which seemed a most inopportune move as we knew that German forces were then advancing to take Cassel. The command post had to close at Premesques at 1030 hours and open at its new location at the same hour. It was arranged that some others and I should remain at Premesques until 1030 hours and then move to the new headquarters. However, the Commander-in-Chief decided that he would stay and fight the battle from Premesques until later in the day, remaining there until 1645 hours when he left for Cassel. We followed in a second convoy some fifteen minutes later.

We had only been on the road about half an hour when we were attacked by half a dozen Messerschmitt 109s which machine-gunned us heavily. I had three holes in my windscreen and wasted little time in jumping into the nearest ditch.

Another member of my group, Colonel Whiteford, threw himself into a drain with dire results. The military policeman immediately behind me was hit seven times in his right leg and some other troops, who were not members of our group, were also hit. I put a tourniquet on the unfortunate man's leg and bundled him into the back of my car before setting off once more, eventually reaching Neuve Eglise where I handed him over to a field ambulance.

Despite the growing peril facing the BEF, Hill found himself in a happy frame of mind:

I was in a great regiment with a long family tradition. We had our own king and country to wave our flag for, a great empire to be proud of and a cause that was entirely just. This outlook proved most important for two reasons: firstly, it gave one the resilience of mind to cast off the mental effects resulting from participating in the retreat of an army ending in heavy loss of life, the self-destruction of its guns, armour, vehicles, ammunition and with the loss of many as prisoners of war and the evacuation of its remaining strength with the clothes in which they stood up and hopefully their personal weapons. To witness and experience such a catastrophe from beginning to end from, you might say, its heart centre at Lord Gort's command post, could not but leave one badly scarred but nevertheless the right reasons for going to war gave one the mental stamina to fight a long war.

Among the scenes Hill witnessed in May 1940 was Lord Gort's meeting with General Sir William 'Tiny' Ironside, who had replaced him in

September 1939 as Chief of the Imperial General Staff (CIGS) when Gort was despatched to France as Commander-in-Chief of the BEF. It was at this meeting that the decision was taken to evacuate all troops from the beaches of Dunkirk and thereafter Hill found himself in charge of the British section of the La Panne beach during the last thirty-six hours of the evacuation. The images of those last few days in France in May 1940 would remain in his memory for the rest of his life:

> The evacuation of the troops from Dunkirk began on Monday 27 May 1940 and was supposed to be completed by Friday the 31st. The troops and ships were subjected, however, to an incessant bombardment by the German air force using both conventional and dive-bombing. I observed many aerial combats during the four days we were at La Panne, and saw two of our own Spitfires brought down on to the beach and one that dived into the sea. A large number of enemy aircraft were also shot down. During the last two days, German artillery also ranged in on the beaches and ships, inflicting heavy casualties among the troops. It would have been quite impossible for the BEF to have been embarked if the mole at Dunkirk had been put out of action. The mole's capacity was 4,000 personnel per hour, whereas that of the beach was approximately 4,000 per day. I eventually embarked on a destroyer at about 1900 hours on the evening of Friday the 31st, just as the Germans were attacking the mole with dive-bombers. Three hours later, at around 1000 hours, we landed at Dover where we were hustled aboard a train, the destination of which was unknown. I discovered however that, very conveniently for me, it stopped at Salisbury at 4.00 am and so I nipped off it and walked home, arriving there at 7.00 am.

In recognition of his exploits in France during the previous six months, Hill was awarded the Military Cross. Shortly after his return, he found himself promoted to the rank of major and posted as Deputy Assistant Adjutant General (DAAG) to Headquarters British Troops in Northern Ireland. His appointment there was only a brief one but once again involved adventure: he was despatched incognito over the border into the Irish Republic where he made his way to Dublin with the task of assisting in planning the evacuation of the capital in the event of a German landing in the south of the country. During his stay, he was accommodated in the Gresham Hotel on O'Connell Street, in the heart of the city, as he subsequently related:

> There followed a very interesting week in which I must have met all the top brass with the exception of de Valera. Plans were drawn up

for the evacuation of refugees to the west and north-west of Dublin and for our main routes to be safeguarded. I returned rather pleased with the results achieved, including two pairs of silk stockings for my wife, and expecting a commendation from the C-in-C, but two weeks later it was reported that pill-boxes were being built facing us on our selected routes. It appeared that any mutual trust between us and the Irish seemed to have flown out of the window.

Two amusing incidents that occurred during my time in Northern Ireland remain in my mind. The first was when I was asked to escort the Commander-in-Chief, General Sir Hubert Huddlestone, who had been invited to tea with Lady Londonderry at Mount Stewart. During the course of the tea, while sitting in comfortable armchairs, Lady Londonderry exposed a modest proportion of inner leg, revealing a snake tattooed thereon and moving in an upward direction. The C-in-C went very red in the face, did not know which way to look but simply had to look again! On the journey home, I was asked, 'Did you see what I saw? Did you know of its existence?' I replied, 'Yes Sir, but I had not personally had the opportunity to observe it.' The Commander-in-Chief's response was, 'Then why the hell didn't you warn me?' Needless to say, I was not called upon again to act in a personal capacity thereafter.

The second incident occurred during the bombing of Belfast and its shipyards when the local population abandoned the city and flooded into the country in every direction. Amidst great ballyhoo and with great publicity, the Dublin Fire Brigade despatched its four smartest fire engines to help fight the fires. Four days later, they were due to motor back to Dublin, receiving a heroes' welcome en route and cementing a happy relationship en route. However, they found that all the brass on their engines, hoses and most of their helmets had been pinched. Needless to say, this was a blow for public relations and the officers responsible for the visit, notably the DAAG!

On returning to England, Hill was posted to Luton as GSO 2 (Operations) at Headquarters Eastern Command, whose area of responsibility covered East Anglia and the Central Midlands. There he remained until 1941 when the next, and most illustrious, stage of his military career began.

Chapter 3

The campaign in France of 1940 had seen a devastatingly effective demonstration of the new German strategy of blitzkrieg, 'lightning war', as Wehrmacht armoured columns surged across France, brushing aside all opposition as they headed for the Channel ports in an effort to cut off the withdrawal of the BEF. At the same time, an additional dimension of blitzkrieg was being unveiled elsewhere – one that would ultimately have a direct bearing on the future of Major James Hill MC of The Royal Fusiliers.

During the mid-1920s, Germany had begun forming a new air force, in complete defiance of the Treaty of Versailles. In 1924, a secret training facility was established in the Soviet Union at an airfield near Lipetsk, a city situated on the banks of the Voronezh River in the Don basin, 438 kilometres to the south-east of Moscow. Known officially as the 4th Squadron of the Red Army's 40th Wing, this facility trained German aircrew during the following nine years, using mostly Dutch and Russian, but also some German, training aircraft before it was closed in 1933.

On 26 February 1935, Adolf Hitler ordered Reichsmarschall Hermann Göring, who had distinguished himself as a flying ace during the First World War, to re-establish the Luftwaffe, in so doing breaking the Treaty of Versailles ban on German military aviation. This violation met with no sanction from Britain, France or the League of Nations, who did nothing to oppose it.

In 1936, Germany began forming a new arm of the Luftwaffe: airborne forces. A parachute training school was established at Stendal, 78 miles west of Berlin, and the first parachute unit was raised early that year from volunteers from the Hermann Göring Regiment, a Luftwaffe unit raised from the Prussian State Police, and was designated *Fallschirmjäger-regiment 1* (FJR-1). An Army parachute company was also formed, shortly afterwards being expanded to a battalion.

Trainee *fallschirmjäger* underwent three months of initial training during which they received instruction in all infantry weapons and equipment, including those of the enemy, and close-quarter battle. On passing this phase, they underwent a sixteen-day parachute course covering aircraft drills, exit techniques, parachute flight control and landing drills. During the last six days, a total of six jumps were carried out from a Junkers Ju-52 transport, the last of which was a company jump. The exit technique appeared somewhat hair-raising to the trainees who were required to dive head first from the aircraft, spreadeagling themselves as they did so.

Each *fallschirmjäger* was also required to learn to pack his own parachute and much emphasis was placed on this aspect of his training. After an extensive period of trials and development, the parachute initially selected for service with the German airborne forces was the RZ-1 (*Rückenpackung Zwangauslösung 1*) which was a static, line-operated, 28-gore model developed by the Luftwaffe's experimental research establishment at Rechlin, in the present-day northern German state of Mecklenburg-Western Pomerania, and designed to meet the operation requirement for a dropping altitude of 300 feet. The RZ-I, however, proved unreliable and was replaced in the spring of 1940 by the RZ-16; that was in turn followed by the RZ-20, which incorporated further improvements. All three versions of the RZ parachute featured a harness that suspended the parachutist from a single point high up on his back, resulting in him hanging forwards and allowing him no facility to steer the parachute.

The *fallschirmjäger* was easily distinguished from other members of the German armed forces by his combat dress. This comprised: a narrow-brimmed, lightweight steel helmet fitted with a triple anchor point harness and normally worn with a camouflaged cloth cover; a weatherproof knee-length, loose-fitting smock (originally plain olive drab but of camouflage pattern fabric from 1940 onwards) worn over the individual's uniform and equipment during a jump; and grey, loose-fitting trousers tucked into high leather rubber-soled boots laced up the sides. Rubber knee protectors and padded leather gauntlets were worn during a jump to protect the hands and knees on landing.

The *fallschirmjäger* jumped with only a 9mm pistol for personal protection. His main personal weapon, be it machine carbine, rifle, light machine gun or mortar, was dropped in one of four containers which carried the weapons of the twelve-strong stick of which he was a member. Each container was fitted with a parachute at one end, and with shock absorbers to reduce the impact of landing.

Fallschirmjäger were equipped with standard small arms as issued throughout the Wehrmacht, including: the MP-38 and MP-40 9mm machine pistols; Mauser 98K 7.92mm rifle; the MG-34 7.92mm light machine gun (subsequently replaced by the MG-42 which featured a higher rate of fire) and light anti-tank weapons. The sole exception was the *Fallschirmgewehr-42* (FG-42), a 7.92mm gas-operated assault rifle capable of semi and fully automatic fire and designed specifically for use by airborne troops. Support weapons included 81mm and 105mm medium mortars, and a 37mm anti-tank gun mounted on a two-wheeled carriage. Artillery units were equipped with the *Gebirgskanon-36* 75mm mountain gun, which became the standard artillery piece for German airborne forces.

July 1938 saw the emergence of the man who was to become the 'founding father' of the German airborne forces of the Second World War, Major General Kurt Student, who had hitherto held the appointment of Inspector General of Luftwaffe training establishments. By September, he had formed the 7th Air Division, a formation comprising: the 1st Battalion FJR-1; the Army's parachute battalion; a battalion of the Hermann Göring Regiment; the 16th Infantry Regiment (on loan from the Army's 22nd Infantry Division); a contingent of parachutists formed from the Nazi para-military Sturmabteilung organisation, better known as the 'Brownshirts'; and supporting artillery and medical units. Aviation support for the newly-formed division was provided by a formation of 250 Ju-52 transports and a small unit equipped with DFS-230 assault gliders.

September 1938 saw the invasion and annexation by Germany of the Czechoslovakian border region of the Sudetenland. The 7th Air Division was stood by to provide follow-up support by carrying out airlanding operations at Freudenthal, in the Czech province of Moravia, but in the event was not deployed. Shortly afterwards, the 16th Infantry Regiment returned to the 22nd Infantry Division and the Sturmabteilung contingent also departed. The 7th Air Division was thus left with only the 1st Battalion FJR-1 and the nucleii of its supporting arms. Student, who was now also appointed Inspector of Parachute Troops, thus set about creating the Division as a fully independent airborne formation with its own artillery, engineer and signals elements.

By the end of 1938, command of all airborne forces had been vested in the Luftwaffe. The Army transferred its parachute battalion which became a Luftwaffe unit designated 2nd Battalion FJR-1. It retained 22nd Infantry Division which was, however, placed under Luftwaffe command as an airlanding formation to form an airborne corps with 7th Air Division. The latter received its own organic aviation support assets in the form of the tactical transport squadrons of a wing of four special-purpose battle groups equipped with a total of 220 aircraft. In the autumn of 1939, a second wing was formed, together with a special group allotted the role of transporting heavy weapons.

The workhorse of both wings was the Ju-52/3m, a tri-motor transport with a maximum tactical radius of 621 miles and a maximum cruising speed of 131 knots (152 mph) at 2,950 feet. Known affectionately as 'Tante Ju', it was flown by a crew of three and could accommodate twelve paratroops, while carrying four weapon and equipment containers in a bomb bay. When carrying out airlanding operations, the aircraft was capable of accommodating seventeen fully equipped infantrymen.

The Ju-52/3m was also capable of towing the DFS-230 assault glider, a high-winged aircraft capable of carrying ten fully equipped troops, including its two pilots who fought in the ground role after landing. With a payload of almost one ton, it comprised a fuselage of tubular steel covered with a canvas skin and wooden wings, the latter featuring flaps on the upper surfaces which, when raised, permitted a steep angle of descent as the glider approached for a landing. The principal advantage of the DFS-230 was its virtually silent approach, thus achieving the element of surprise, coupled with its capability of delivering heavy weapons and light vehicles.

In the summer of 1939, by which time 7th Air Division was based in western Germany in the towns of Tangermünde, Hildesheim, Gardelegen and Braunschweig, two additional parachute regiments, designated FJR-2 and FJR-3, were formed. Each comprised three battalions, each of which consisted of three rifle companies and a support company equipped with mortars and machine guns. Artillery support, in the form of anti-tank and *Gebirgskanon-36* light mountain guns, was provided by separate companies allotted to battalions as required. Plans were also put in hand for the formation of divisional troops comprising signals, reconnaissance, anti-tank and medical units.

The Division was still undergoing expansion when, on 1 September 1939, Germany invaded Poland. Reinforced by 16th Infantry Regiment in the airlanding role, it was deployed to Lower Silesia and on three occasions was stood by for action: initially to carry out landings over the River Vistula, in the area of Pulawy, with the task of denying crossing points to Polish forces and to cut off the latter's reserves; secondly, to seize and hold the bridge across the River San at Jaroslaw ahead of advancing German armour; and thirdly, to capture the Polish government and military high command who had established themselves in Krzemieniewice, in south-eastern Poland.

In the event, the speed of the German advance through Poland was such that 7th Air Division was not required, although the 16th Infantry Regiment was flown forward to take part in fighting to the north of Lodz. It was not long, however, before Student's *fallschirmjäger* would undergo their baptism of fire.

On 9 April 1940, Germany invaded Norway and Denmark. Overall command of the operation, code-named WESERÜBUNG, was vested in General Nikolaus von Falkenhorst, the commander of XXI Corps, whose plan called for two of his divisions to invade Denmark while a further six were launched into Norway.

In addition to his own corps, Falkenhorst was allotted the 1st Battalion FJR-1. Denmark was the initial target, with two airfields at Aalborg in North Jutland being among the objectives to be seized on the first day, along with a number of Norwegian airfields. These would be taken by the battalion whose No. 4 Company was tasked with seizing the airfields at Aalborg and capturing another key objective: the 2-mile-long Vordingborg bridge connecting the Danish island of Falster with Zealand, on which is located the Danish capital of Copenhagen. In support of No. 4 Company would be three battalions of the 305th Infantry Regiment.

Meanwhile the Battalion's Nos 1 and 2 Companies would drop on the Norwegian airfield at Fornebu, being followed by two battalions of the 324th Infantry Regiment, together with elements of Headquarters XXI Corps once the airfield had been secured. In the meantime, No. 3 Company would drop on an airfield at Sola, near Stavanger; once it had been taken and secured, two battalions of the 193rd Infantry Regiment would be airlanded.

Operation WESERÜBUNG began in the early hours of 9 April with the No. 4 Company platoon successfully seizing and securing the two airfields at Aalborg. In the meantime, however, heavy cloud and poor visibility had forced the transports carrying Nos 1 and 2 Companies to Fornebu to divert to Aalborg, where they landed shortly after the airfields had been taken. Meanwhile, the aircraft carrying the two battalions of the 324th Infantry Regiment were still heading for Fornebu, only to find it still in Norwegian hands. The leading formation of aircraft received a radio message ordering it to turn back but, believing it to be a hoax by the Norwegians, pressed on regardless; in fact, the message was genuine as the decision had been taken to abort the airlanding since the airfield was still held by enemy forces. On coming under fire as it made its approach, the leading aircraft was hit but swung away and led the formation to Aalborg where it landed.

By 0900 hours, however, all resistance at the airfield at Fornebu had been neutralized following an attack by German aircraft. Shortly afterwards, Nos 1 and 2 Companies took off from Aalborg and were dropped successfully at Fornebu, securing and holding the airfield until the arrival of the leading elements of the two battalions of the 324th Infantry Regiment.

Meanwhile at Sola, near Stavanger, No. 3 Company dropped at 0900 hours and immediately came under fire from machine guns sited around the airfield. Air support soon appeared, however, in the form of two Messerschmitt Me-110 fighter-bombers and it was not long before all resistance was overcome. Having stormed and overrun the defenders' positions, the *fallschirmjäger* cleared the runway of obstacles and a few minutes later the first of the transports carrying the leading elements of the 193rd Infantry Regiment touched down.

In the meantime, the Vordingborg bridge had been seized by the rest of No. 4 Company which succeeded in taking the Danish defenders completely by surprise, swiftly disarming them and capturing the bridge without a shot being fired. Shortly afterwards, the *fallschirmjäger* were joined by troops of the 325th Infantry Regiment who pushed on towards Copenhagen.

Thus the initial phase of Operation WESERÜBUNG proved to be a total success and Student's *fallschirmjäger* received their baptism of fire. Four days later, the 1st Battalion FJR-1 participated in the second phase: the capture of key objectives further north. On 15 April, No. 1 Company was dropped near Dombas, 90 miles north-west of Oslo, its task being to block a narrow pass through which ran the railway line linking the Norwegian capital with Trondheim, and to cut the line of withdrawal of Norwegian troops pulling back from Oslo to join up with British forces which had landed at Andalsnes. The operation was not a success: the company was scattered during the drop which resulted in some men being killed as they were dropped from too low an altitude, allowing insufficient time for their parachutes to deploy fully. Most of the survivors landed among Norwegian defensive positions and suffered heavy casualties, the remainder fighting on for four days before their ammunition was exhausted and they were forced to surrender.

The final airborne operation in Norway saw the 1st Battalion FJR-1 being deployed to Narvik, in the northern part of the country, to reinforce German forces under Lieutenant General Eduard Dietl which were under siege from the British and Norwegians. On 26 May, the Battalion was dropped on the Björnfeld Heights along the border with Sweden. Following the drop, it advanced along the railway line into Narvik where it linked up with Dietl's forces. In the meantime, sorely-needed light artillery, in the form of *Gebirgskanon-36* mountain guns, was flown in by transports which landed on a frozen lake at Bardufoss; there was no way the aircraft could take off again, however, and thus they had to be sacrificed. A few days later, two companies of the 3rd Mountain Division's 137th *Gebirgsjäger-regiment*, having undergone a crash course in parachuting, were also dropped. Despite being scattered during the drop and a number suffering injuries, most of the mountain infantrymen linked up with Dietl's still hard-pressed forces, which subsequently withdrew by sea from Narvik at the end of May and were transported to Oslo. A week later, on 7 June, the Allies retreated from Norway and two days later all organized resistance to the German invasion collapsed.

Shortly afterwards, the 1st Battalion FJR-1 returned by sea to Germany where Lieutenant General Kurt Student, promoted to that rank on 1 June, expressed his satisfaction at its performance and that, apart from the loss of No. 1 Company at Dombas, it had suffered relatively light casualties. The Luftwaffe's 10th Air Fleet, however, had suffered severely during the campaign in Norway, losing over 100 of its Ju-52 transports.

Student and his *fallschirmjäger* were not permitted to rest on their laurels for long, however, because Hitler was already turning his attention towards Belgium and Holland, these being his initial targets in Western Europe. The British and French, meanwhile, were well aware that an attack was in the offing and had made their dispositions accordingly. The latter placed their faith in the seemingly impregnable Maginot Line, comprising three interdependent belts of fortifications stretching from Luxembourg to Switzerland along the French border with Germany. Key elements of these were 108 large forts situated 9 miles apart, each housing 1,000 troops; interspersed between them were a number of smaller fortified bases, each garrisoned by 200–500 troops. These and their larger brethren in turn formed the backbone for a large number of additional fortifications manned by companies and platoons. All fortifications throughout the line were heavily protected by minefields and barbed-wire defences, with observation posts positioned well forward to provide early warning of any attack.

In 1939, the *Oberkommando der Wehrmacht* (OKW) (German High Command) had produced a plan to invade the Low Countries by outflanking the Maginot Line to the north and, thrusting through southern

Belgium, head straight for the Channel ports with the aim of cutting off the British Expeditionary Force. It was approved in February 1940 and adopted, following modifications which envisaged the advance into Belgium as a secondary move designed to draw off British and Belgian forces from the main German thrust through the semi-mountainous forests of the Ardennes, heading past Sedan and on to the estuary of the River Somme.

The Dutch defences consisted of three lines. The first, only lightly fortified and following the Rivers Maas and Ijssel, was merely intended to delay any attacking force. The second – called the Grebbe-Peel Line and extending for 80 miles from the southern shore of the Zuider Zee south-east to the Belgian border near Weert – comprised extensive defences combined with natural obstacles, which included the floodable Geld Valley, the Peel and Maas marshes and the Noorder Canal. The third line of defence, known as Fortress Holland and stretching from Den Helder to the Holland Deep, was a fully prepared defensive area embracing the cities of Amsterdam, Rotterdam, The Hague and Utrecht. To the south it was protected by the Rhine-Maas estuary, while to the east lay the Ijsselmeer and the area between the estuary and Nuiden which could be flooded if necessary.

Belgium's defences incorporated a delaying position on the Albert Canal and a main defensive line extending along the Dyle, the latter covering Brussels and the port of Antwerp. The delaying position was protected along its entire length by a number of forward positions with the exception of one area known as the Maastricht Appendix where the canal ran close to the Dutch border, running through a deep cutting over 100 yards in width and spanned by three bridges at Veldvezelt, Vroenhofen and Canne. An infantry division was deployed to defend this area, a brigade being allotted to the defence of each of the bridges. Defensive emplacements included blockhouses lining the canal for 600 yards on either side of each bridge, all of which were prepared for demolition with explosives.

Artillery support for the garrisons at the bridges was provided by the guns of the vast and seemingly impregnable fortress of Eben Emael. Measuring some 200 by 400 yards, it had been built in the mid-1930s by being blasted out of granite. In appearance just a huge grassy mound, its reinforced concrete roofs and walls were 6 feet thick. It was manned by a 1,185-strong garrison and was equipped with the following artillery: six 120mm guns with a range of 10 miles, two of which possessed a 360° traverse; sixteen 75mm quick-firing guns; twelve 60mm anti-tank guns; 25

twin-mounted machine guns; and a number of anti-aircraft machine guns mounted on the roof in four retractable casemates. One side of the fortress towered 120 feet above the Albert Canal, while the others were protected by minefields, deep ditches, a 20-feet-high wall and blockhouses equipped with machine guns, anti-tank guns and searchlights.

The entire defensive system was based on a strategy calling for the Belgians to hold their positions along the Albert Canal until such time as British and French forces could come to their aid. The Germans, however, were well aware of this and had laid their own plans accordingly. Their assault on the Low Countries would be led by 7th Air Division and 22nd Airlanding Division. The former, consisting of three parachute regiments and the 16th Infantry Regiment, was allotted the task of carrying out a series of drops to seize and secure bridges over the rivers and canals leading from the south to Fortress Holland. Among these were the bridges spanning the Holland Deep at Noerdijk and the Oude Maas near Dordrecht. Other targets included an airfield at Waalhaven and two bridges over the Nieuwe Maas at Rotterdam.

Meanwhile the 22nd Airlanding Division, comprising the 47th and 65th Infantry Regiments and the reinforced 1st Battalion FJR-2, would seize a number of airfields in the area of The Hague at Valkenburg, Ockenburg and Ypenburg. The 1st Battalion FJR-2 would carry out a parachute assault, with the rest of the Division landing once the airfields had been secured, thereafter advancing on Amsterdam with the intention of capturing the Dutch High Command and the Royal Family. In addition, the Division was to interdict all railway lines and roads to prevent the movement of Dutch reserves.

The overall aim was to lay a carpet of airborne troops to secure a corridor along which elements of the German Eighteenth Army, comprising 9th Panzer Division, an SS motorised regiment, a division of cavalry and six infantry divisions, would advance over the water obstacles and into Fortress Holland.

In the early hours of 10 May 1940 the 1st Battalion FJR-2 took off in sixty-five Ju-52 transports and headed westwards for The Hague. An hour later they were followed by a further 100 aircraft carrying the airlanding troops and advance divisional headquarters of Lieutenant General Hans Graf von Sponeck. At 0630 hours the *fallschirmjäger* companies were dropped over the airfields at Valkenburg, Ockenburg and Ypenburg, encountering fierce resistance from three battalions of Dutch infantry who drove them off before mounting strong counter-attacks. At the same time, the anti-aircraft artillery at all three locations inflicted heavy casualties on the transports, shooting down eleven out of twelve aircraft carrying the leading elements of the 65th Infantry Regiment. The second wave of aircraft thus had to be diverted to Katwijk where they landed on the beach, roads and any areas of open ground large enough to accommodate a Ju-53. This did not prove simple as the Dutch had foreseen such an eventuality and erected obstacles which inflicted heavy casualties among the aircraft and airlanding troops alike. Those of the latter who survived were killed or captured by Dutch forces.

22nd Airlanding Division's situation continued to deteriorate throughout the rest of that day, the Dutch recapturing the airfields at Ockenburg and Ypenburg, and mounting a series of strong counter-attacks at Valkenburg. Meanwhile, the third wave of aircraft had been diverted to Waalhaven, near Rotterdam, where it landed virtually unopposed.

At the same time, 7th Air Division was enjoying greater success. A 438-strong force, designated Storm Group Koch and comprising troops of the 1st Battalion FJR-1 and a company of the divisional engineer battalion, had been tasked with attacking and knocking out the fortress at Eben Emael. It was divided into four assault sub-groups: Granite, comprising eighty-five men in eleven DFS-230 gliders whose objective was the fortress itself; Steel, consisting of ninety-two men in nine gliders who were tasked with taking the Veldvezelt bridge; Concrete, with a strength of ninety-six men in eleven gliders who were to capture the Vroenhoven bridge; and Iron, whose ninety-strong force in ten gliders was to seize the Kannes bridge.

Just prior to the landings by the 1st Battalion FJR-2 and 22nd Airlanding Division, Steel, Concrete and Iron would land at their respective objectives which they were to seize and secure. Forty minutes later, a platoon of reinforcements would be dropped at each location, together with additional machine guns and ammunition. In the meantime, Granite would land on top of the fortress and attack its casemates with 50 kilogram shaped-charge explosives capable of penetrating the 6-feet-thick reinforced concrete.

Storm Group Koch took off at 0415 hours on 10 May in forty-one gliders towed by Ju-52 tugs. The flight proved uneventful, albeit two of Granite's gliders were lost en route: one because of a snapped tow rope and the other due to a premature release. Steel and Iron cast off from their tugs some 20 miles inside Germany and flew on undetected, but Concrete was towed over the Dutch border where its tugs were detected by anti-aircraft artillery which opened fire, alerting the defences in the area to the imminent threat.

Nevertheless Concrete and Steel, each comprising five sections of infantry and four of engineers, touched down successfully at their predetermined landing points and immediately went into the assault. While the parachute infantry sections launched their attacks on the bridge defences, the engineers used flamethrowers and explosives to knock out the blockhouses and gun emplacements before turning their attention to cutting the firing circuits of the demolition charges set into the bridge structures. In the meantime, Iron had failed to seize the bridge at Kannes because it had landed late and the element of surprise had been lost. It came under heavy fire from the defenders who blew the bridge shortly afterwards.

Granite meanwhile had landed safely on the roof of Eben Emael, the gliders using arrester parachutes to halt within 20 yards of touching down. The *fallschirmjäger* lost no time in attacking the fortress casemates, blasting their way through the roofs and then dropping grenades into the chambers below.

At 0610 hours, formations of Ju-52s appeared over each of the three bridges and dropped the reinforcements, coming under fire from the ground and suffering heavy casualties. At the Kannes bridge, Iron eventually overcame all resistance and seized its objective.

The leading elements of the Eighteenth Army were meanwhile advancing into Holland and at 1015 hours began providing artillery support for Storm Group Koch. By 1300 hours, the leading units had linked up with the *fallschirmjäger* companies at the bridges.

Elsewhere, the remainder of 7th Air Division had also been playing its part in the invasion. The 2nd Battalion FJR-1 was dropped in the area of the three bridges over the Holland Deep and secured its objectives after fierce fighting. At the bridge at Dordrecht, however, the 1st Battalion FJR-1 managed to seize only part of its objective before the Dutch counter-attacked, recapturing the bridge. At Waalhaven, the 3rd Battalion FJR-1 had been dropped to the east of the airfield and encountered stiff resistance from the defenders. Shortly afterwards, however, the 3rd Battalion 16th Infantry Regiment landed to their rear in Ju-52s and, following a brief battle, the airfield was soon in German hands.

On the outskirts of Rotterdam, meanwhile, a 120-strong company of the 16th Infantry Regiment, which was under command of 7th Air Division, was landed in twelve Heinkel 59 seaplanes close to the two bridges on the Nieuwe Maas, both of which were seized and their demolition charges removed. The company was reinforced shortly afterwards by a force of fifty *fallschirmjäger* who were dropped south of the bridges, but joined up with the infantry company in time to help it repel a strong Dutch counter-attack.

Fierce fighting continued throughout 11 May, a counter-attack by the French Seventh Army being beaten back by swarms of JU-87 Stuka dive-bombers. The following day, the leading units of 9th Panzer Division arrived at the Moerdijk bridges where they linked up with the *fallschirmjäger*. By nightfall on 14 May, Lieutenant General Kurt Student had established his command post in the headquarters of the Dutch High Command. Shortly after doing so, however, he was wounded in the head by a stray bullet and was evacuated to Germany, command of 7th Air Division being assumed temporarily by Major General Richard Putziger, commander of the Luftwaffe formations which had provided air support during the entire operation.

On 15 May, the surviving elements of 22nd Airlanding Division linked up with the ground forces; out of the 2,000 men of the division who had been landed on 10 May, casualties were particularly heavy among the 47th and 65th Infantry Regiments. Losses had also been high among the Luftwaffe transport squadrons, with 170 Ju-52s destroyed and almost the same number badly damaged. Furthermore, a large number of aircrew had also been lost.

Following its return to Germany, 7th Air Division was expanded to incorporate three parachute regiments, each of three battalions, with Storm Group Koch becoming the 1st Battalion of the *Luftlande-Sturmregiment* 1 (LSR-1) (1st Airlanding Assault Regiment). This was a new formation comprising four battalions of *fallschirmjäger* trained as a glider-borne assault force. Together with 22nd Airlanding Division, 7th Air Division was incorporated into another newly-created formation, XI Air Corps, which was established in the summer of 1940.

The development of the German airborne forces, and the strategy and tactics in their use in Scandinavia and the Low Countries during the first half of 1940, had been studied with keen interest in Britain by a number of high-level observers, among them the Prime Minister, Winston Churchill. On 22 June, he wrote the following minute to General Sir Hastings Ismay, head of the Military Wing of the War Cabinet Secretariat:

> We ought to have a corps of at least 5,000 parachute troops, including a proportion of Australians, New Zealanders and Canadians, together with some trustworthy people from Norway and

France. ... advantage of the summer must be taken to train these troops, who can then nonetheless play their part meanwhile as shock troops in home defence. Pray let me have a note from the War Office on the subject.

In fact, the creation of a fledgling airborne capability was already under way. Following the creation by the RAF of a parachute training establishment, the Central Landing School, at Ringway, near Manchester, the Army took the decision to convert one of its newly-formed commando units to the new role. No. 2 Commando was selected and moved to a new location at Knutsford, near Ringway. On 3 July 1940, Lieutenant Colonel C.I.A. Jackson assumed command of the unit and six days later B and C Troops reported to the Central Landing School for training. By August, a further 500 troops had been selected to undergo parachute training from a total of 3,500 volunteers. By the end of September, a total of 961 descents had been carried out by 290 trainees.

During the period of its conversion, No. 2 Commando was organized into a headquarters and a number of troops, each numbering fifty men, with an overall established strength of 500 all ranks. In November 1940, it was redesignated 11th Special Air Service (SAS) Battalion and reorganized into a headquarters, a parachute wing and a glider-borne wing. Two months earlier, the Central Landing School was expanded and redesignated the Central Landing Establishment, incorporating No. 1 Parachute Training School (PTS), as it was now called, and a glider training squadron.

In early 1941, the members of 11th SAS Battalion received their baptism of fire when the decision was taken to stage an operation in southern Italy, the aim of which was to disrupt water supplies to the ports of Taranto, Bari and Brindisi, all of which were embarkation points for Italian forces in North Africa and Albania, and thus show the rest of the world that Britain was still very much a force with which to be reckoned. The real purpose of the operation, however, was to test the new airborne unit and the effectiveness of its training and equipment, as well as the capability of the RAF to deliver paratroops at a predetermined location and time.

A thirty-eight-strong force, designated X Troop and commanded by Major T. A. G. Pritchard, was selected from the Battalion for the operation, which was code-named COLOSSUS; attached to it for the operation were three Italian-speaking interpreters. On 7 February 1941 the troop, which included a party of eight sappers, emplaned at RAF Mildenhall in Suffolk aboard eight Whitley bombers of No. 91 Squadron RAF, and flew to Malta from where the operation would be launched. Three days later, at 1830 hours, six of the aircraft took off from Malta and headed for southern Italy and X Troop's target: the Tragino Aqueduct, which provided the main water supply route for the province of Apulia and its population of over two million. The aqueduct crossed the Tragino, a small watercourse, at a location some 30 miles north-east of the small town of Salverno in the province of Campania.

Five of the aircraft dropped their sticks in close proximity to the dropping zone, but the sixth, carrying six of the troop's sappers, was unable to locate it and eventually dropped its stick and equipment in a valley 2 miles north-east of the target.

Despite problems experienced in locating and retrieving some of the equipment containers in the dark, due to the lights on them being inoperable, X Troop succeeded in attacking and destroying the aqueduct at 0030 hours on the morning of 11 February. Half an hour later, it split up into three groups which began making their way independently over mountainous terrain, moving by night and lying up by day, towards the coast and the mouth of the River Seale over 50 miles away, where a Royal Navy submarine, HMS *Triumph*, would be waiting to take them off on the night of 15/16 February.

In the event, all three groups and the party of sappers, which failed to join up with them, were captured on 12 February. Had any of them succeeded in reaching the coast, however, they would have found no submarine waiting for them. While the operation was under way, one of the two aircraft carrying out the diversionary bombing raid on the railway marshalling yards at Foggia had suffered engine trouble. The pilot had radioed the operational base on Malta, reporting that he was heading for the River Seale estuary where he intended to ditch his aircraft, being completely unaware that this was the planned rendezvous for the evacuation of X Troop. Concerned that his radio message had been monitored and that the submarine would be detected by enemy naval forces, the decision was taken not to send HMS *Triumph*.

While Operation COLOSSUS was of little value in terms of its effect of the disruption of water supplies to the three Italian ports, it nevertheless provided valuable experience which was subsequently put to good use.

In May 1941, the Chiefs of Staff directed that a parachute brigade was to be formed as swiftly as possible, with 11th SAS Battalion as the nucleus. Two months later, authority was given for the formation of a brigade headquarters, four parachute battalions and a troop of sappers. Requests for volunteers were sent throughout the Army and recruiting teams visited units, although the latter were limited to sending a maximum of ten men in order to avoid undue depletion.

In September, Headquarters 1st Parachute Brigade was formed at Hardwick Hall under the command of Brigadier Richard Gale; attached to it was a signals section and No. 1 Air Troop Royal Engineers.

In the meantime, the decision had been taken to disband 11th SAS Battalion and distribute its strength among the four new parachute battalions. After meeting its new commanding officer, Lieutenant Colonel Eric Down, however, Brigadier Gale decided instead that it should be retained and redesignated as 1st Parachute Battalion.

This early formative period was not an easy time for 1st Parachute Brigade, which now comprised the 1st, 2nd and 3rd Parachute Battalions. There were insufficient numbers of good warrant officers and NCOs so that there were occasions when officers in the new units had to make their presence felt in order to enforce discipline. Furthermore, many of the volunteers were unsuitable, either because of their physical inability to meet the exacting demands of the parachute selection course, or due to their disciplinary records leaving much to be desired. Despite such problems, however, the enthusiasm of those volunteering for Airborne Forces helped to overcome many difficulties.

In October 1941, 1st Airlanding Brigade was formed and shortly afterwards was grouped with 1st Parachute Brigade to form the 1st Airborne Division under the command of Major General F.A.M. 'Boy' Browning, who was also appointed Commander Paratroops & Airborne Troops. December of that year witnessed the formation of The Glider Pilot Regiment so that by the end of the year, Airborne Forces were well and truly established in the British Army's order of battle. They did not, however, possess a corporate identity and it was thus decided by the War Office that all parachute battalions and The Glider Pilot Regiment should become part of a new formation designated the Army Air Corps, which was officially formed on 24 February 1942.

Three days later, a second airborne operation took place when on the night of 27/28 February twelve Whitley bombers of No. 51 Squadron RAF dropped a 120-strong force – comprising C Company, 2nd Parachute Battalion, nine sappers of 1st Parachute Squadron Royal Engineers, four signallers and an RAF radar specialist – on the coast of northern France. The target was a German radar post, one of a chain situated along the French coast.

By the end of 1941, the RAF was suffering increasing losses of bombers on raids over Europe due to the efficiency of German radar, which tracked the incoming formations and guided the Luftwaffe's night fighters in to intercept them. British radar experts already possessed a great deal of technical data on the German target acquisition radar, code-named Freya, but were anxious to acquire details of the Würzburg, the narrow-beam radar used by the Luftwaffe to vector in its night fighters for interception.

One of these radar posts, equipped with the Würzburg, had been located by RAF aerial reconnaissance a short distance north of the village of Bruneval, situated 12 miles to the north of Le Havre, and the decision had been taken to mount an operation to seize key components for examination.

After a period of training on Salisbury Plain in Wiltshire, followed by two further periods spent on Loch Fyne in Scotland and on the Dorset coast rehearsing night embarkations in landing craft, a final dress rehearsal was carried out on 23 February 1942. At 2230 hours on the night of 27/28 February, C Company, commanded by Major John Frost, and its attached personnel took off from an airfield at Thruxton in Hampshire.

As the Whitleys crossed the coast, they came under anti-aircraft fire but none were hit and shortly afterwards dropped their sticks, all of whom landed on the DZ safely with the exception of one which was dropped 2 miles short.

Within ten minutes, the entire force had rallied and set off for its objective. Frost's men were divided into five groups designated Nelson, Jellicoe, Hardy, Drake and Rodney. Nelson was tasked with clearing and securing the beach from which the force would be evacuated after completing its mission, while Rodney would take up a position between the site and the likely main enemy approach to block any counter-attack. Jellicoe, Hardy and Drake, under the command of Frost himself, was the assault element which would attack and capture the radar site and a nearby villa housing the Luftwaffe technicians; it would be accompanied by the party of sappers and the RAF radar specialist, Flight Sergeant E.W.F. Cox, whose task it would be to supervise the dismantling of the Würzburg radar.

The small German garrison at the radar site was divided into three elements: the site itself was manned by Luftwaffe technicians, protected by a detachment of guards, bringing the total number there to approximately thirty men. Some 300 yards to the north lay Le Presbytère, a group of buildings surrounded by woods and occupied by more technicians and troops, whose strength was estimated at over 100 men; in Bruneval itself there were a further forty troops.

The attack was launched on a signal from Frost and his men soon overran the radar site, where Flight Sergeant Cox and the sappers swiftly set to work. As they did so, however, the site came under heavy fire from the area of Le Presbytère, but it was not long before the radar had been dismantled and Frost and his men were heading for the beach. Unfortunately it had not been cleared of the enemy so it was not until 0215 hours that all enemy opposition had been overcome and the entire raiding force was ready for evacuation.

Meanwhile, there was no sign of the landing craft and all attempts to establish contact using radio, signal lamp and flares proved fruitless. Frost decided to redeploy his men in positions to defend the embarkation point and had just finished doing so when the landing craft suddenly appeared. The entire force therefore began embarking under fire from the enemy who opened fire on the beach with mortars and threw grenades down from the cliff top. By 0330 hours, Frost and his men were safely out to sea and transferring to a fleet of motor gunboats which took the landing craft in tow and headed for home. It was at this point that Frost learned that the delay in the appearance of the landing craft had been due to the sudden appearance of an enemy destroyer and two E-boats passing less than a mile away; fortunately, the small flotilla of gunboats and landing craft had avoided detection by remaining motionless until the enemy vessels had disappeared into the darkness.

The Bruneval raid had been a huge success: not only had the mission of capturing the Würzburg radar been accomplished, but Frost and his men had provided further proof of the effectiveness of Britain's new Airborne Forces.

Chapter 4

In April 1942, the Airborne Forces Depot & Battle School was formed. Initial selection for parachute training was conducted at Hardwick Hall, near Chesterfield in Derbyshire, with all volunteers, regardless of rank, being subjected to a gruelling two weeks of aptitude tests which included intensive physical tests in the gymnasium and on the assault course, as well as over the surrounding countryside. Organized in small squads, each under an Army Physical Training Corps instructor, they did everything at the double while being observed closely for any sign of weakness. The aim of the selection course was to find those who possessed the high degree of stamina and self-discipline essential in a paratrooper. The number of failures on the course was high, and the fate that all volunteers dreaded was to be 'returned to unit'.

Located beside the depot was the Battle School. Training, including field-firing exercises with live ammunition, was conducted by day and night in the Derwent Valley and on the surrounding moors. It was intensive and tough as from the very start it was appreciated that airborne troops would be required to be capable of fighting and surviving against larger, more heavily armed formations until they linked up with ground forces. Their lack of armour and firepower would have to be counter-balanced by very high standards of physical fitness and personal skill, while each man would be required to possess a very high degree of courage, self-discipline and self-reliance. Exercises, by day and night, frequently culminated in long marches back to barracks and the ability to cover long distances at high speed in full battle order soon became a matter of pride in the newly-formed parachute battalions – 10 miles in two hours, 20 in four and 50 miles in twenty-four.

Those fortunate enough to pass the selection course went on to No. 1 PTS at Ringway where they underwent the two-week parachute course. In the first week, troops underwent ground and synthetic training during which they were instructed in how to exit the aircraft, control their parachutes in the air and land correctly. Fuselages of different aircraft were sited in the hangars and the trainee parachutists learned to jump from all of them, using the correct exit procedure for each.

Other aids included the fan trainer, an apparatus mounted on a platform some 20 to 30 feet above the ground and comprising a drum around which was wound a steel cable, the end being attached to a parachute harness. When a trainee jumped from the platform, his weight caused the drum to revolve; its speed, however, was controlled by two vanes which acted as air brakes and thus the trainee landed with an impact similar to the one he would experience when using a parachute.

Trainees progressed from the fan trainer to a 100-foot high tower, from the top of which protruded a long steel arm. Suspended from this by a cable was a parachute canopy stretched over a large metal hoop. On launching himself from the tower, a trainee found himself hanging below the parachute. Having practised his flight drills and then adopted the correct position for landing, he was released and floated to the ground.

The end of the first week of the parachute course saw trainees carrying out their first two jumps from a cage suspended at a height of 700 feet beneath a barrage balloon. These were followed during the second week by five jumps from a Whitley bomber, initially in sticks of five and ultimately ten. On successful completion of the course, the newly-qualified parachutists received the much-coveted wings to be worn on the right shoulder.

James Hill had volunteered for Airborne Forces, in later years blaming his batman:

> Shortly after Winston Churchill issued his directive for the formation of an airborne force of 5,000 men, my batman, whom I had retained with great difficulty, asked permission to volunteer. I said I would give the matter due consideration and after three days said I would let him go. However, the thought of being looked after in perpetuity by anyone else was too much for me so I also volunteered in order to get him back.

He successfully qualified as a parachutist in the spring of 1942 and in May joined the 1st Parachute Battalion, as Captain Miles Whitelock, the Adjutant of the Battalion at the time, later recalled:

> In the middle of May 1942 the battalion, which was stationed at Bulford on Salisbury Plain, needed a new second-in-command. This would be an important appointment because the current

Commanding Officer, Lieutenant Colonel Eric Down, was due for promotion and thus the new second-in-command would be likely to succeed him. We were informed by Headquarters 1st Airborne Division that two officers would pay us a visit, the object of the exercise being for us to vet the prospective candidate and for him to assess the battalion. Both officers held the rank of Major and both had won the Military Cross – one in Palestine before the war, and the other in France in 1940.

I was invited by the Commanding Officer to meet both of them. It did not take me long to realise that the tall, fit-looking figure of Major James Hill would suit us well and I was able to say so when asked my opinion by the Commanding Officer. It was apparent that James had experienced heavy fighting during the battles in France: he had served on the staff of Lord Gort who had sent him to organize the evacuation of Calais, and he had been one of the last to leave Dunkirk. He was suitably modest about these exploits, but on account of them commanded much respect.

In due course, Hill was appointed as Second-in-Command of the Battalion, which shortly afterwards was briefed to take part in a large raid on the French port of Dieppe, its mission being to attack and destroy the coastal batteries guarding the entrance to the harbour. The Battalion would be operating alongside Canadian troops, as he later recounted:

> The Battalion was chosen to take part with the Canadians and, in order to enable them to recognize British paratroops, a company was sent to train with them one month before the operation was due to take place. To my consternation, however, on its return I found that the Canadians had told my chaps that the target was Dieppe! As far as we were concerned, I was the only person meant to know! Fortunately, however, I have no reason to believe that the German intelligence ever benefited from this leak.

Hill soon became heavily involved in the planning, his energy and attention to detail seemingly inexhaustible. One of the major tasks in planning the operation was the compilation of the aircraft loading schedules which involved listing the contents and positioning the numerous containers of arms, ammunition, rations, medical supplies and a large variety of items of equipment. He excelled at such work and proved tireless in his efforts to ensure that the schedules were completed down to the last detail.

In the event, however, the attack on Dieppe was cancelled due to bad weather. It did take place a month later, by which time the decision had been taken to use commandos instead of paratroops. The operation proved to be a disastrous failure resulting in a high number of casualties.

Following the cancellation of the operation, Lieutenant Colonel Eric Down was promoted to the rank of brigadier and given the task of forming 2nd Parachute Brigade. Hill was promoted to lieutenant colonel and assumed command of 1st Parachute Battalion. In the wake of the cancellation of the Dieppe operation, morale in the Battalion was low. A perceptive man, Hill was well aware of this and decided that the cure lay in a change of scenery combined with a regime of ruthless fitness. Accordingly, the Battalion found itself moving by train to Exmoor where it disembarked at Dulverton, only to be told it was to march to Exford in full battle order. Eventually, following a gruelling march across Exmoor with Hill leading the way, it finally arrived at a tented camp that would be its home for the next four weeks.

The training was conducted without respite but the weather was fine and 1st Parachute Battalion began to recover its morale and esprit de corps, all ranks taking great pride in their physical achievements. At the end of the four weeks, Hill decided that a fitting test of the Battalion would be for it to march the 110 miles back to Bulford in full battle order. No one was spared – not even the medical orderlies, cooks, clerks and other members of the Battalion's administrative element. The march would take two and a half days with the Battalion sleeping rough en route. Many years later, Miles Whitelock's memories of Hill during that march were still vivid:

> We set off early in the morning, James Hill once again at the head of the column. He inspired us all by his physical fitness and enthusiasm. During the regulation ten-minute rest halts every two hours, he would walk back down the column encouraging and exhorting his officers and men – no halting or rest for him. He reminded us that in fluid battle conditions our lives might easily depend on fitness – both mental and physical. Like everyone else, he carried full battle order and slept under a groundsheet. The whole battalion, with the exception of one or two isolated cases, benefited from the experience of this exhausting test of fitness. James was determined to ensure that his battalion was capable of sustained stamina because he had experienced the importance of combating battle fatigue in 1940. He made sure, not least by his own example, that the officers and men under his command were equipped with the

physique and determination necessary to withstand long periods under fire without sleep and on the move. His efforts were appreciated and understood, and in future would stand all who served under him in very good stead.

The summer of 1942 proved to be a fine one and 1st Parachute Battalion's rigorous training programme was interspersed whenever possible with opportunities for sport, with matches and competitions being played against other Army and RAF units. On one occasion the members of the Battalion's cricket team, accompanied by a number of spectators including the Commanding Officer and members of the divisional staff, arrived at Winterbourne Gunner to play the Royal Artillery Training Centre. To their dismay, they observed that the Gunners' captain was wearing an England cricket overseas touring team blazer; on enquiring as to his identity, their morale sank even lower when they learned that he was none other than Maurice Nicholls of Essex and England – indeed the England opening fast bowler! The first innings saw 1st Parachute Battalion bowled out for under twenty while Winterbourne Gunner made 150 for six and then declared. During the second innings, however, Nicholls was kind enough to take a rest and thus the Battalion was able to play out time and so avoid an innings defeat.

In August, another important milestone was reached in the creation of British airborne forces with the formation on 1 August 1942 of The Parachute Regiment; this became the parent entity for the new parachute battalions, comprising part of the Army Air Corps along with The Glider Pilot Regiment.

At the end of August, a plan was conceived by Headquarters Combined Operations for an attack on the island of Ushant, situated off the coast of Brittany, at the mouth of the English Channel. It possessed considerable strategic importance as not only did it command the entrance to important approaches, and in particular to the port of Brest, but was also the command centre and control point for German U-boat operations in the North Atlantic. Intelligence reports indicated that it was well defended and, even more importantly, that there was a technically advanced radar station sited on it. It was thus decided to mount an airborne operation to attack the island and seize the radar.

The task was given to 1st Parachute Battalion and accordingly Hill and his adjutant were summoned to London where they reported to Headquarters Combined Operations. Such was the secrecy surrounding the operation that both men were in complete ignorance of the reason for their summons as Captain Miles Whitelock later recalled:

> We were shown into a room in which a long table displayed an intricate model of the island. Maps and charts lined the walls and it was not long before a Royal Navy captain arrived to 'put us in the picture'. Very attractive and specially trained WRNS and WAAF secretaries and typists produced typed drafts of orders and security was impressed on us at all times: a code word and the correct response to it was issued to us – no one could enter the room or talk about the operation without giving it. There was much to think about and plan. As far as I can recall, there were to be three phases to the operation: Phase 1 – the assault; Phase 2 – the occupation of the radar station, removal of the radar equipment and destruction of the site; and Phase 3 – withdrawal and evacuation.
>
> Minute details of aircraft, landing schedules, drop times, support plans, pick-up arrangements – all these were prepared and gradually the plan for the raid took shape. We were summoned to the office of the Chief of Combined Operations, Admiral Lord Louis Mountbatten himself. He reviewed our plans and personally overruled objections from his own naval chief-of-staff who was somewhat naturally anxious about the potential danger of provoking an all-out sea battle at a time when the Royal Navy's resources were fully stretched in countering the U-boat menace as well as conducting operations in the Middle and Far East.
>
> James Hill was in his element, his keen eye for detail and inspiring personality made an impression on all whom he met, particularly when dealing with the Royal Navy. During the three days we were at Combined Operations, away from the day-to-day running of the Battalion, I came to know him well. It became clear to me that I had the good fortune to be closely associated with an exceptional character. I recall vividly an occasion when he took me out to dinner at Pruniers Restaurant in St James Street; at that time, even in wartime, an excellent fish restaurant. Madame Prunier herself received us and welcomed James as an obviously valued customer.
>
> Committed to the pursuit of excellence, his clarity of thought, utter determination and professionalism became more evident every day. He was ambitious, selfless, understanding and compassionate. These characteristics blended with his steely resolve to succeed and to play his own part in beating the enemy. I think I realised, at the

time, that I was dealing with someone who, if spared, would be likely to make a name for himself. How right that judgement proved to be!

Hill and Whitelock returned to Bulford, taking with them Top Secret orders for the operation and being followed in due course by two young Royal Navy sub lieutenants who had just completed a special three-jump course at No. 1 PTS. They were attached to Battalion Headquarters and would drop with the Battalion to assist in organizing its evacuation by landing craft and destroyer. With the date of operation fast approaching, excitement mounted as the Battalion moved to an airfield at Hurn, near Bournemouth, where it made its final preparations.

At the last minute, however, the weather intervened and the operation was cancelled, as Hill later recalled:

> We were literally in our aircraft, lined up on the runway of Hurn airfield, ready for take-off when the operation was cancelled. It transpired that the reason for this was that the Flying Fortresses tasked with bombing the German fighter airfields covering the Cherbourg Peninsula had entered a weather front and became lost. They in turn were covered by a new squadron of our latest high altitude Spitfires who had been ordered to tail the Fortresses. When lost, the Fortresses had the necessary fuel to return home but the Spitfires did not and I understand they landed all over France! Although the pilots knew nothing of our operation, it was feared that security might have been compromised. You can well imagine the 'fed-upness' and frustration following this let-down.

The cancellation of the Ushant operation inevitably had a major effect on morale but once again Hill's encouragement and enthusiasm did much to counteract this considerable blow to his Battalion. In any case, he and his men did not have to wait long before another opportunity arose to test their resolve and courage.

During September, the decision was taken to include an airborne unit in the Allied forces that would take part in the forthcoming campaign against Axis forces in North Africa. The unit initially allotted was American: the 2nd Battalion 503rd Parachute Infantry Regiment which had arrived in Britain in mid-June 1942 and had been placed under command of 1st Airborne Division. Major General 'Boy' Browning, however, successfully argued that a single battalion would prove insufficient for the task and consequently 1st Parachute Brigade was detailed, in addition to the 2nd/503rd, being placed under command of the Supreme Allied

Commander, General Dwight D. Eisenhower. He in turn allocated it to First British Army under Lieutenant General Sir Kenneth Anderson. However, 1st Parachute Brigade was not up to full strength nor fully equipped to war scales, and thus men and equipment had to be taken from 2nd Parachute Brigade and other units within 1st Airborne Division.

Prior to their departure from Britain, however, the men of 1st Parachute Brigade had to learn to jump from the C-47 transports of the US Army Air Force's (USAAF) No. 60 Troop Carrier Group, which had arrived in Britain at the end of September, as the RAF was unable to spare any aircraft for airborne operations in North Africa. Until now, all British parachutists had been accustomed to jumping from converted bombers, making their exits through apertures in the floors of the aircraft fuselages. The C-47, however, was equipped with a door in its port side through which parachutists or containers were despatched.

The initial jump from the C-47 was carried out by 250 men of 3rd Parachute Battalion on 9 October. Tragically, four of them were killed during the drop and an immediate investigation revealed that the static line on the British 'X' Type parachute was too short for use with the C-47, causing two of the canopies to become entangled with the aircraft's tail wheel. It was found that raising the tail of the aircraft during a drop eliminated the risk of this happening again.

The C-47s returned to Salisbury Plain and Headquarters 1st Airborne Division suggested that the next jump might be carried out by 1st Parachute Battalion, to be watched by 2nd and 3rd Parachute Battalions and the rest of the Division. As Captain Miles Whitelock later recalled: 'James Hill leaped at the chance and responded by saying that not only would the Battalion be delighted to do so but also that he would lead the jump with his adjutant as No. 2 in the stick.'

The day of the jump dawned bright and clear as 1st Parachute Battalion marched from Bulford to the airfield at Upavon. Emplaning aboard the C-47s, it dropped successfully without experiencing any problems or injuries. Thus faith was restored in the C-47 which went on to become one of the workhorses of British airborne forces.

In early October, the Battalion received a warning order to prepare for overseas service, and excitement mounted once more as tropical clothing and equipment were issued. Finally, all ranks were given forty-eight hours' embarkation leave. There was no indication as to the Battalion's destination and inevitably there was much speculation, the Middle East, Carpathian Mountains, Turkey and North Africa being among those areas rumoured to be where the Battalion was to be despatched.

Chapter 5

During the latter part of October 1942, 1st Parachute Brigade, less Battalion Headquarters, two rifle companies and mortar platoon of 3rd Parachute Battalion, left its bases on Salisbury Plain and entrained at Amesbury for Greenock in Scotland. On 29 October, it sailed for an unknown destination with 1st Parachute Battalion embarked aboard the troopship *Arundel Castle*, as James Hill later recalled:

> We boarded on the Clyde and set sail in convoy for Algiers. I was then permitted to brief the Battalion on its role in the North African landings: in essence, we were to take off from Maison Blanche airfield at Algiers and fly some 450 miles to capture an airfield at El Aouina in Tunisia. We had all the necessary maps and aerial photographs to enable us to plan and prepare for the task.

Conditions on the ship were cramped and exercise space very limited. Nevertheless, it was essential that physical fitness was maintained at a very high level so much of each day was devoted to physical training.

The *Arundel Castle* was part of a large, very heavily protected convoy of troop ships and freighters. At that time, all convoys to the Middle East and North Africa were routed far out into the Atlantic to keep them well away from the French, Spanish and Portuguese coastline. This convoy was no different and sailed south and west, those aboard the troopships still in complete ignorance of their final destination as they kept a constant watch for U-boats and enemy aircraft, although fortunately none appeared. Gradually, the convoy's course took a more easterly direction and soon it passed through the Straits of Gibraltar into the no less dangerous waters of the Mediterranean. On 13 November it reached North Africa and Algeria where 1st Parachute Brigade disembarked at Algiers.

The commander of First British Army, Lieutenant General Sir Kenneth Anderson, had originally intended to mount an airborne operation to seize a key road junction at Beja and the El Aouina airfield at Tunis – 1st Parachute Battalion had been allotted these tasks but by the time 1st

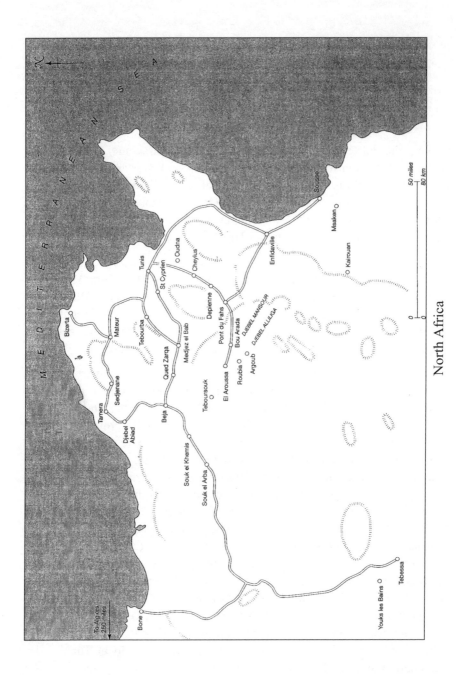

North Africa

Parachute Brigade arrived at Algiers there were reports of some 10,000 German troops being flown in to Tunis. It was thus decided that the Battalion, supported by detachments of 1st Parachute Squadron RE and 16th Parachute Field Ambulance, would be dropped at Souk el Arba with the tasks of seizing the crossroads there, establishing contact with French forces stationed at Beja 43 miles to the north-east, and conducting harassing operations to the east.

Initially, 1st Parachute Battalion found itself bivouacked in the Algiers Botanical Gardens from where a strong reconnaissance patrol was despatched by Hill to reconnoitre an airfield situated some 5 miles inland at Maison Blanche and held by French troops. At this juncture, following the Allied landings further west at Oran that had been opposed by the French, there was some uncertainty as to whether the French forces in Algeria were pro-Allied or pro-Vichy in their sympathies. In the event, the patrol returned to report that the French at Maison Blanche seemed cooperative and so on the following morning 1st Parachute Battalion left the botanical gardens and marched to the airfield where, over the next two days, while awaiting the arrival of its transport aircraft, it prepared itself for the drop at Souk el Arba.

Not least among the problems facing the Battalion in preparing for the operation was insufficient time. Added to that was the lack of transport because 1st Parachute Brigade had not been permitted to bring any of its own vehicles, owing to the limited amount of shipping space available. This hampered the movement of equipment unloaded from the ships in Algiers harbour to Maison Blanche airfield where many of the stores did not appear until the afternoon of 14 November. These had to be broken down and packed into containers, while parachutes had to be unpacked from the crates in which they had been shipped, and then inspected by the parachute packing section of the RAF's No. 38 Wing attached to 1st Parachute Brigade.

Souk el Arba was a small village in the mountainous country to the west of Tunis. The location of a suitable drop zone (DZ) had not been confirmed at that juncture but the French had assured Hill that one could easily be identified from the leading aircraft. 1st Parachute Battalion was to be flown in C-47s of the No. 64 Troop Carrier Group of the USAAF's 51st Troop Carrier Wing. There were, however, only thirty-two aircraft and thus only one of Hill's rifle companies could be carried in the first lift. Added to these shortcomings was the absence of any charts of the area, other than French quarter-inch-to-the-mile maps designed for use by motorists, which made it highly unlikely that the aircrews would be able to locate the DZs. Consequently, Hill decided to travel in the cockpit of the leading aircraft flown by the commander of the 51st Troop Carrier Wing and with him select the most suitable DZ in the area of the objective. Having done so, he would then retire to the rear of the aircraft and jump with the other members of his stick.

The aircraft duly arrived and, at dawn on 13 November, took off for Souk el Arba. Hill's thirty-strong group was in the leading aircraft, as Captain Miles Whitelock later described:

> We flew low eastwards over the sea for about one and a half hours; through the side windows we could see our escort of four Lightning fighters criss-crossing the sky above us. I could not but help wonder what a flight of determined Messerschmitts would do if they caught this fat prize. Our Dakotas were unarmed and we would be sitting ducks. I might add that fifteen other ranks, who had been deliberately left behind as a rear party, were so disappointed that at the last minute they rushed across the tarmac and were hauled aboard by their comrades. Such was their spirit!

The aircraft flew on and at a point approximately 200 miles off the coast turned inland. At this juncture, however, weather conditions deteriorated markedly and the cloud base descended to a point where the pilot of the leading aircraft advised Hill that it would be too dangerous to attempt to fly through the mountainous terrain ahead. Bitterly disappointed, the Battalion turned back and returned to its base, much to the displeasure of Lieutenant General Anderson, as Hill later recalled:

> The Army commander was not pleased. He knew nothing about paratroops and did not much like us. I was thus told that the next time we set sail, if cloud intervened we were to drop as near the enemy as possible. We decided in that eventuality we would drop on the beach some 50 miles to the north of our flight line.

That night Maison Blanche was bombed by enemy aircraft, but suffered little damage. The following morning, 16 November, dawned bright and clear; at 1100 hours 1st Parachute Battalion took off for Souk el Arba once more and followed the same route, but its mission had now been changed: it was to seize the town of Beja, persuade the French garrison there to join the Allied cause, and conduct probing and harassing operations.

Weather conditions were good as the C-47s flew over the mountains and Hill was soon able to pick out a suitable DZ. In each of the aircraft, men stood up and checked each other's static lines, waiting as the aircraft approached the DZ. Red and green lights went on in quick succession and then each stick was piling out of the door of its aircraft as 1st Parachute Battalion carried out the first ever battalion operational drop in the history of British airborne forces.

The drop was unopposed but there were a small number of casualties, with one fatality, Private Webster, who was strangled by one of his parachute's rigging lines that somehow became wound around his neck. Among those injured were Major Sir Richard des Voeux, a liaison officer accompanying the Battalion, who suffered a broken leg on landing, and a medical officer, Captain Charles Robb, in command of the detachment of 16th Parachute Field Ambulance, who sprained an ankle. In addition, four men were slightly wounded by an accidental discharge from a Sten gun. An additional problem was the local Arabs who attempted to spirit away some of the equipment containers.

No sooner had the drop taken place than a patrol was despatched into Souk el Arba, a Union Jack waved from the roof of the local *mairie* soon indicating that the village was clear. Shortly afterwards, however, a French officer appeared, as Captain Miles Whitelock later related:

> I think he was an officer in the Spahis or colonial troops. He reassured us that the French were with us but suggested that the sooner we rolled up and concealed our parachutes the better because German reconnaissance aircraft were active in the area. He also informed us that he thought we should push on to Beja without delay, and that there were some local buses, powered by charcoal, nearby which could be commandeered. We found these and at around 1700 hours set off eastwards into the mountains. At about 2100 hours, by which time it was dark, we halted about a mile short of the town and camped out on the hillside. It was wet and miserably cold.
>
> The Commanding Officer decided that he would attempt to contact the commander of the French forces in the area who numbered some 3,000, and so, accompanied by myself and a handful of our men, he set off into the town to find him. This was easily achieved and we bearded the Frenchman, a colonel named Bergerou, in his own headquarters. At the outset, he regarded us with suspicion and at one point during the conversation, which was conducted in French and English, I felt we might be taken prisoner. Eventually, however, we convinced him we meant business and promised to parade our entire force through Beja the next day so that he could

judge its strength for himself. This we did, after hitting upon the ruse of marching through the town wearing steel helmets and then doing so again attired in our maroon berets, thus giving the impression that we were twice our actual strength. It seemed to work because from then on the French were cooperative.

Beja, an important road and rail junction, was now in the hands of 1st Parachute Battalion, which began probing eastwards towards Mateur and Tunis, and to the south in the direction of Medjez el Bab. At this juncture, Hill received accurate intelligence that the Germans were conducting a rapid build-up of their forces in Tunisia. Unbeknownst to the Allies, German agents in Spain had earlier reported the large convoy, of which the *Arundel Castle* had been part, sailing through the Straits of Gibraltar; with American landings already taking place at Oran, the Germans had swiftly deduced that Tunisia would be next and had despatched forces to counter the Allied threat. Among Axis forces despatched from France, Greece, Sicily and Germany were *fallschirmjäger* units of the *Luftwaffen-Jäger-Brigade.*

Hill arranged with Colonel Bergerou for one of his companies to take over the French positions covering Beja. Soon afterwards, however, he learned that the Germans were in the habit of sending a patrol of eight armoured cars to the railway station at the village of Sidi N'Sir, situated some 20 miles from Beja and occupied by a French company of Senegalese infantry. Arriving each morning around 1000 hours, the Germans would exchange pleasantries with the French before returning to their base on the coast at Bizerta.

Hill decided to show the Germans that they were not invincible, while also winning over the French even further by ambushing the patrol. The following day, having persuaded Colonel Bergerou to permit him to send a company through the French lines to Sidi N'Sir, he despatched S Company, commanded by Major Peter Cleasby-Thompson, and a small party of sappers to make contact with the French company commander at Sidi N'Sir. As S Company moved out in the commandeered charabancs, the rest of the Battalion moved into Beja and took over the positions covering the roads from Sidi N'Sir to Medjez el Bab. Hill established his Battalion Headquarters in the local slaughter house which, situated at the eastern edge of the town, gave good views of the surrounding countryside, while the detachment of 16th Parachute Field Ambulance established itself in the town's hospital.

During this period, the Battalion was attacked by a force of Ju-87 Stuka dive-bombers which caused considerable damage to the town. Looting by local Arabs ensued, being brought to a halt when two of their number were arrested and, on the orders of the French mayor, summarily executed, their bodies being left where they fell as a warning against any further looting.

In the meantime, Hill continued to converse with the French from whom he discovered that the enemy had positioned a force of some 300 men along the river line to the east of Medjez el Bab but had made no attempt to cross the river, having made it clear to the French that they would not do so unless fired upon first. By this time, the spearhead element of First British Army had linked up with 1st Parachute Battalion in the form of Blade Force. Commanded by Lieutenant Colonel Richard Hull of the 17th/21st Lancers, this was a 2,600-strong force comprising elements of 6th Armoured Division, including Hull's regiment equipped with Valentine tanks, a squadron of Daimler armoured cars of the Derbyshire Yeomanry, a motorized company of the 10th Battalion The Rifle Brigade, a battery of 25-pounders of 12th Regiment RHA (HAC), a battery of 72nd Anti-Tank Regiment RA equipped with 6-pounder anti-tank guns, a troop of Bofors 40mm anti-aircraft guns and a troop of sappers.

Having reviewed the situation with the commander of Blade Force, Hill despatched No. 7 Platoon, commanded by Lieutenant Stanley Wandless, and the Derbyshire Yeomanry squadron to counter any attempt by the enemy to cross the river.

In the meantime, Major Cleasby-Thompson and S Company duly arrived at Sidi N'Sir, where they received a warm welcome from the French, and lay up for the night before deploying into ambush positions the following morning. The German patrol, comprising four large armoured cars and four smaller reconnaissance vehicles, duly appeared on time, driving through the ambush area and on towards Sidi N'Sir. S Company and its sappers then proceeded to lay a necklace of No. 75 Hawkins anti-tank grenades across the road before settling down to await the Germans' return.

On one side of the road was a steep slope; on the other was a large bog. Cleasby-Thompson sited a 3-inch mortar on a nearby hill and two Bren light machine guns in the bog, while positioning his main ambush group on the hillside some 80 yards from the road. Lieutenants Philip Mellor and Arthur Kellas, equipped with a number of Gammon bombs, were hidden in a ditch at the side of the road.

S Company did not have long to wait. The enemy convoy reappeared, Cleasby-Thompson and his men holding their fire until the grenades were detonated. As the last vehicle entered the killing area, a second necklace of Hawkins grenades was pulled on to the road to prevent any attempt at escape by vehicles reversing out of the ambush. The leading armoured car, however, passed over the first necklace without rolling over any of the grenades and disappeared from sight around the corner. The second was not so fortunate and detonated a grenade, swerving over to one side and blocking the road. S Company opened fire immediately, two of the reconnaissance vehicles being destroyed and their crews killed by grenades thrown by Lieutenants Mellor and Kellas in the ditch. Just then the leading armoured car reappeared but was immediately disabled by a Hawkins grenade. Meanwhile, S Company's 3-inch mortar was bringing down fire on the tail of the column, forcing the remaining vehicles to move forward into the centre of the killing area. All four armoured cars were destroyed and their crews captured by the time the remainder of the enemy surrendered.

Casualties among S Company were light; among them were Lieutenant Kellas, who had been wounded in the eye, and Company Sergeant Major Steadman. Loading the wounded on to the two reconnaissance vehicles that were still intact, the company withdrew to Sidi N'Sir before returning to Beja.

Keen to demonstrate further to the French and local population that the Germans were far from invincible, Hill gave orders for the two vehicles and prisoners to be driven around Beja. S Company's action did much to convince the French in the area to rally to the cause, not least because it gave rise to the belief that the British possessed a secret anti-tank weapon capable of destroying German armour.

While S Company had been engaged in its successful ambush, further casualties had been suffered elsewhere. A fighting patrol commanded by Lieutenant Mickey Stewart had been sent out to probe in the direction of Medjez el Bab, but it encountered some enemy and in the ensuing action Stewart and three of his men were killed.

In the early hours of the following morning, 20 November, the enemy attacked the French forces at Medjez el Bab. The previous day, at a meeting with the commander of Vichy French forces in Tunisia, General Barré, the Germans had insisted that they be permitted to assume control of the bridge there. Barré, who had been warned by Hill that any attempt by the Germans to cross the bridge would meet strong opposition from 1st Parachute Battalion, had rejected this demand.

In the meantime, 1st Parachute Battalion had been joined by Blade Force. Having reviewed the situation with Lieutenant Colonel Hull, James Hill had reinforced Lieutenant Wandless's No. 7 Platoon by despatching R Company, under Major Josh Conron, to provide further support for the French. Departing at 1300 hours, the Company was attacked en route to the bridge by enemy aircraft, two of its vehicles being wrecked and two men severely wounded. On its arrival at the bridge, Major Conron swiftly deployed some of the company in positions to protect a battery of French 75mm guns sited in the anti-tank role, and the remainder of his men around the village itself.

In the meantime, Hill had decided to commit the whole of his Battalion and set off for Medjez el Bab. The Battalion's Second-in-Command, Major Alastair Pearson, meanwhile, embussed the remainder of the Battalion and headed for Oued Zarga where he was met by Hill who informed him that the Germans had crossed the river in strength at several locations and therefore it was no longer possible to reach Medjez el Bab. Hill ordered Pearson to mount S and T Companies on the backs of the tanks and armoured cars of the 17th/21st Lancers and Derbyshire Yeomanry, and take them 10 miles down the Beja road. He himself then set about commandeering all available transport to extricate R Company and No. 7 Platoon.

The Germans had launched their attack at 0100 hours but met stiff resistance. Two of their tanks had been destroyed in the initial phase of the assault, exploding and setting fire to some soft-skinned vehicles carrying fuel. The fighting had then died away, only to flare up again when R Company and No. 7 Platoon launched a counter-attack during which they encountered *fallschirmjäger* of the 2nd Battalion FJR-5. The initial breakthrough by the Germans failed as the French launched equally determined counter-attacks supported by artillery and encouraged by the presence of R Company and No. 7 Platoon. Although the French suffered heavy casualties, the enemy were beaten off and subsequent aggressive patrolling by Major Conron and his men helped to prevent any further attempts by the Germans to advance westwards.

In due course, Hill appeared with his commandeered transport and withdrew R Company and No. 7 Platoon to Beja where they rejoined the rest of 1st Parachute Battalion, whose positions there were taken over by a battalion of The Northamptonshire Regiment, while Hill and his men took a day's well-earned rest.

The following day, Hill received a report from the French that an enemy armoured column was advancing west of Sidi N'Sir and immediately despatched S Company in support, while also sending R Company to reinforce the French holding the bridge at Oued Zarga; in the meantime, a battalion of The East Surrey Regiment moved up to Beja to reinforce the Northamptons. S Company arrived at Sidi N'Sir to find that the French had been attacked that morning by Italian lorried infantry supported by tanks. This attack, however, had been beaten off, with all the tanks being destroyed and the enemy infantry suffering heavy losses.

It was noticeable that by this time the French were fighting with increased confidence and commitment. This was due in no small measure to Hill who had achieved in no uncertain terms the two objectives given to him at the outset: to harass the enemy at every opportunity, and to bring in the French forces on the Allied side.

Two days later, Battalion Headquarters received a visit from the commander of 78th Infantry Division, Major General Vivian Evelegh, who informed Hill that he was planning to mount an attack on Medjez el Bab the following day. Nevertheless, he gave permission for 1st Parachute Battalion to mount a night attack in the early hours of the following morning on a small hill called Gué situated 9 miles to the south-east of Sidi N'Sir where, according to intelligence just received by Hill, a 300-strong force of Italians, supported by tanks, was harboured up at the base of the feature.

Accordingly, at 1800 hours that evening, the Battalion moved along the valley to Sidi N'Sir and its small railway station, where it was joined by a thirty-strong detachment of the French Senegalese infantry who were to assist in carrying the ammunition for the Battalion's 3-inch mortars. At approximately 2230 hours, S and T Companies, accompanied by Battalion Headquarters, the Mortar Platoon and the French company, thereafter headed across country along a narrow track which followed the railway line. On either side of the track the mountainous terrain was rocky and difficult as the Adjutant, Captain Miles Whitelock, later described:

> We could only march in single file. Two scouts, in the form of the Commanding Officer's and my batmen, were sent on about 100 yards ahead. We followed with the rest of the Battalion, the Senegalese and the sappers streaming along behind us. It was a moonlit night and it was absolutely essential that, in order to achieve complete surprise, that we were as quiet as possible. We crept along the valley, weapons at the ready. The only sound was the muffled sound of our feet and the howling and barking of the dogs in the tiny Arab settlements on the hillsides.

After about two hours, we halted at a high point from where, across a small flat piece of terrain, we could just discern in the moonlight the hulls of armoured vehicles on a lightly wooded hillside. There was a small river running across the bottom of this small flat area, and there were some trees and undergrowth concealing a small Arab settlement of mud huts. Shortly afterwards we pressed on, leaving R Company in reserve with the Mortar Platoon which began to set up its baseline position from which it would bring down supporting fire.

The plan was that one platoon from T Company and a composite platoon formed from members of Battalion Headquarters, under the command of Captain Vic Coxen and Lieutenant Bob Lloyd, attacked from the west, while another platoon of T Company did likewise from the south. Meanwhile two platoons of S Company, together with Hill and his tactical headquarters, would mount an assault from the east. The remaining S Company platoon was given the task of attacking some anti-aircraft guns positioned on the high ground north-west of the main position. R Company would remain in reserve until required while the Mortar Platoon, under the control of the Second-in-Command, Major Alastair Pearson, would bring down a concentration of fire of high explosive from the bridge area south of the river, while the French Senegalese infantry company, having completed its task of bringing up the mortar ammunition, withdrew into reserve. Meanwhile, a twenty-seven-strong detachment of sappers of 1st Parachute Squadron RE would move round Gué and mine the road to the rear of the objective to hinder any attempt at withdrawal or reinforcement by the enemy.

Slowly and silently, Hill and his assault force worked their way down to the river, forded it and moved forward into the undergrowth beyond. By this time the enemy tanks were above them but Hill and his men remained unobserved and so far appeared to have gained the vital element of surprise. Advancing through the undergrowth, they succeeded in reaching the top of the feature and the centre of the enemy position, creeping in amongst a number of vehicles.

H-Hour had been set for 0300 hours, but suddenly, fifteen minutes beforehand, there were three loud explosions. There was pandemonium as the enemy, a mixed force of Italians and Germans, opened fire in the darkness as 1st Parachute Battalion's assault groups immediately launched their attacks. Hill himself was in close proximity to the enemy as he later related:

I soon realised that the enemy were firing one-in-seven tracer from the hill just above my battalion headquarters. After four minutes or so I could not stick it any longer so took three good chaps and climbed up to see what the form was – only to find three light tanks dug into the side of the hill, firing apparently at random. On close inspection in the moonlight, I saw they had small peepholes let into the side.

I put the barrel of my .38 revolver through one of the holes and pulled the trigger. The bullet went whanging round inside, whereupon the turret hatch shot open and some Italians leaped out shouting, 'Italiano! Italiano!' The same thing happened with the second tank – this was far too good to be true! However, when I went to try the same procedure on the third tank the peephole was shut so I banged on the turret with the thumbstick I always carried. This time, when the turret shot open, a great big German came out. I sensed he had a weapon and as he jumped down, he shot me through the chest, neck and shoulder. He was a brave man.

The German paid dearly for his courage because he was immediately mown down by a burst of fire from one of Hill's men nearby.

Knocked unconscious, Hill apparently had an out-of-body experience and found himself looking down at three bodies on the ground:

I recognised the centre one as myself, the one on the left was the German and there was another on the right. In due course, on coming to, I lifted myself on to my elbows and sure enough there was the German and a third body on my right. I then had what can only be termed a flash: 'You need never be afraid to die.' This was a great comfort as I had never anticipated I would live; indeed, quite frankly, it was a comfort for the remaining years of the war.

Just prior to Hill being wounded, Captain Miles Whitelock had been sent to investigate the source of the three explosions that had initiated the attack prematurely. On reaching the bottom of the hill, he discovered that one of the sappers' primed Hawkins anti-tank grenades, which were being carried in sandbags, had exploded and triggered the remainder, killing most of the sapper detachment. Making his way back to the top of the feature to report what had happened, Whitelock ran into some of the fierce close-quarter fighting and was struck down by a grenade exploding at his feet, suffering severe wounds to his face, head and limbs.

As Hill and Whitelock lay seriously wounded, the battle continued to rage fiercely around them for just under two hours before 1st Parachute Battalion finally overran the enemy position. The Battalion's casualties, in addition to Hill and Whitelock, numbered three men killed (two of them Hill's and Whitelock's batmen) and three wounded, in addition to eighteen members of the sapper detachment killed when their Hawkins grenades exploded. Enemy casualties were heavy, with a large number of Germans and Italians seriously wounded.

At this juncture the Battalion's medical officer, Captain Michael Haggie, and his team of medical orderlies appeared on the scene and began treating the wounded. Hill then handed over command of the Battalion to Major Alastair Pearson before he and Whitelock were carried off the objective and down the hill to the railway line and the Regimental Aid Post. Shortly afterwards, they were laid side by side on a railway truck on which they were pushed by a team of Senegalese infantrymen and medical orderlies towards Beja. Meanwhile, 1st Parachute Battalion set about clearing the objective of any remaining enemy before abandoning it, with T Company covering the withdrawal.

The journey back to Beja was not without incident for Hill and Whitelock as at one point the truck and its pushers were strafed by enemy aircraft, the pushers diving for cover and leaving the two semi-conscious officers helplessly exposed to a hail of fire which mercifully they survived unscathed. Thereafter, Beja was eventually reached without further incident, and Hill and Whitelock were taken to the 16th Parachute Field Ambulance field dressing station where Captain Charles Robb carried out emergency surgery.

The following day, the Germans exacted their revenge for the attack on Gué by launching a series of bombing raids by Stukas on the town. These inflicted an enormous amount of damage and a large number of casualties among the civilian population. Captain Charles Robb was among those wounded but continued to treat the injured, performing hundreds of operations completely undeterred.

Following surgery, Hill and Whitelock were accommodated in the town's school where fortunately they escaped further injury, remaining in Beja for three or four days before being evacuated by road to a convent at Souk el Arba. The combination of the marvellous treatment given to them by the nuns, good food and rest in comfortable beds resulted in a marked improvement in their condition by the time they were moved to a military hospital which was being established at Bone. The journey by train to

Bone, however, proved to be a nightmare as Whitelock later recalled:

> Our travels on the push truck on the Mateur railway were nothing compared to that in the hospital train which took us from Souk el Arba to Bone. The Commanding Officer and I were laid out opposite each other across the carriage.
>
> Unfortunately, civilian wounded were also travelling on the train and one gentleman of mixed origin decided to perch himself on the top bunk above the Colonel. He then started to spray himself with foul-smelling scent, which of course soon covered the Colonel in the lower bunk. We were not amused!
>
> In due course, we arrived at Bone. Initially, the hospital was in some kind of building and the Commanding Officer and I were accommodated together in a small room with a number of others. He was allotted a bed and very kindly gave me, who was still laid out on a most uncomfortable stretcher, a sorbo rubber cushion or pillow. I have no idea where he acquired such a luxury which up to that time he had been able to retain, but he gave it up for me – a gesture of comfort and concern which I never forgot.

Hill and Whitelock were subsequently moved to another hospital in Algiers, the latter remaining there for a long sojourn before being evacuated back to Britain by hospital ship. It was during his time in Algiers that Hill, still hospitalized, was awarded the Légion d'Honneur by the French, as he later remembered with some amusement:

> I was lying in bed, rather badly winged, in a sunny room in the Algiers general hospital when suddenly in came a sister with a team of ladies. I was given the equivalent of a new pyjama top and top sheet, and the room was dusted throughout, and then they shot out. A few minutes later, I heard the sound of marching feet approaching down the passage. The door was thrown open and in was ushered General Giraud who had recently arrived by submarine to take over the duties of Commander-in-Chief of French forces in North Africa from Admiral Darlan. He was accompanied by his ADC and a number of flunkies, all highly bemedalled. He bussed me on both cheeks, then summoned his ADC, a Capitaine Bazaine, and removed the poor fellow's Légion d'Honneur which he pinned on my pyjamas. After salutes all round, in which I could not very well participate, the entourage turned about and marched out.

In early January 1943, Hill discharged himself from hospital and made his way back to 1st Parachute Battalion which, following the action at Gué, had moved to a new location 10 miles south of Mateur from which it had carried out a programme of vigorous patrolling for the next ten days before withdrawing to Algiers, where it went into reserve. On his return, Hill found that a new Commanding Officer had arrived in the person of Lieutenant Colonel G.P. Gofton-Salmond, replacing Major Alastair Pearson who, at 27 years of age was considered too young to command a battalion. Hill consulted the commander of 1st Parachute Brigade, Brigadier Ted Flavell, who agreed that it would be a travesty for Pearson, who had led the Battalion with great ability and distinction during Hill's absence, to be removed from command. The problem of Lieutenant Colonel Gofton-Salmond was solved by 1st Parachute Battalion's medical officer, Captain Michael Haggie, who declared him medically unfit for active duty on the grounds that he suffered from severe piles. Major Alastair Pearson was subsequently promoted and remained in command of the Battalion.

In December 1942, Hill was flown home to Britain to recover further from his wounds. His performance while commanding 1st Parachute Battalion in North Africa is perhaps summed up best by Lieutenant Doug Charlton, who served under him throughout that campaign:

> Throughout his short command of 1st Parachute Battalion, James Hill was gifted in kindling and holding the confidence of the men he led. In both training and action, his mind was always active and acute, his ideas clear, decisive and expressed with precision and brevity. In the early battles in North Africa, he showed a remarkable presence of mind, a flexibility in responding to unexpected events and an unshakeable firmness born out of sheer resolution and belief. He was a man of clear vision, ingrained leadership and humility, with an unshakeable Christian faith. He showed us how to combine the very heights of courage with a depth of compassion which is, and always has been, the stamp that is the noblest and best in the British parachute soldier.
>
> It was a sad loss to the battalion when he was seriously wounded at Gué Hill in Tunisia, but he left us with an indelible memory of a truly combative and decisive leader of determined fighting men.

Chapter 6

In early 1942, due to the insufficient number of volunteers successfully qualifying as parachutists, the War Office had decided that further parachute units would be formed by converting infantry battalions to the role. Among the first of these were the 7th Battalion The Queen's Own Cameron Highlanders and 10th Battalion The Royal Welch Fusiliers, which were redesignated the 5th (Scottish) and 6th (Royal Welch) Parachute Battalions, both of which were incorporated into 2nd Parachute Brigade.

In November 1942, during the absence of 1st Parachute Brigade on operations in North Africa, two further formations had been added to the order of battle of Airborne Forces: 3rd and 4th Parachute Brigades commanded by Brigadiers Gerald Lathbury and John Hackett respectively. 3rd Parachute Brigade would be raised in Britain and incorporate the 7th (Light Infantry), 8th (Midland) and 9th (Eastern & Home Counties) Parachute Battalions to be formed from the 10th Battalion The Somerset Light Infantry, 13th Battalion The Royal Warwickshire Regiment and the 10th Battalion The Essex Regiment respectively.

On 11 February 1943, while still recuperating from his wounds, James Hill was awarded the Distinguished Service Order (DSO) for his 'inspiring leadership and undaunted courage' while commanding 1st Parachute Battalion on operations in North Africa. At the same time, he was given command of 9th Parachute Battalion, which was in the process of forming. Although physically still not completely fit, he immediately made a great impression on all ranks of the Battalion as Captain Cliff Norbury, the Battalion's Intelligence Officer, later recalled:

> He moved everywhere at great speed and very quickly was christened 'Speedy' Hill, soon establishing himself and becoming respected and loved by us all – officers and other ranks. When he thought he was fit again, he asked our Medical Officer, Teddy Church, to upgrade him but Teddy refused, saying that he considered that James had still not recovered fully from his wounds. James

responded by saying, 'Come with me, Teddy,' and took him in his jeep to the foot of Beacon Hill, just outside Bulford Barracks where we were stationed. Setting off up the hill, James easily won the race to the top and when a puffing Teddy joined him, said, 'Now say I'm not fit!' Needless to say, Teddy immediately signed him off A1!

Most of the members of the 10th Battalion The Essex Regiment had volunteered to stay with their unit in its new role. However, after undergoing selection at the Airborne Forces Depot at Hardwick Hall, and successfully completing the parachute course at No. 1 Parachute Training School at Ringway, only 150–160 qualified parachutists returned to the Battalion to become the nucleus of 9th Parachute Battalion.

Hill's tenure of command was very brief because later that same month he was promoted to the rank of brigadier and appointed to command 3rd Parachute Brigade, which he now had the task of forming. Like 9th Parachute Battalion, the 7th and 8th each numbered 150–160 all ranks on completion of their parachute training, their ranks thereafter being swelled by volunteers from other units. Hill later commented on them:

The men I commanded were of two entirely different types: firstly, the soldiers of fortune, many such men were in my original 1st Parachute Battalion – i.e. spoiling for a fight and thus had to be very well disciplined; secondly, those who had volunteered to join the paratroops because they thought it was their duty to do so – i.e. those in the 8th and 9th Battalions. In addition, I found that the battalions were as different as chalk and cheese – different outlooks and each with a soul of its own. The men of the 8th Battalion were rugged, relentless, tough and not too fussy. Those of the 9th, on the other hand, were masters of detail, fussy, very dedicated and could be relied upon to tackle any problem with precision and professionalism.

From the very start, Hill instituted a programme of intensive training throughout his brigade, including the headquarters, as Captain Tony Woodgate, the Staff Captain, later recalled:

James expected his staff to do as much as ordinary soldiers as well as their staff work. Every morning, he took us on PT before breakfast on the grass outside the brigade headquarters. After breakfast, we would have the brigade commander's conference at which he would produce a small black notebook in which he had recorded everything he had noted down when going around units on the previous day – he liked to spend most of his time out with them.

Hill placed great emphasis on physical fitness, believing that this would be a crucial factor in achieving success any future operations, as he later explained:

> I insisted that everyone had to be 100 per cent fit. I also ensured that every officer was capable of performing two jobs. Furthermore, each battalion and company had an A and B headquarters so that if one was knocked out the other would take over command and control. All the soldiers were trained to operate the different weapons in a battalion and to drive vehicles such as Bren carriers. I also rammed home my four principles of battle: firstly, speed – the brigade had to move fast at all times; secondly, control – discipline and control at all times; thirdly, simplicity – in thought and action; and fourthly, firepower – maximum effective firepower.

Early 1943 saw the departure from Britain of 1st Airborne Division, less 3rd Parachute Brigade, two battalions of 1st Airlanding Brigade and the Airborne Light Tank Squadron, for operations in North Africa. On 23 April, the War Office issued authorization for the creation of a second airborne division incorporating 3rd Parachute Brigade and two formations yet to be formed: 5th Parachute Brigade and 6th Airlanding Brigade. The new grouping was designated 6th Airborne Division and its commander was Major General Richard Gale, who had founded and commanded 1st Parachute Brigade before being appointed Deputy Director of Air at the War Office.

Initially, the nucleus of 6th Airborne Division was provided by 3rd Parachute Brigade, but the latter was weak in numbers as a consequence of having supplied reinforcements for 1st Parachute Brigade. In late May, its strength was decreased further with the transfer of 7th Parachute Battalion to become the nucleus of 5th Parachute Brigade. Hill was thus left with 8th Parachute Battalion under Lieutenant Colonel Alastair Pearson, his former Second-in-Command in 1st Parachute Battalion, and 9th Parachute Battalion commanded by Lieutenant Colonel Terence Otway. In place of 7th Parachute Battalion he would receive the 1st Canadian Parachute Battalion, which would arrive from Canada within three months. Hill was delighted with this news as he later recorded:

> I was summoned to the divisional headquarters by Major General Richard Gale who said to me: 'James, we have been given the one

and only Canadian parachute battalion to be part of this division, and I want it to go to your brigade. You will, however, have to lose one of your battalions.' I was, of course, absolutely delighted at having the Canadians, albeit very sad that I would have to relinquish the 7th Parachute Battalion which henceforth would form part of 5th Parachute Brigade.

During May, 6th Airlanding Brigade was formed under the command of Brigadier The Honourable Hugh Kindersley, incorporating the 2nd Battalion The Oxfordshire & Buckinghamshire Light Infantry, the 1st Battalion The Royal Ulster Rifles and the 12th Battalion The Devonshire Regiment.

5th Parachute Brigade was formed on 1 July 1943 under Brigadier Ted Flavell, who shortly afterwards was succeeded by Brigadier Nigel Poett. In addition to 7th Parachute Battalion, it incorporated two newly-raised units: 12th (Yorkshire) Parachute Battalion, formed from the 10th Battalion The Green Howards; and 13th (Lancashire) Parachute Battalion, formed from the 2nd/4th Battalion The South Lancashire Regiment.

July also witnessed the arrival of the 1st Canadian Parachute Battalion, commanded by Lieutenant Colonel George Bradbrooke, which soon after its arrival proceeded to No. 1 PTS to undergo training in British parachuting techniques. On 11 August, it joined 3rd Parachute Brigade. Hill later recalled its arrival:

The battalion was very similar to my old 1st Parachute Battalion, in that it comprised men who wanted to fight and the sooner the better. They didn't want to sit out the war in Canada, so they had joined the 1st Canadian Parachute Battalion, which consisted of volunteers from all walks of Canadian life. One parachute battalion on its own, however, is of no use to anyone so the Canadians had very wisely decided to give it to us. These men had flown from their homes 3,000–4,000 miles away to stand in our midst and share our burdens in what was our hour of need.

Hill continued with the task of training his brigade and turning it into a first-rate fighting force. Those not already qualified as parachutists had to undergo selection and training at Hardwick Hall and then the parachute course at Ringway. Throughout the second half of 1943 all units in the Brigade, and indeed throughout 6th Airborne Division, concentrated on training at all levels, from the individual soldier through section, platoon and company levels. Training took place day and night, exercises frequently commencing with parachute drops and glider landings, and nearly always finishing with a 20-mile march back to barracks. Much emphasis continued to be placed on physical fitness, with every member of the Brigade, including Hill and his headquarters staff, jumping, landing, exercising and marching. This endless round of training soon resulted in the creation of a tremendous esprit de corps within the Brigade and the rest of the Division. Hill later described this period of intensive activity:

During that period, we lived our training, and this was not hard to do. In fact, it was handed to Commanding Officers on a plate for three reasons. Firstly, if a man did not make the grade we could chuck him out and this possible threat provided a salutary stimulant to all and sundry. Secondly, every parachutist in the brigade was under the age of 30, I being the antique of the party at the age of 32.

Thirdly, there wasn't a woman to be found in the place. It was marvellous! Bulford Camp provided a home for hermits. Looking back, I cannot recollect being confronted with a bad disciplinary problem in this connection.

The training in 3rd Parachute Brigade, which I would say was typical, was based on four cardinal points. All old chestnuts but vital to us, and the emphasis placed on them had a great bearing on whatever success we may have achieved in later battles. The first of these was speed. We counted on moving across country twice as fast as anyone else. Our standards for those days were very high: there were the usual 50 miles in a day and 10 miles in two hours, carrying 60 pounds per man, and I used to judge a battalion physically fit for battle if it could move from the Exford training area in Somerset to Bulford, a distance of 112 miles. In order to emphasise the importance of speed, everyone doubled from point A to B in barracks in working hours.

The second was that of physical fitness. I have often been asked if this tremendous emphasis on fitness, with its consequent elimination of many good men, was necessary. I wondered that too on one occasion when I found myself being reported to myself by an astonished woman representing the Women's Institute at Cholderton who had observed Brigade Headquarters struggling with their 10 miles in two hours. Fitness did, however, give us an invaluable asset, namely that of endurance, without which I think we would have had difficulty in producing the stamina required of us in the coming months.

The third cardinal point was that of simplicity. A parachute brigade was a very simple organisation. Simplicity breeds speed and eliminates mistakes. We tried to preach the vital importance of this at every turn.

The fourth and last point was that of control. We had numerically small battalions, numbering some 500 fighting men, and little ammunition. Tight control was thus essential in order to extract the maximum out of limited resources. At night, we would risk the danger of concentration and link our men with toggle ropes. We always duplicated battalion and company headquarters in parachute operations, on the move and in battle.

By the end of November 1943 3rd Parachute Brigade, along with the rest of 6th Airborne Division, was declared fit for role, but only just in time because on 23 December, less than eight months after its formation, the Division was ordered to mobilize and be prepared for operations by 1 February 1944.

Chapter 7

On 17 February 1944, Lieutenant General Sir Frederick 'Boy' Browning, the Commander Airborne Troops, arrived at Headquarters 6th Airborne Division to brief Major General Gale on the role which 6th Airborne Division would play in Operation OVERLORD, the forthcoming invasion of Nazi-occupied Europe. Gale later summed up his feeling of excitement:

> Our great moment had arrived. I was now to be told what we had been so impatiently wanting to know. All our training, all our endeavours, all our beliefs were at last to be put to the test. We had tried to think of every contingency. We, the whole team, had studied, laboured, pondered and deduced. We knew what we could do and what we wanted. We knew just how far the bow would stretch.

He was dismayed, however, when Browning revealed the plan and then gave details of 6th Airborne Division's tasks, which called for one of its parachute brigades and an airlanding anti-tank battery to be placed under command of 3rd Infantry Division that would land from the sea. The Brigade was to seize two bridges over the Caen Canal and River Orne at Benouville and Ranville, both approximately 15 miles north of Caen. The limitation placed on the size of the airborne force was due to the number of aircraft available for the operation.

Gale allotted the task to 3rd Parachute Brigade. Hill, however, realized immediately that parachute troops were not ideal for the coup de main force for the bridges due to the risk of their being scattered during the drop. He requested that a company of airlanding troops be placed under his command for the task, and Gale agreed.

In addition to being bitterly disappointed that his division was not to be committed in its entirety, Gale was also worried that a single parachute brigade would not be sufficient for the task. His arguments obviously impressed others because on 23 February, five days after Browning's visit, the decision was taken to allocate Nos. 38 and 46 Groups RAF to the operation, and thus the whole of 6th Airborne Division would be committed under command of I Corps.

Gale and a small group of his staff immediately threw themselves into the planning of the operation, moving to Headquarters I Corps in London, which was co-located with Browning's Headquarters Airborne Troops. In due course, the more detailed planning was carried out at The Old Farm at Brigmerston House near Milston, situated in Wiltshire between Netheravon and Bulford. Each element of the Division, including the 1st Special Service Brigade, which would be under command, and Nos. 38 and 46 Groups RAF, had its own planning cell there. During the final stages, Gale and his staff moved to Scotland to coordinate plans with 3rd Infantry Division.

The overall Allied invasion plan called for an assault on the coast of Normandy in the area between the Cherbourg Peninsula and the River Orne, the Americans on the right and the Second British Army on the left. The British assault would be carried out by I and II Corps, on the left and right respectively. 6th Airborne Division would be under command of I Corps, commanded by Lieutenant General Sir John Crocker, its role being to protect the left flank of the British assault, which would be bounded by the Caen Canal and the River Orne, and to dominate the area east of Caen, whose features themselves dominated the British left flank.

The Division was allotted three tasks: firstly, the capture of the two bridges at Benouville and Ranville and the establishment of a bridgehead to hold them; secondly, the destruction of a coastal battery at Franceville Plage (known as the Merville Battery) prior to seaborne forces coming within its range; and thirdly, the destruction of the bridges over the River Dives at Varaville, Robehomme, Bures and Troarn in order to delay any advance by enemy forces from the east.

Two secondary tasks were also given to the Division: firstly, the mopping up and securing of the area between the Orne and Dives, including the capture of the towns of Sallenelles and Franceville Plage, as well as the clearing of the strip between these two towns and Cabourg at the mouth of the Dives; and secondly, having secured a firm base east of the Orne, to operate against any enemy reserve formations attempting to move towards the covering position from the east and south-east.

The sum total of the tasks given to Gale was formidable, involving as it did the seizing of an area of 24 square miles and holding it; to accomplish them, he had one airborne division and a brigade of commandos. His plan, however, was governed by the number of aircraft available to him, these being insufficient to transport the Division in one lift. He thus had to decide

63

which of his three brigades and divisional troops should be flown in and which should be transported by sea. The tasks of seizing the bridges at Benouville and Ranville, and the destruction of the Merville Battery, required speed and surprise, but these essential factors could not be guaranteed in a parachute operation. Furthermore the troops seizing the bridges had to be capable of resisting German counter-attacks, which might include armour. This meant that some of the Division's anti-tank assets would have to be landed as soon as possible.

Bearing these factors in mind, Gale decided that 6th Airlanding Brigade and its more heavily armed units would carry out the operation to capture the two bridges, while the attack on the Merville Battery and other more dispersed tasks would be allotted to 3rd Parachute Brigade. 5th Parachute Brigade, the 6th Airborne Armoured Reconnaissance Regiment and divisional troops would be brought in on a second airlift. Divisional Headquarters, together with elements of the Division's artillery and anti-tank units, would land after 6th Airlanding Brigade.

Enemy forces in the Division's planned area of operations comprised the 711th and 716th Infantry Divisions, possibly two squadrons of armour and a number of infantry and artillery units formed from training establishments. Both divisions were classed as low-category formations whose efficiency was assessed, in comparison to a first-class division, as being 40 per cent in static defence and 15 per cent in a counter-attack role. The 711th Infantry Division, which was deployed east of the Orne with its headquarters at Pont L'Évêque, numbered approximately 13,000 to 14,000 men, equipped with a number of anti-tank guns and approximately sixty infantry, field and medium artillery pieces. It was reported as also being equipped with thirty-five French Renault tanks. The 716th was of a similar size, its artillery comprising twenty-four gun-howitzers, twelve medium howitzers and a number of anti-tank guns, while its armour consisted of a few obsolete German and French tanks.

A far more serious threat was posed by the 12th SS Hitler Jugend Panzer Division which, numbering 21,000 men and equipped with Panther Mk V tanks, was deployed 30 miles to the south-east of Lisieux. Likewise the 21st SS Panzer Division, approximately 20,000 strong and also equipped with Panthers, was based in the area of Rennes and was considered a major threat by Gale and his planners.

Finally, the 352nd Infantry Division, fully manned and well equipped, was also situated within striking distance. It was estimated that it could be ready for operations in the Caen-Bayeux area by H+8 hours and that the 12th SS Panzer Division could arrive east of Caen by H+12.

On 18 March, Gale issued orders to his brigade commanders. 6th Airlanding Brigade would land just after midnight on 5 June and capture intact the bridges over the Caen Canal and the Orne, securing both before dawn. Thereafter, it was to establish defensive positions to the east and south-east, and hold a small bridgehead on the west of the canal pending the arrival of 3rd Infantry Division. 3rd Parachute Brigade meanwhile was to silence the Merville Battery by not later than an hour and a half before the seaborne landings, destroy the bridges over the River Dives and deny the Bois de Bavent ridge to the enemy. 5th Parachute Brigade and the major element of the divisional troops were to land on the evening of D-Day. 1st Special Service Brigade was to seize the towns of Sallenelles and Franceville Plage, and clear as much as possible of the coastal area between them and Cabourg. The remainder of the Division, comprising the 53rd (Worcestershire Yeomanry) Airlanding Light Regiment RA (less one battery) and the balance of divisional troops, would come by sea.

During the following month, however, RAF aerial reconnaissance revealed that the Germans had erected anti-glider defences in the form of poles and pits on the landing zones (LZs) and dropping zones (DZs) selected by Gale and his staff. Initially, it was feared that the Division's plans had been compromised but further reconnaissance revealed that similar measures had been put into effect in all open areas of terrain along the entire French and Belgian coasts. These defences posed a problem and it was agreed among the planners that a mass glider landing was no longer feasible until the LZs had been cleared.

Major General Gale was thus forced to modify his plans. The task of capturing the bridges at Benouville and Ranville was now given to 5th Parachute Brigade. The coup de main operation itself would, however, still be carried out by a glider-borne force comprising a reinforced company of six platoons under the command of 5th Parachute Brigade, which would land shortly afterwards and clear the area of the Division's LZs after first securing the area of Benouville, Ranville and Le Bas de Ranville. The tasks of 3rd Parachute Brigade and 1st Special Service Brigade remained unchanged, and 6th Airlanding Brigade would land on the evening of D-Day.

Now that each brigade's tasks had been confirmed, training became even more intense. 7th Parachute Battalion, which would relieve the coup de main force, consisting of D Company 2nd Battalion The Oxfordshire & Buckinghamshire Light Infantry, went off with the company to Devon where it exercised and rehearsed on two similar bridges spanning the River

Exe and a canal nearby. Meanwhile, 13th Parachute Battalion and sappers of 591st Parachute Squadron RE practised LZ clearance with explosives.

In 3rd Parachute Brigade, James Hill had given the task of attacking and destroying the Merville Battery to 9th Parachute Battalion, commanded by Lieutenant Colonel Terence Otway, while allotting the destruction of the bridges over the Dives at Varaville and Robehomme to Lieutenant Colonel George Bradbrooke's 1st Canadian Parachute Battalion, which thereafter was to hold the centre of the Bois de Bavent at Le Mesnil. 8th Parachute Battalion, commanded by the redoubtable Lieutenant Colonel Alastair Pearson, was tasked with blowing the bridges over the Dives at Bures and Troarn, subsequently denying the dense woods along the southern part of the ridge to the enemy.

A dummy replica of the Merville Battery, complete with gun emplacements, minefields, anti-tank ditch and barbed-wire defences was constructed near the village of West Woodhay on the Berkshire Downs, below and between Newbury and Hungerford, to aid 9th Parachute Battalion in training for its task, while bridges similar to the objectives of the other two battalions were found in the south of England.

While the brigades and battalions trained and rehearsed intensively, 6th Airborne Division's administrative staff under the Assistant Adjutant & Quartermaster General (AA & QMG), Lieutenant Colonel Shamus Hickie, along with the Deputy Assistant Quartermaster General (DAQMG) in each brigade headquarters, was grappling with such matters as the supply of weapons, ammunition, equipment, fuel, rations and water, as well as the organization of casualty evacuation and other aspects of logistical support for all the Division's units. In addition to the load carried by each soldier and glider, all Halifaxes, Stirlings and Albemarles being used as transports and tug aircraft would carry containers of ammunition and equipment in their bomb bays. These would be dropped after each aircraft's stick of paratroops had been dropped or its glider released. Once the planned link-up with I Corps had taken place, additional supplies and support would be moved forward by road.

On 19 May, 6th Airborne Division and No. 38 Group RAF were visited by His Majesty King George VI, accompanied by Queen Elizabeth and Princess Elizabeth. It was a great occasion for the Division, which was able to demonstrate its skills to the royal party, who watched a mass landing by gliders at Netheravon and a drop by 1st Canadian Parachute Battalion.

The Division also received a visit from General Sir Bernard

Montgomery, the commander of 21st Army Group. He addressed the members of each brigade and spoke to them of the forthcoming invasion, expressing his confidence in them and emphasizing the need for them to have confidence in themselves and their commanders. Following his visit, he expressed his approval of what he had seen in a signal sent to Major General Gale. This was reinforced by a letter from Lieutenant General Browning in which he stated:

> To confirm our conversation last night, I should like to congratulate you on the very fine appearance of your division, not only the type of officers and men, but also the turnout and the state of weapons and equipment. It showed a standard which I have always hoped airborne forces would attain and maintain; whatever anyone else thought, I, at any rate, was fully satisfied.

To those who knew General 'Boy' and his exceedingly high standards, this was very high praise indeed.

The training for Operation OVERLORD culminated in a four-day test exercise for the Division, held between 21 and 25 May during which the 'enemy' was provided by elements of 1st Airborne Division and the 1st Polish Independent Parachute Brigade. Although very few members of 6th Airborne Division were aware of the fact, this was the final rehearsal. On 25 May, the Division moved into transit camps surrounded by barbed wire and guarded by armed sentries. During this time, James Hill took the opportunity of visiting all elements of his brigade, as he later recalled:

> Well, the great day was arriving and all my battalions were penned in their camps, which they weren't allowed to leave. This period was very interesting to me. All day long the Canadians, with whom I'd pitched my tent, were playing games – baseball, throwing balls about – and I thought what tremendous vitality they had. Then in the afternoon, I would visit my English battalions and find half a dozen chaps desultorily kicking a football, and the rest asleep. I thought to myself: here is the difference between the Old World and the New – the élan and joie de vivre of the New World Canadians, and the maturity and the not worrying, not bothering and having a good nap while you can, of the British.

It was only now that all was revealed concerning the Division's tasks, with detailed briefings being held at all levels. On 30 May, Commanding Officers briefed their company commanders, the latter in turn holding orders groups for their platoon commanders, who then briefed their men. Highly detailed and realistic models of objectives, supported by maps and aerial photographs, were used at each level of command to ensure that every officer taking part knew exactly what was required of him and his men. Included in each briefing were outline details of the Division's tasks so that each soldier was not only aware of his role but also of the background and reasons for it.

Initially, take-off for 6th Airborne Division was scheduled for the evening of 4 June. On the morning of 3 June, units paraded in full battle order and moved in transport to the mounting airfields. Containers were loaded aboard aircraft while parachutes were drawn and fitted. Around midday, however, a signal was received, postponing the operation for twenty-four hours.

That evening, Hill went round all his units again for a final briefing of his officers and men, finishing with these words which were to stand many in good stead during the coming days: 'Gentlemen, in spite of your excellent training and your splendid briefings, you must not be daunted if chaos reigns. It undoubtedly will!'

Years later, he reflected on the Herculean task facing his brigade:

Looking back on my brigade's task for D-Day, I think I would have accepted it as well nigh impossible for 2,000 young men with an average age of 22 years who, with the exception of three officers, had never seen a shot fired in anger before, to be asked at dead of night, in a foreign field, to put out of action an enemy battery and destroy five bridges across the River Dives, in a flooded river valley, interspersed with deep irrigation ditches. These tasks covered a span of 7 miles. Thereafter, as near first light as possible, the brigade was required to capture and hold the ridge which was the dominating feature overlooking the Orne valley where the main divisional objective was the capture intact of the bridges over the River Orne and the canal so that a bridgehead for a future break-out by 21st Army Group could be established.

When regarded in retrospect and the cold light of day, that was a formidable task in any circumstances. The extraordinary thing was that not one of us doubted our ability to carry it out. During our months of training we had built up faith in each other and faith in ourselves – this was what training was all about!

The following morning, 5 June, a further signal was received, confirming that take-off would be later that day. That evening, 3rd and 5th Parachute Brigades left their transit camps again for the mounting airfields. First to take off were the pathfinders of the 22nd Independent Parachute Company, whose task it would be to mark the DZs. Meanwhile, the coup de main force of D Company 2nd Battalion The Oxfordshire & Buckinghamshire Light Infantry, under Major John Howard, was already airborne and heading for Normandy in its six gliders.

It was a fine night with a clear sky, the moon shining as the armada of aircraft carrying 3rd and 5th Parachute Brigades took off. They were followed by the tugs and gliders carrying Major General Richard Gale's tactical headquarters and divisional troops.

Chapter 8

The aircraft carrying 3rd Parachute Brigade, less 8th Parachute Battalion, comprised a total of 108 C-47 transports. 1st Canadian (less one company) and 9th Parachute Battalions were to be dropped by seventy-one C-47s on DZ 'V', while the brigade headquarters and 8th Parachute Battalion would be dropped by thirty-seven C-47s on DZ 'K'; also landing on DZ 'K' would be six Horsa gliders.

Each DZ was to be marked out by a stick of pathfinders from 22nd Independent Parachute Company with holophane coloured lamps laid out in the form of a 'T': an orange lamp was placed at the end of each arm of the 'T' and a green one at the base. The aircraft would be guided to the DZ by Eureka ground-to-air radio beacons transmitting to a Rebecca receiver fitted in each C-47.

The drop itself did not go well because things had already begun to go wrong as was later explained by Sergeant Matt Wells of 22nd Independent Parachute Company, who had been dropped earlier:

> I landed in some sort of orchard which was flooded to a depth of about two or three feet. The first things that struck me were the eerie silence and the searchlights that were sweeping the sky. I had just got up out of the water and taken off my harness when there was a loud splashing noise coming through the water towards me. As I prepared for the worst, five or six cows came out of the darkness. I decided that they had obviously been disturbed by some of us, so I went around and along a hedge until I came to a gate. I climbed over this and as I did so, someone came marching along the lane in which I now found myself. I challenged whoever it was with the password 'Punch' and he replied 'Judy'. It was Corporal Frank Knowles from my stick.
>
> We had obviously been scattered, so we set off in the same direction from which the cows had come and met up with the others who were in the process of laying out the DZ marking aids. We had

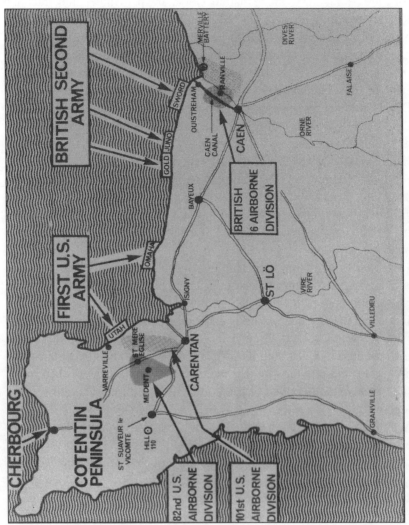

Allied Landings on D-Day

71

been allowed thirty minutes to find the correct DZ; under the conditions prevailing at that time, we could have done with ten minutes longer.

Unfortunately, nearly all the radio beacons and lamps for DZ 'V' had been lost or were damaged. To make matters worse, the pathfinder stick intended for DZ 'K' was dropped on to DZ 'N', which was allocated to 5th Parachute Brigade. This resulted in fourteen of the aircraft carrying 3rd Parachute Brigade's headquarters and 8th Parachute Battalion dropping their sticks on to DZ 'N' instead of DZ 'K'. Some time later 5th Parachute Brigade's pathfinders, who had themselves been dropped some distance away, arrived on DZ 'N' and set up the correct radio beacons and lamps. 3rd Parachute Brigade's advance party comprised elements of Brigade Headquarters and each battalion, together with a company of 1st Canadian Parachute Battalion, was tasked with clearing obstructions from DZ 'V'. Their drop also proved chaotic: of the fourteen Albemarles carrying them, two dropped only three and nine men respectively; six men made their exit from a third aircraft as it crossed the coast and only four jumped over the DZ; a fourth aircraft, under fire, was forced to make a second approach and thus dropped its stick late.

Two more aircraft reported technical problems, one losing time, the other being forced to return to base after being hit by anti-aircraft fire while on its seventh approach to the DZ, which it could not locate. Major Bill Collingwood, the Brigade Major, was travelling in this last aircraft when it was hit. He was knocked through the aperture and remained suspended beneath the fuselage, hanging by his static line which had become wound round his leg. Despite the fact that there was a 60lb kitbag attached to his leg, he was eventually pulled back into the aircraft during the return flight to England.

Accompanying 3rd Parachute Brigade's main body were the forward observation parties from 53rd Airlanding Light Regiment RA, a section of 4th Airlanding Anti-Tank Battery RA, 3rd Parachute Squadron RE, one troop of 591st Parachute Squadron RE and 224th Parachute Field Ambulance. Nine aircraft dropped their sticks in the marshy areas on either side of the River Dives, 2 or 3 miles from DZ 'V', while the remainder were scattered over a wide area.

James Hill was dropped about a quarter of a mile to the south of Cabourg, alongside the submerged bank of the River Dives, as he later related:

Shortly after midnight on D-Day, I dropped into 4 feet of water in the flooded valley of the Dives. Shortly afterwards, I heard an exchange of shots which proved to be one member of my bodyguard shooting the other in the leg. Fortunately, we found a mound with a hut on it. We had no option but to leave him there, giving him some of our ration of Mars Bars, and I'm happy to say he lived to tell the tale. We reckoned we could fight for forty-eight hours on two Mars Bars, and took them instead of rations in order to carry extra ammunition.

Many good chaps were drowned that night. It took me four hours to reach dry land adjacent to my brigade DZ. The country in question had been wired prior to flooding and there were deep irrigation ditches that could not be seen and in which many drowned. I was able to collect about forty-two other soldiers in the same predicament. The reason we survived was because we fastened ourselves to one another by the toggle ropes we all carried, which meant that if someone fell into an irrigation ditch, we could pull him out. In addition, we could tackle the wire obstacles together. Being a professional soldier, I had a large number of tea bags sewn into the tops of my trousers and rather annoyingly spent four hours making cold tea!

Upon arrival on dry land, I collared a Company Commander of 1st Canadian Parachute Battalion who told me of the Canadians' success in clearing the DZ for those who eventually arrived. They had captured the enemy command post and were now engaged in mopping up Varaville. As the time was about 0600 hours, I decided to proceed to Sallenelles to see how 9th Parachute Battalion had fared at the Merville Battery. I collected some forty-two very wet stragglers; among them were a Royal Navy bombardment officer and rating, as well as an Alsatian messenger dog and its handler, and I then proceeded down a narrow lane which ran parallel to the coast. I remember the sight of the naval bombardment which opened up prior to the landings and which had to be seen to be believed. It was the greatest and noisiest fireworks display of all time!

Suddenly I heard a noise that I recognized, and shouted to all the men to get down. There were no ditches in the road, only a hedge and then water. My party found itself in the middle of an attack by low-flying aircraft coming in from the sea and dropping anti-personnel bombs. I threw myself to the ground and lay on top of Lieutenant George Peters, the Mortar Officer of 9th Parachute Battalion. I looked around and knew I had been hit. The lane was covered in dust, and the smell of death and cordite prevailed. In the middle of the track I saw a leg and thought it must be mine but then realised it belonged to George Peters on whom I was lying, and who now was dead. I myself had been saved worse injuries by my water bottle, which was smashed to pieces, and my spare underwear which I carried in the tail of my jumping smock.

I found that there appeared to be only two survivors capable of getting to their feet – myself and my defence platoon commander. An immediate problem then arose: what do you do? Do you look after the many wounded and dying, or press on? There was of course only one answer – press on. The two of us therefore injected the wounded with our own morphia, taking the morphia from the dead and handing it to those who needed it the most. I will never forget the cheer that was given to us as we left by those who were soon to die!

While James Hill and those with him were struggling to find their way across the flooded terrain surrounding the Dives, the advance elements of 9th Parachute Battalion had been successfully dropped on DZ 'V' and subsequently reached the Battalion RV without difficulty. These comprised two parties commanded respectively by Majors Alan Parry and George Smith. Parry's party, made up of himself and a representative from each of the Battalion's companies, was to assist the Battalion in rallying at a rendezvous (RV) point before leading it to a firm base near the battery. In the meantime, Smith's party, comprising himself and two company sergeant majors, and accompanied by eight members of B Company under Captain Paul Greenway, was to reconnoitre the battery and cut a gap in any barbed wire. Greenway and his men, equipped with mine detectors, were then to crawl into the minefield surrounding the battery and clear three lanes through it. Once they had done so, Smith's party would return to the assembly area and bring the Battalion forward.

Barbed-wire obstacles and an anti-tank ditch formed part of the battery's defences on the far side of the minefield, so Bangalore torpedoes and lightweight portable bridging material would be needed to deal with these. These, together with two 6-pounder anti-tank guns, three jeeps and trailers, and further supplies of 3-inch mortar bombs and ammunition for the Battalion's medium machine guns, would be brought in by five gliders.

The attack on the battery would be led by fifty men of A Company, commanded by Captain Robert Gordon-Brown. Accompanied by a team of eight sappers, they would land inside the battery itself. Once the wire obstacles had been breached, C Company would join Captain Gordon-

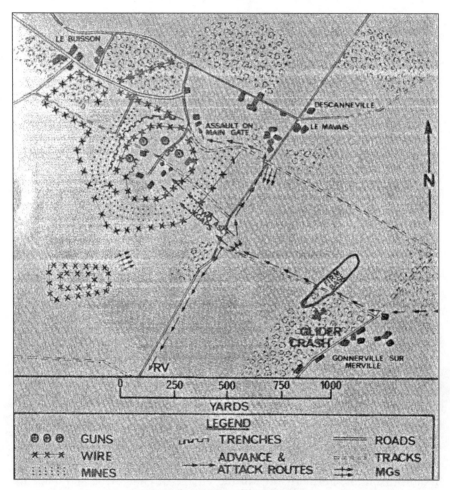

Attack on Merville Battery

Brown's force in attacking the reinforced-concrete casemates in which the battery was housed, followed by B Company. The other half of A Company, meanwhile, would remain in the firm base as the Battalion's reserve.

9th Parachute Battalion had to complete its task of neutralizing the battery and withdraw by 0510 hours, by which time, in the event no success signal had been received by a naval bombardment officer who was to drop with the Battalion, the light cruiser HMS *Arethusa*, lying out to sea in the English Channel, would commence shelling the battery with her 6-inch guns.

Having landed safely on DZ 'V', Major Alan Parry and his men made their way to the RV point and set out the lights marking the company locations, while Major George Smith's party, accompanied by Captain Greenway and his mine-clearance team, set off towards the battery which lay about a mile and a quarter away. Shortly afterwards, RAF Lancasters attacked the battery but missed it, most of their bombs falling to the south and nearly hitting Smith and his party. The C-47s bringing the main body of the Battalion were by this time approaching the French coast. Unfortunately, due to the fact that most of the pathfinding equipment for DZ 'V' had been damaged, only a few lamps were marking the zone by the time the aircraft arrived overhead. Moreover, visibility from the air was bad due to smoke from the bombing raid on the battery blowing across the DZ. Consequently, only a few sticks landed on the DZ while others were dropped into the Dives marshes or on the high ground between Cabourg and Dozulé.

By 0250 hours, only 150 members of 9th Parachute Battalion had arrived at the RV point, and none of the eleven gliders bringing in the Battalion's vehicles and heavy stores had appeared. Moreover, the Battalion was without its 3-inch mortars and only one of its Vickers medium machine guns and a few Bangalore torpedoes had been retrieved after the drop. Nevertheless, bearing in mind that the battery had to be destroyed and the Battalion clear of the objective by 0510 hours, Lieutenant Colonel Otway decided to press on. Led by Major Alan Parry, the Battalion followed a route skirting the northern edge of the village of Gonneville and made its way to a road junction where it met Major George Smith. Shortly afterwards, Captain Greenway and his team appeared and reported that lanes had been cleared through the minefield. Due to the shortage of Bangalore torpedoes, it was decided to blow only two gaps in the wire obstacles with two groups moving through each. It was now 0430 hours. As the Battalion was redeploying, six enemy machine guns outside the battery opened fire, three from either flank. The Battalion's single Vickers medium machine gun engaged the enemy guns on the left while a section of six men under Sergeant Knight engaged those on the right as they headed for the main entrance to the battery.

Led by Major Alan Parry, the assault force moved along the two lanes through the minefield and took up its position just short of the wire obstacle. At that moment two gliders flew low overhead, the second coming under fire from a 20mm anti-aircraft gun inside the battery position, and disappeared into the darkness beyond. One glider, piloted by Staff Sergeant Bone, eventually landed in a field 2 miles to the south. The other, flown by Staff Sergeant Kerr, touched down and was heading for a large hedge at the edge of the minefield. Spotting a mine warning sign, Kerr managed to haul his glider up over the hedge and a lane beyond it, streaming his arrester parachute and crashing into an orchard beyond. The platoon inside, commanded by Lieutenant Hugh Pond, made a somewhat dazed exit only to hear the sound of men approaching. Deploying swiftly into positions on either side of the lane, Pond and his men opened fire as enemy troops appeared.

At that precise moment, the Bangalore torpedoes were detonated and the assault on the battery itself began. The four assault groups raced through the breaches blown in the wire obstacles, each heading for its designated casemate. Lieutenant Alan Jefferson, the commander of No. 12 Platoon in C Company, led the attack on No. 1 Casemate, as he later recounted:

> In action for the first time, I found my angle of vision to be severely limited. I knew that we were on the right flank though whether Sergeant Knight's diversionary party was round by the gate to give us a modicum of cover and support, I neither knew nor considered.
>
> The hard, squat shape of No. 1 Casemate was now visible, and I could see that it was encrusted with moulded concrete lozenges like scales on a huge beast. Its sheer mass was formidable, and the dark entrance large enough to drive a tank through – had they closed the steel doors we'd been told about – I seemed to feel something nick me between the shoulder blades and was aware of Private Morgan, my batman, falling down, just behind me. Our number was dwindling. Then I felt a lash across my left thigh. I stumbled and fell. There was no pain but I couldn't get up again.

The remainder of No. 12 Platoon continued heading for their objective, and shortly afterwards Jefferson could hear muffled explosions coming from inside Nos 1 and 2 Casemates and observed smoke pouring from the doorways.

Major Alan Parry, who was in command of the assault, was also heading for No. 1 Casemate when he was hit in the leg and fell into a large bomb crater. After a few minutes, he recovered sufficiently to clamber out and hobble towards No. 1 Casemate where he encountered a scene of carnage with dead and wounded men lying around the entrance. Among them was Captain Hal Hudson, the Battalion's Adjutant, who had been shot in the stomach.

One of the assault groups was commanded by Colour Sergeant Long who later vividly recalled leading the attack on No. 4 Casemate:

> The assault was all hell let loose. The wire had been cut for us by an advance party and, firing from the hip and throwing grenades, we went forward to the guns. Our attack was a complete surprise to the Germans but they soon recovered and gave a very good account of themselves. In the end, however, we overcame them.

Whereas the enemy gunners in No. 4 Casemate suffered the worst, all of them being killed, the Germans in the other three casemates and the command bunker were putting up a fierce defence. Twelve men of 9th Parachute Battalion inside No. 1 Casemate were captured, and three more killed, during the assault. In the meantime, one of the battery's forward observers, located in an observation post on the beach at Franceville, had called for fire support from artillery batteries located to the east of Merville. These responded and shortly afterwards several salvoes of shells began falling around the casemates.

Not long afterwards, what remained of the attacking force began to withdraw from the area of the battery and regrouped at the Calvary, a statue depicting Christ on the Cross, which was situated less than a mile to the south. The battery had been silenced temporarily but its four guns remained undamaged inside the casemates. Later that morning, the battery opened fire on targets at Ouistreham, on the Orne estuary and along the Caen Canal but was immediately subjected to an overwhelming heavy bombardment by Allied ships and aircraft. The battery survived this and a subsequent attack by No. 3 Commando before eventually being withdrawn on 17 August with its four guns intact.

9th Parachute Battalion had suffered heavy casualties: of the 150 men who had attacked the battery only about eighty were unscathed; some sixty-five were killed, wounded or missing. Lieutenant Colonel Otway decided to attack and seize the village of Le Plein so at 0600 hours the remnants of the Battalion moved off from the Calvary, leaving its wounded there. After being mistakenly attacked by high-flying RAF bombers, Otway and his men reached a crossroads between Le Plein and the neighbouring village of Hauger where the remnants of B Company, led by Major George Smith, came under fire. Smith mounted an attack, forcing a platoon of enemy back into Le Plein and into the church, killing some fifteen of them. As the Battalion cleared and secured a number of houses at the northern end of the village, however, another platoon of Germans mounted a counter-attack, but this was met by the Battalion's single Vickers MMG which wreaked havoc at close range, killing twelve enemy and forcing the rest to withdraw.

A platoon of B Company, under Lieutenant Thomas Halliburton, attacked a large house from the rear. Situated near the church and surrounded by a 6-foot-high wall, it appeared to be the main enemy defensive position in the village. As the platoon negotiated the wall, however, it came under fire, Halliburton was killed and the platoon was forced to withdraw.

At this juncture, Lieutenant Colonel Otway decided to establish a defensive position in the Château d'Amfreville and await the arrival of the commandos of 1st Special Service Brigade. Early that afternoon, No. 6 Commando appeared and took up positions within the village.

In the meantime James Hill had been following 9th Parachute Battalion:

I eventually turned up at the first aid post of 9th Parachute Battalion, and an officer told me that the battalion had successfully dealt with the battery and, although only eighty strong, was now trying to dislodge the enemy from the Sallenelles feature. As I passed the battalion's Regimental Aid Post, Doc Watts, the Medical Officer, unwisely told me that I looked bad for morale – to which I replied, 'My bloody man! If you had spent four and a half hours in cold water making tea, and then had much of your left backside removed, you would not be looking your best either!' No doubt to keep me quiet, and to assist in temporary patching-up operations, Doc Watts put me out for a couple of hours. Being a good soldier, he then produced a lady's bicycle and a soldier to push it. Thus, at 1100 hours, I wobbled off to see the divisional commander, who had now established his headquarters in Ranville, and tell him what I knew of the Canadians and 9th Parachute Battalion. This involved me in a downhill ride of some 2 miles and it was amusing because sometimes Germans ran

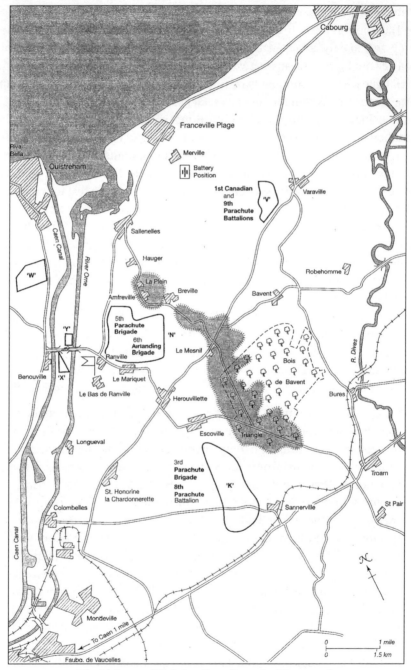

6th Airborne Division Landings in Normandy

across the road and at other times British, and I never knew whom I was going to meet next!

8th Parachute Battalion meanwhile had suffered a similar fate to the 9th, being scattered during the drop. With half its pathfinders dropped on to the wrong DZ and several aircraft being forced by the anti-aircraft fire to take evasive action, the result was that only a fraction of the Battalion was dropped on or near DZ 'K' to the west of Touffreville. In addition, of the Battalion's six gliders, only two landed in the correct location; these contained jeeps and trailers loaded with explosives. Three others landed on DZ 'N', while the sixth glider, also carrying a jeep and trailer carrying explosives, landed 4 miles south of Touffreville, at La Vieille Église in Le Marais de Vomont.

The Battalion was tasked with destroying the bridges at Bures and Troarn, the plan calling for it to secure and hold Troarn, with one company providing cover and support for the sappers of 3rd Parachute Squadron RE who would blow the bridges. When Lieutenant Colonel Alastair Pearson reached the Battalion RV at a track junction near Touffreville at 0120 hours, he found only thirty men plus a jeep and trailer belonging to the Engineer squadron. By 0330 hours, this number had increased to eleven officers and 130 other ranks, but there was no news of the rest of the sappers who had dropped with the Battalion.

Pearson decided to send a small force to destroy the bridges at Bures, while he waited at a crossroads a mile to the north of Troarn, until he had sufficient men with which to attack the town. At 0400 hours, his group moved off to the crossroads that lay in heavily wooded terrain to the east of the main road between Troarn and Le Mesnil. En route, he set up an ambush comprising two PIAT detachments under the command of a junior NCO, Lance Corporal Stevenson, to cover the Battalion's rear.

On reaching the crossroads, Pearson despatched a patrol under Captain Kelland to reconnoitre the two bridges at Bures, one of which was a steel girder railway bridge and the other a similar but shorter one carrying a trackway. At 0630 hours, No. 2 Troop of 3rd Parachute Squadron RE, commanded by Captain Tim Juckes, reached the bridges. By 0915 hours, both had been destroyed and the troop joined up with Pearson and his men.

Meanwhile more members of 8th Parachute Battalion were arriving, among them Lieutenant Thompson, the Mortar Platoon commander, who was accompanied by some fifty men of A Company, and the majority of the Machine Gun and Mortar Platoons, bringing with them three Vickers medium machine guns and two 3-inch mortars. He had earlier met Major

J.C.A. 'Tim' Roseveare, the commander of 3rd Parachute Squadron RE, and some of his sappers who were on their way to blow the bridge at Troarn. Roseveare had ordered Thompson to establish a firm base at a road junction while he went forward to deal with the bridge. While reconnoitring the area, Thompson had encountered the PIAT ambush party and thus learned of the Battalion's whereabouts.

Not long afterwards, six enemy half-tracks drove into the PIAT ambush and were destroyed, three enemy being killed. The remainder of the latter, subsequently identified as being from a unit of the 21st Panzer Division, withdrew on foot towards Troarn.

Pearson sent out patrols to reconnoitre the areas to the north and west of Troarn. He had so far received no confirmation that the bridge there had been destroyed, so he despatched Captain Tim Juckes and his sappers, together with No. 9 Platoon of B Company under Lieutenant Colin Brown, to check whether the bridge had indeed been blown and, if necessary, to increase the damage to it.

The sappers and No. 9 Platoon made their way to the outskirts of Troarn and then headed for the bridge where they came under fire from a house near the church. A brief skirmish ensued, resulting in the capture of a small group of seven Germans who turned out to be members of a 21st Panzer Division reconnaissance unit. Soon afterwards, however, Brown and his men came under fire again from enemy troops positioned in other houses in the area of the church. After these had been cleared by the platoon, more prisoners being taken in the process, Captain Juckes and his sappers went forward and inspected the stone bridge in which they found a gap had been blown – this they assumed, correctly, to be the work of Major Tim Roseveare. Placing further charges, they increased the gap to a width of 70 feet. Having completed its task, and having been plied with food and wine by local townspeople, the small party made its way back to the Battalion.

Lieutenant Colonel Alastair Pearson had heard the explosions caused by the bridges being blown, as he later recalled:

> The first was from the direction of Bures and the larger one from Troarn, and I concluded that the demolition had taken place. Major Roseveare was the sapper squadron commander. He'd landed on the wrong DZ at Ranville but commandeered the first jeep he came across and filled it with all the explosives he could find. Together with seven of his men, he made his way down the road towards Troarn which he reached just as it was getting light. The bridge was at the bottom of a steep hill about 600 yards outside the village.

Driving on to the bridge, he abandoned the jeep and laid his charges which blew a big hole in the bridge.

In the meantime, the Battalion had moved to La Grande Bruyère where it took up a position in all-round defence covering the four roads leading to the crossroads. That afternoon an attack was launched on B Company by a small group of enemy, but this was beaten off without difficulty. Throughout the rest of the day, members of the Battalion continued to appear and by 1800 hours that evening its strength had risen to seventeen officers and 300 other ranks. By the end of D-Day, despite a disastrous drop, 8th Parachute Battalion had achieved all its objectives, the two bridges at Bures having been blown along with the one at Troarn. It had, however, suffered heavily with casualties amounting to forty-two killed and fifty-four missing. In addition, a large number had been injured during the drop, or wounded in action.

1st Canadian Parachute Battalion, which had been tasked with destroying the bridges at Varaville and Robehomme, found itself with the majority of its troops dropped some distance from DZ 'V'. C Company had departed from England as part of the advance group along with Brigade Headquarters, elements of 22nd Independent Parachute Company and a stick of 9th Parachute Battalion. The Company Second-in-Ccommand, Captain John Hanson, found himself and his stick some 10 miles from the DZ, while Lieutenant John Madden and his men landed on the opposite side of the River Orne and only 1,200 yards from the invasion beaches.

Being dropped miles from the DZ was not the only problem facing C Company as Corporal Hartigan, who came down 500 yards from the DZ, landing in an apple tree in a French villager's back yard, later recalled:

C Company was on the ground only a few minutes when we knew that disaster was at hand. Many of the 4,000 pound bombs dropped by Lancasters, and meant for the Merville Battery, came down too far inland and were landing in and around the DZ. Only a dozen or so men showed up at the RV. Major Murray McLeod set off for the enemy positions with the handful who were there. They managed to engage the enemy at Varaville within thirty minutes, so that the main drop could not be interfered with. In the next half an hour or so, about twenty more men of C Company showed up.

Eventually, other members of the company appeared before heading off to Varaville to attack the garrison there. Meanwhile the pathfinders set up the two serviceable Eureka radio beacons and laid out their lamps to mark the DZ and guide in the main force.

When the rest of the Battalion arrived, however, A Company was dropped over a wide area and some of its men linked up with elements of C Company preparing to attack Varaville. At the same time the rest of the Company was covering the withdrawal of 9th Parachute Battalion. On arriving at A Company's RV, Lieutenant Jack Clancy found only two or three men waiting there. When no one else appeared, he decided to reconnoitre the nearby village of Gonneville-sur-Merville but found no signs of the enemy. On returning to the RV, he met an officer and twenty other ranks who had arrived in his absence. Taking them under command, he led them towards the Merville Battery. En route, he and his small force encountered no enemy but were forced to take evasive action from the heavy bombing of Gonneville-sur-Merville by the RAF.

After clearing a château of some enemy who had been firing on 9th Parachute Battalion, and after acting as a rearguard for the Battalion's withdrawal, Clancy and his small force eventually reached 1st Canadian Parachute Battalion's positions at Le Mesnil at 1530 hours.

Meanwhile, B Company had also been scattered over a large area, two of its platoons landing in marshy flooded terrain 2 miles from the DZ. One stick, under Lieutenant Philippe Rousseau, landed several miles to the north-east near Villers-sur-Mer. Five others landed in the flooded areas near Robehomme which were criss-crossed with large drainage ditches, many of them up to 7 feet deep. Several men were forced to jettison their equipment to avoid drowning, while others were unable to free themselves of their heavy loads and perished.

Lieutenant Norman Toseland, the commander of No. 5 Platoon, was one of the few fortunate enough to land on firm ground. After joining up with another member of his platoon, he met Sergeant Lacasse who was accompanied by a small group and together they headed for the Robehomme bridge which was one of the Battalion's objectives. Assisted by a young French girl who acted as a guide, they made their way to the bridge, gathering up a number of men from other units along the way, including ten men from No. 5 Platoon, others from 8th and 9th Parachute Battalions, and some sappers.

On reaching the Robehomme bridge, they met Major Clayton Fuller who had landed in the River Dives nearby. By 0300 hours, when the sappers tasked with blowing the bridge had not appeared, Sergeant Poole of No. 3 Troop of 3rd Parachute Squadron RE, one of the sappers who had joined up with Lieutenant Toseland, collected all the plastic explosive carried by the paratroops for making Gammon bombs, amounting to some 30lb in all. He attempted to blow the bridge but the relatively small charge only succeeded in weakening it. At about 0600 hours, however, Lieutenant Jack Inman and five sappers of No. 3 Troop appeared with 200lb of explosive and destroyed the bridge.

In the meantime, the Commanding Officer, Lieutenant Colonel George Bradbrooke, had landed in a marsh to the west of the River Dives. Making his way to the battalion RV, he met his Second-in-Command, Major Jeff Nicklin, together with the Intelligence Officer, Lieutenant R. Weathersbee, and the Signals Officer, Lieutenant John Simpson. Others at the RV included a number of men from 8th and 9th Parachute Battalions, and an anti-tank detachment of the 2nd Battalion The Oxfordshire & Buckinghamshire Light Infantry whose glider had landed in the wrong location. Shortly afterwards, a small group from Headquarter Company and a section of 224th Parachute Field Ambulance also appeared.

Deciding he needed information about C Company's progress with its task at Varaville, Lieutenant Colonel Bradbrooke despatched Lieutenant Weathersbee and two men to find out and report back on the situation. Meanwhile, he led the rest of his small force towards the crossroads at Le Mesnil. En route, they came under fire and were forced to clear a number of enemy out of houses along the road before they could continue. Following an attack by men of Headquarter Company, the enemy withdrew and at 1000 hours Bradbrooke and his men reached the crossroads where he established his Battalion Headquarters.

C Company meanwhile had been undertaking the four tasks allotted to it, but with a fraction of its normal strength. These consisted of: clearing the enemy garrison from Varaville; destroying a 75mm gun emplacement at a road junction near the Château de Varaville just east of the town; blowing the bridge over the River Divette; and the destruction of a radio transmitter station near Varaville.

This was a formidable array of tasks, even for a full-strength company. As it was, when the Company Commander, Major Murray McLeod, arrived at his company RV, he found only a small group of his men. He himself, together with several others, had been on the DZ when the RAF Lancasters bombing the Merville Battery had flown over the zone, some of them emptying their bomb loads on to it as they did so. Along with everyone else on the DZ at the time, he had been left badly shocked.

Enemy deployments in Normandy as at 6 June 1944

By 0030 hours, McLeod's group numbered only fifteen men and between them could muster only three Sten guns, eight rifles and his own pistol. Nevertheless, he led them off to take on the enemy force at Varaville. As he did so, he met a small group of No. 9 Platoon, led by Private Rudko, who had survived the bombing of the DZ. Despite being severely shocked, they were unhurt and in possession of all their equipment.

With just twenty-five minutes left before the drop of the 3rd Parachute Brigade main force, McLeod and his men made their way through the darkness to Varaville. Passing through the village undetected, they came to the gatehouse of the Château de Varaville which was some way from the château, and which overlooked the enemy defensive positions. These consisted of a long trench fortified with concrete and earthworks, with machine-gun positions located at intervals; at each end of the trench was a bunker. Unbeknownst to McLeod, there was a 75mm gun emplacement to the rear of the trench.

Entering the gatehouse, some of McLeod's men found that it was being used as a barracks for about 100 men. He positioned some of his small force around the building while Lieutenant 'Chug' Walker placed twelve men in a shallow ditch. McLeod, accompanied by Private Thompson, then made his way up to the second floor of the gatehouse but shortly afterwards came under fire from the 75mm gun. An attempt was made by Corporal Oikle to knock it out with the group's one and only PIAT, but this failed. Before a second bomb could be fired at it, the gun opened fire again on the gatehouse, setting off the PIAT bombs laid out beside Corporal Oikle, which exploded, killing Lieutenant Walker and fatally wounding Major McLeod.

At that point the Company Second-in-Command, Captain John Hanson, arrived with two men, bringing the force's strength to thirty in total. Although the PIAT had been lost, there was now a Bren gun, which was augmented shortly afterwards by the arrival of a 2-inch mortar carried by Corporal Hartigan, who appeared with Private Mallon. These two managed to reach cover just in time as enemy machine guns opened fire.

At 0830 hours, the enemy showed a white flag and requested they be permitted to send out their wounded and Captain Hanson, who had assumed command, gave permission for them to do so. Shortly afterwards a large explosion was heard away to the south-east, indicating that other members of the Company had succeeded in completing one of C Company's other tasks: the destruction of the Varaville bridge. At 1000 hours, Corporal Hartigan succeeded in working his way into a position from which he could bring down effective fire with his 2-inch mortar on the German position. He fired four high-explosive bombs, all of which hit their target. A few minutes later, a white flag was waved from one of the bunkers and the Germans, numbering forty-three men in total, surrendered.

Swiftly occupying the enemy position, Captain Hanson and his men braced themselves for an enemy counter-attack, but none came. In mid-afternoon, having been relieved by commandos of 1st Special Service Brigade, they and their prisoners set off on a 3-mile march to Le Mesnil. En route, they came under fire on several occasions and two sections had to be detached each time to deal with the problem. Eventually, at 1800 hours, they reached Le Mesnil and rejoined their battalion.

3rd Parachute Brigade's two supporting arm units, 3rd Parachute Squadron RE and 224th Parachute Field Ambulance, had also found themselves dropped wide of the DZ. Shortly after landing, Major Tim Roseveare realized that he was on DZ 'N' instead of DZ 'K'. Within a few minutes, however, he encountered one of his subalterns, Lieutenant David Breeze, and a section of No. 1 Troop; they were soon joined by other members of the Squadron who had succeeded in collecting some of the special 30lb explosive charges designed to demolish the Brigade's bridge targets. Shortly afterwards a team from the parachute field ambulance, complete with jeep and trailer, also appeared.

Roseveare decided to head for Troarn without further delay, rather than search for 8th Parachute Battalion, and so he and his small force set off, subsequently making their way through the enemy-occupied villages of Herouvillette and Escoville undetected. As recounted earlier in this chapter, when they were 3 miles from Troarn, they met the group from 8th Parachute Battalion under Lieutenant Thompson. Deciding to send his main party of sappers on to the bridge at Bures, Roseveare commandeered the 224th Parachute Field Ambulance team's jeep and trailer and, loading it with the explosives and Lieutenant Bridge's section of sappers, headed at high speed for Troarn. On nearing the town, Roseveare ran into a barbed-wire barrier positioned across the road which took a few minutes to cut as it had become entangled with the front axle of the vehicle, before continuing to the edge of the town. At that point, a German soldier on a bicycle blundered into the small party and was shot by Lieutenant Breeze. Roseveare drove through the town at breakneck speed, pursued by a hail of small-arms fire. As he drove downhill out of the town, one of the party, Sapper Peachey, who was sitting on the trailer, was thrown off and subsequently captured.

On reaching the bridge, Roseveare and his men set to placing their charges before positioning the trailer containing the rest of the explosives, in the centre of the bridge itself. Minutes later they detonated them, blowing a 15-foot-wide hole in the bridge, before heading northwards on a track running along the river. Abandoning the jeep at the end of the track, they set off on foot towards 3rd Parachute Brigade's headquarters at Le Mesnil.

In the meantime other elements of the Squadron had encountered enemy troops almost immediately on landing in the area of Ranville. In several instances, sappers were initially cornered but succeeded in fighting their way out and eventually rejoining the Squadron, which regrouped at Le Mesnil.

During the following few days, the Squadron was employed in the infantry role, while also laying minefields and carrying out demolitions tasks. On one occasion, a section of sappers, supported by a platoon from one of the battalions, infiltrated behind German lines and blew two craters in the road leading out of Breville; as they withdrew, they heard the satisfying sound of an enemy half-track falling into the first crater.

Lieutenant John Shave, commanding a section of No. 2 Troop, later recalled events during that period:

> During a lull in our first battle, I was ordered to take my section 2 miles down the Troarn road to be attached to 8th Parachute Battalion. At low strength, the Battalion held the end of a salient spread from the Bois de Bures on the left, across the Troarn road and to the edge of the escarpment falling away to the right. We dug in on part of the Battalion perimeter where our first task was to booby trap a wood in front of the platoon on our right. We spent the day of the 10th June laying trip wires connected to charges of plastic explosives in this wood.
>
> On the following day, the 11th June, we lifted the mines that we had laid on D-Day in order to allow the 1st Battalion The Gordon Highlanders to pass through as the initial move by 51st Highland Division to extend the salient. During the night, along with a platoon of 8th Parachute Battalion, we patrolled through the Bois de Bures to crater the Bures-Bavent road which was the only route open to the Germans on our side of the River Dives. In the depths of the woods, we encountered sustained machine-gun fire and the platoon commander ordered a withdrawal.

Angered by this incident, Lieutenant Colonel Alastair Pearson led us out in company strength on the following night, cleared out the enemy and held the road while my sappers and I cratered it over a culvert. During that day, we had also removed the booby traps laid earlier as the platoon on our right was disturbed by straying cattle setting off the charges. We also suffered a serious casualty when Corporal Powell was badly wounded by mortar fire. His loss was a great blow to us all and I promoted Sapper Hurst to be my Second-in-Command.

Patrols ordered for the night of the 13th included sapper reconnaissance of the River Dives to discover what the Germans were doing about crossings. Accompanied by Sapper Martin, I ventured through the woods to Bures. The railway bridge was as we had left it on the 6th June. Following the river, we disturbed some cows who alerted a German patrol. Leaving Martin with orders to return to the battalion if I ran into trouble, I swam the river near the road bridge. To avoid the steep reed-covered bank, I climbed up the broken steelwork of the bridge where I was greeted by indistinct shapes and a shout of 'Hande hoch!' ['Hands up!'] I ducked down and fed them the 36 Grenade that we all carried. In so doing, I fell back into the water and was able to escape. Whilst running back through the woods, I was fired upon by what later turned out to be the crew of a self-propelled gun laagered up on the road. We measured its track width on the following night when we repeated the patrol. On this occasion, with two others, I approached close enough to the Troarn bridge to be able to hear and see, in the moonlight, that it was being rebuilt with timber.

Unlike that of 3rd Parachute Brigade, the deployment of Headquarters 6th Airborne Division went without a hitch. The gliders carrying Major General Richard Gale and his advance headquarters took off after the aircraft carrying the two parachute brigades. Gale himself travelled in glider No. 70, flown by Major Billy Griffiths, accompanied by his ADC, Captain Tom Haughton, and Major David Baird, his GSO 2 Operations, together with his signaller, personal escort, driver, and Rifleman Grey who was Captain Haughton's batman. Gale later gave an account of the flight to Normandy and the subsequent landing:

In the glider we all wore our Mae Wests, and taking our places we all fastened ourselves in and waited for the jerk as the tug took the strain on the tow-rope. Soon it came and we could feel ourselves hurtling down the smooth tarmac. Then we were airborne and once again we heard the familiar whistle as the air rushed by and we glided higher and higher into the dark night.

I suppose all men have different reactions on these occasions. I went to sleep and slept soundly for the best part of an hour. I was woken by a considerable bumping. We had run into a small local storm in the Channel. Griffiths was having a ticklish time and the glider was all over the place.

Between the glider and tug there is an intercom line, so that the two pilots can talk to one another. In this bumping we received, the intercom line broke; the only means of speech contact from the tug to the glider and vice versa was lost. The problem of cast-off would have to be solved by judgement. Griffiths merely said, 'The intercom has bust.'

Only a few minutes after that he said, 'We will be crossing the French coast shortly.' We were flying at about 5,000 feet and we soon knew the coast was under us, for we were met by a stream of flak. It was weird to see this roaring up in great golden chains past the windows of the glider, some of it being apparently between us and the tug aircraft. Looking out, I could see the canal and the river through the clouds; for the moon was by now fairly well overcast and the clear moonlight we had hoped for was not there. Nevertheless, there we were.

In a few moments Griffiths said, 'We are over the landing zone now and will be cast off at any moment.' Almost as soon as he said this, we were. The whistling sound and the roar of the engines suddenly died down; no longer were we bumping about but gliding along on a glorious steady course. Away went the tug aircraft back to England. Round we turned, circling lower and lower; soon the co-pilot turned round to tell us to link up just as we were about to land. We all linked up by putting our arms around the men next to us. We were also, as I have said, strapped in. In case of a crash, this procedure would help us take the shock.

I shall never forget the sound as we rushed down in our final steep dive, then we suddenly flattened out and soon, with a bump, bump, bump, we landed on an extremely rough stubble field. Over the field we sped and then with a bang we hit a low embankment. The forward undercarriage wheel stove up through the floor, the glider spun round on its nose in a small circle and, as one wing hit one of those infernal stakes, we drew up to a standstill. We opened the door. Outside all was quiet.

About us now the other gliders were coming in, crashing and screeching as they applied their brakes. It was a glorious moment.

In the distance, from the direction of the bridges, we could now hear bursts of machine-gun fire. Except for the arrival of more and more gliders around us, all seemed to be still. It was eerie. Had Ranville been cleared of the enemy? Were the bridges taken? Were they intact and safely in our hands? How was Terence Otway and his gallant battalion faring at the Merville Battery? We could still hear intermittent fire from the direction of the bridges.

While they were attempting to unload the glider the passing moments seemed like hours. It was still dark and the unloading was proving to be more difficult than we had anticipated. The crash we had had, though not serious, resulted in the nose being really well dug into the ground and the problem of getting the jeep out was defeating us. Eventually we had to give it up, and so on foot we set out for Ranville.

By 0430 hours, the entire advance headquarters was moving off the LZ in its jeeps and trailers and by 0600 hours was established in the Château de Heaume in Le Bas de Ranville. An hour later, at 0700 hours, the Allied air and sea bombardment of the assault beaches began. This was the signal for radio silence to be lifted and the signallers busied themselves establishing communications with the two parachute brigades. Later that morning, having visited 5th Parachute Brigade, Major General Gale started to receive reports of 3rd Parachute Brigade and in particular the details of 9th Parachute Battalion's assault on the Merville Battery. This was a relief to him because until then he had not received any news of the Brigade's progress and was becoming anxious.

It was later that morning that James Hill arrived at Divisional Headquarters, being pushed along on a bicycle. He subsequently recounted the welcome he received from Major General Gale:

On my arrival, General Richard Gale said: 'Well James, I am happy to tell you that your brigade has succeeded in all its objectives.' This was marvellous news, making me gloriously happy! At that juncture, however, I was seized by the ADMS, Colonel McEwan, whom we reverently called Old Technicolour because of the enormous number of medals he had accrued during the First World War and other conflicts, who insisted I must leave for the Main Dressing Station for an operation. This I refused to do unless he guaranteed to drive me personally to my brigade headquarters after I had been operated on. This he undertook to do. It was about 1300 hours and the last thing I knew was a heavy artillery concentration coming down on Ranville as 21st Panzer Division launched a counter-attack on our bridgehead.

When I awoke at around 1530 hours, McEwan was as good as his word and sat me on the back seat of his jeep and, with his driver, we set off for my brigade headquarters at Le Mesnil. As we were leaving Ranville, however, six Germans ran across the road ahead of us. McEwan, to my amazement, shouted at his driver to pull up and, taking a revolver out of the jeep pocket, with his driver set off in hot pursuit of the Germans, leaving a very irritated brigade commander sitting gingerly in solitary state on the back seat! However, three minutes later they sheepishly returned and continued on their mission to Le Mesnil, which was reached at 1600 hours in the afternoon. I found that Alastair Pearson had temporarily taken over the brigade and had been shot through the hand, but it took more than that to render him hors de combat. After briefing me, Alastair then returned to his battalion.

I then took stock. 9th Parachute Battalion, about ninety strong, was still on the La Panne feature and had not arrived in the brigade area as they had not been relieved by the Commandos as planned. The Canadians were at Le Mesnil as ordered and about 300 strong, while 8th Parachute Battalion was 2 miles down the road and numbering some 250 in strength.

I found that I had no Brigade Major. I learned later that he had been blown out of the door of his aircraft by enemy fire and hung suspended with a 60-pound kitbag attached to his leg before they could pull him in as the aircraft limped back to Odiham in England. Although his leg was pretty well dislocated and stuck out sideways, he was able to get a lift over in a glider the same evening with the airlanding brigade and arrived at my headquarters at Le Mesnil at 0900 hours the next morning. However, the Brigade Major must have two legs that work and so he was taken to the Main Dressing Station some forty-eight hours later; it is of such stuff that good Brigade Majors are made.

Neither did I have my DAA QMG, Major Alec Pope. I learned later that he had been dropped some 15 miles to the north of the River Dives and gathered together a small band of men, including two glider pilots. Cornered by the Germans, they refused to surrender, died fighting and were later buried in a delightful little churchyard at St Vaast en Auge. How easy it would have been for them to surrender, but they didn't.

There was no Roman Catholic padre. Before the battle, I had given Padre McVeigh a shillelagh for self-defence. He had been dropped wide and was taken prisoner. He got fed up with being interrogated by six Germans and, setting about them with his shillelagh, escaped. He was in due course recaptured, but the Germans refused to accept he was a priest and stripped him of his dog collar. He spent the rest of the war in the toughest prisoner-of-war camp on the Baltic.

Nor was there a Commando Liaison Officer – Peter Haig Thomas, for three years stroke of the Cambridge boat and Olympic oarsman. He was killed within half an hour of landing, and lies buried in the village churchyard at Bavent.

We had had a bad night drop with arduous tasks to carry out. We had suffered heavy casualties, had little sleep and possessed only the small amount of food we carried. This was not an auspicious way to start the Normandy campaign and thus imposed severe physical and mental strain on young soldiers inexperienced in battle. Nevertheless, their careful preparation enabled them to pass their initiation with flying colours.

Chapter 9

As dawn was breaking on 6 June, Major General Gale met the commander of 5th Parachute Brigade, Brigadier Nigel Poett, who reported that the bridges over the River Orne and Caen Canal had been taken, and that 7th Parachute Battalion was deployed on the west bank, while 12th and 13th Parachute Battalions were in positions holding Le Bas de Ranville and Ranville respectively.

The first member of his brigade to land on DZ 'N', Poett was a man who believed in leading from the front. He had dropped with the pathfinder team from 22nd Independent Parachute Company so that he would be well placed to take the appropriate action in the event that the assault on the Caen Canal and River Orne bridges by the glider-borne coup de main force was unsuccessful. He landed precisely in the right place, as he later related:

> I was very well dropped. When I landed, it was in complete and absolute blackness. There was not a soul in sight and not a sound apart from the noise of the aircraft going away. I could see the exhausts of the aircraft and knew the direction in which it was flying, which was towards Ranville. I moved up the line in the direction in which it was heading and met a private soldier from my defence platoon. A few seconds later, the attack on the bridges went in and we could see the flashes and hear the sounds. I immediately headed for the bridges, not waiting for anyone else, where I expected my wireless operator who was an officer. Unfortunately, he had been killed on the DZ.

Poett's radio operator was Lieutenant Gordon Royle of 6th Airborne Divisional Signals. Shortly after landing, he had encountered a number of enemy with a machine gun and attacked them single-handed, but was killed.

On reaching the Orne bridge, Poett discovered that Major John Howard's company had taken both its objectives and subsequently had beaten off a German counter-attack. As he was being briefed, he could hear the sound of the aircraft bringing in his brigade; in addition to his three battalions, this comprised forward observer parties from 53rd Airlanding Light Regiment RA, 591st Parachute Squadron RE (less one troop) and 225th Parachute Field Ambulance.

7th Parachute Battalion's advance party had dropped with the pathfinders but took a long time to rally. Consequently, no one reached the Battalion RV at Le Horn, near the Orne bridge, and mark it prior to the arrival of the main drop. Although the dropping of the Brigade generally went well the Battalion was scattered, this largely being due to each man being very heavily laden with equipment which resulted in slow exits from aircraft and inevitable dispersal of sticks.

By 0230 hours, only 40 per cent of the Battalion had reached the RV and only a few of the containers packed with 3-inch mortars, Vickers medium machine guns and radios had been located. The sound of Major John Howard's whistle, signalling the successful capture of the bridges, could be heard and so the Commanding Officer, Lieutenant Colonel Geoffrey Pine-Coffin, decided to make for the bridges without any further delay, leaving his Second-in-Command, Major Eric Steele-Baume, at the RV to collect up any stragglers.

C Company, under Captain Bob Keene, led the way at the double, followed by Major Nigel Taylor's A Company, which crossed the bridges and took up positions in houses in the southern part of Benouville. B Company, under Major Roger Neale, meanwhile moved into positions in the wood and hamlet of Le Port at the northern end of Benouville.

The Battalion was well established in its positions by dawn, but Lieutenant Colonel Pine-Coffin still had only some 200 of his own men and Major John Howard's seventy-strong company which, together with its attached party of sappers, was holding the eastern end of the canal bridge.

In Le Port, B Company was positioned with its platoons in some of the houses and on a wooded spur between the village and the canal bridge. Initially it came under fire from the church nearby but this was countered by a well-placed PIAT bomb that decapitated the church tower, silencing any opposition.

Shortly afterwards, some light tanks appeared and halted in full view of one of C Company's platoons positioned in an outpost at the Château de Benouville. The crews dismounted and gathered in a group at the head of the column, at which point the platoon opened fire, hitting a number of the crewmen and scattering the remainder who fled back to the safety of their vehicles, which were soon heading away across the fields in the direction of the coast.

Throughout the morning the enemy probed A Company's positions in the southern part of Benouville which came under fire from self-propelled guns at close range, forcing the withdrawal of a platoon deployed on either side of the main road on the southern edge of the village. Meanwhile Lieutenant David Hunter's platoon, positioned in a farm just to the west of the road, found itself dealing with groups of enemy infantry attempting to carry out a flanking movement to its left. Later that morning, enemy infantry and armour succeeded in reaching the southern edge of Benouville but were prevented from advancing any further. At one point a Mark IV tank did reach the centre of the village from the rear but was knocked out and set ablaze with Gammon bombs.

During the morning two enemy patrol craft were observed approaching the canal bridge, which was still held by a platoon of Major John Howard's company. When they were at a range of some 100 yards, Howard's men opened fire and hit one of the craft with a PIAT, disabling it. This vessel was captured but the other succeeded in making good its escape.

Throughout the morning of 6 June, 7th Parachute Battalion's positions were probed by the enemy who were operating in approximately company strength, in some cases supported by tanks. Attempts were made to infiltrate the Battalion's positions but these were thwarted by aggressive patrolling. The Battalion was still hampered by the lack of its radios and at times Lieutenant Colonel Pine-Coffin found the situation becoming somewhat obscure, much to his concern.

At noon, however, the welcome sound of bagpipes heralded the arrival of the leading elements of Brigadier The Lord Lovat's 1st Special Service Brigade which, having bypassed the enemy, had pushed inland as swiftly as possible to link up with 5th Parachute Brigade.

The arrival of the commandos did not result in any respite for 7th Parachute Battalion, which continued to be subjected to pressure from the enemy. The late afternoon saw A Company bearing the brunt of the fighting, at one point being cut off from the battalion. Despite being wounded in the thigh, Major Nigel Taylor continued to command his company while propped up in the window of a building until eventually forced to hand over to his Second-in-Command, Captain Jim Webber, who had also been wounded. By mid-afternoon, however, the Company had been reduced to some twenty men, with all of its officers either killed or wounded. Nevertheless, despite its heavy losses, it held its positions in Benouville for seventeen hours.

At 2115 hours the leading elements of 185th Infantry Brigade, in the form of the 2nd Battalion The Royal Warwickshire Regiment, reached the bridges. The relief of 7th Parachute Battalion, however, proved difficult as it was still in contact with the enemy but it was eventually achieved by an attack which relieved the Battalion's forward company and permitted the evacuation of the wounded. By 0330 hours on 7 June, the Battalion had withdrawn over the bridges to a position in reserve after being in action for a period of twenty-one hours of continuous and hard fighting.

12th Parachute Battalion, along with the 13th, had found itself scattered during the drop. Its RV was at a quarry below the road linking Ranville and Sallenelles near the Orne, approximately half a mile north of the river bridge. The first to arrive at the RV were the Commanding Officer, Lieutenant Colonel Johnny Johnson, the commander of A Company, Major Gerald Ritchie, the Second-in-Command of B Company, Captain Jerry Turnbull, and the Regimental Sergeant Major.

The majority of the Battalion, however, had been dropped in some woods and orchards on the eastern side of the DZ and it was about three-quarters of an hour before some began to arrive at the RV. The Battalion's Second-in-Command, Major Ken Darling, and the Adjutant, Captain Paul Bernhard, meanwhile found themselves on one of 3rd Parachute Brigade's DZs, while the Signals Officer and his signallers, together with the commander of Headquarter Company, Major George Winney, were dropped some distance away as the result of the pilot of their aircraft mistaking the River Dives for the Orne.

By the time it left its DZ, the Battalion was at 60 per cent of its full strength. Nevertheless it moved swiftly to take its objective, which was the area of Le Bas de Ranville. A Company took up positions in the area of a road junction to the east of the Orne bridge, while B Company, on the forward left, was positioned on the southern edge of the village. C Company was located on the rising ground to the south, facing in the direction of Caen with its right flank on the canal and a twelve-man standing patrol deployed 300 yards forward of the main company position.

The enemy's reaction to 12th Parachute Battalion's arrival was not long in coming. Two attacks on Ranville were mounted by elements of the 125th Panzer Grenadier Regiment but these were repulsed, the enemy losing a number of men taken prisoner, along with three self-propelled guns and a tank knocked out by the guns of 4th Airlanding Anti-Tank Battery RA.

During the fighting, C Company's standing patrol was attacked by enemy infantry supported by two self-propelled guns as the patrol commander, Captain John Sim, later recalled:

My particular task was to command a forward screen in a hedgerow some 300 yards from C Company's position. It had been planned that I was to have a section from No. 4 Platoon, two LMGs, two PIATs, a 17-pounder and 6-pounder anti-tank gun, a Forward Observer Bombardment (FOB) officer to direct the fire of a cruiser lying offshore, and a wireless set for my own use. The flanks of my position were to be covered by machine guns from a position in the rear.

By first light my party, less the 17-pounder anti-tank gun, the two PIATs and my wireless set, was dug in and well camouflaged. The FOB party was busily engaged in ranging the cruiser's guns on likely targets while one of my snipers scored a hit on a man inspecting a container some 400 yards away. At about 1000 hours, we spotted some men who appeared to be positioning a gun on a hill towards Caen. My FOB directed fire on to them and they vanished. Then came a long wait without a movement to be seen.

At about 1100 hours, we were surprised to see a company of about fifty men straggling across our front from the left flank. They appeared to be some of our own men as they were wearing parachute-style steel helmets and camouflage smocks. They were about 300 yards away across a large open field and I thought perhaps B Company, on my left, was sending out a patrol in force. However, I soon changed my mind when they changed direction and advanced in line towards us. I asked the FOB to direct the cruiser's guns on them and then switch to the woods behind. A little while later, however, he informed me that this could not be done as they were firing on a priority target.

Meanwhile, the enemy continued to advance, knee-deep in long grass. Only my sniper was active, further down the hedgerow, as our plan was not to open fire until the enemy had come to within 50 yards of us where there was a barbed-wire cattle fence. We watched and waited as the enemy came closer and closer. When they reached the fence, I fired a Verey light straight at them and my men opened fire. The enemy went straight to ground in the long grass.

Simultaneously, two self-propelled guns lumbered up from behind a ridge to our front and opened fire while on the move. They stopped 70 yards away from us, a sitting target for our 6-pounder anti-tank gun but it did not open fire. Shortly afterwards, a soldier crawled up to me on hands and knees and saluted! He was sorry but the 6-pounder could not fire as the breech block had slipped and must have been damaged in the glider landing. I could not be angry with him for not telling me earlier as he was so apologetic, but the knowledge that I had no weapon with which to engage the self-propelled guns was rather frightening.

We were by now suffering casualties rather quickly. The man on my right was dead. Another of my men, while crawling up to me moaning and groaning, slumped over before he could reach me and lay still. I noticed that the FOB had been badly wounded.

Meanwhile the enemy, under the covering fire of the self-propelled guns, were crawling round to my right flank. I sent up two red Verey lights in their direction, a pre-arranged signal to my company commander that I was being attacked from that direction. I hoped that he would get the 3-inch mortars into action and do something to help me. No response, however.

As so often happens in action, all fire suddenly ceased and silence reigned for a bit. I felt fogged and mentally dulled, incapable of realising that I was in danger. Peeping through the thick hedge, I saw a German soldier standing up in another hedge running at right angles to ours. I ordered my batman to have a shot at him, which he did. The self-propelled guns had quietened down – one of them was firing only spasmodically into our position. To my amazement, I saw the hatch of one open and a German officer, splendidly arrayed in polished jackboots, stiff cap and Sam Browne belt, leisurely climbed down and lit a cigarette. He was allowed only two puffs. I don't think we killed him as we did not find his body later.

Again we were subjected to fire but this time by mortars, the bombs airbursting in the hedgerow trees. Most uncomfortable – and we could do little but keep our heads down and hope for the best while the hell lasted. Again that sudden silence. One of my sergeants came to me and informed me that there were only four of us left alive and asked me what we were to do. The question, I am ashamed to say, made me very aware of my personal danger and I decided that, rather than wait in the ditch to be killed, it was worth the risk to dash back to our company position and perhaps live to fight another day. We could do no more good where we were, in my opinion.

The four of us – my sergeant, my batman, a sniper and myself – made use of a shallow ditch that ran alongside a ditch into the main position. We covered each other leapfrog fashion, running a few yards, crawling, firing and so back to our company; the Germans firing wildly at us most of the time. Soon after we had evacuated the forward position, it was subjected to 3-inch mortar fire and reoccupied by another section from C Company, the Germans having had enough and withdrawn. The FOB, who had been badly wounded in the thigh, and two other badly wounded men were taken away by stretcher-bearers; the remainder lay dead at their posts.

The two self-propelled guns had followed up Sim's withdrawal but both were knocked out by a 6-pounder anti-tank gun sited on B Company's position. No further fighting occurred until 1700 hours when the standing patrol reported enemy activity on an area designated the 'Ring Contour'. Later that evening, an attack on it was mounted by A Company which despatched a platoon forward under cover of artillery fire from the guns of 3rd Infantry Division, but came under very heavy fire and was forced to withdraw.

By the time 13th Parachute Battalion had moved off from its RV, it also numbered no more than 60 per cent of its full strength. It was tasked with securing Ranville and covering both bridges from the approaches to the south-east, between the Orne and the wooded ridge of the Bois de Bavent.

A Company, commanded by Major John Cramphorn, had the task of protecting the sappers of 591st Parachute Squadron RE and assisting them in clearing the anti-glider poles from the LZ on which Major General Richard Gale and his advance headquarters were due to land, along with some of the divisional troops at 0330 hours. The task was completed with half an hour to spare, despite the area coming under mortar and machine-gun fire, and the gliders landed successfully at 0335 hours.

By 0400 hours on 6 June, the Battalion had cleared a number of defensive positions on the northern edge of Ranville that overlooked the DZ, as well as some groups of enemy troops in various houses. By dawn, it had secured the village that hitherto had been garrisoned by a company of enemy infantry of which the main body was apparently away from its billets during the hours of darkness. Thereafter, A Company was put to work laying a minefield to the east of the village.

Later that day, four self-propelled guns appeared from the direction of Herouvillette but all were knocked out by 6-pounders. During the afternoon, the enemy mounted a company attack on Ranville from the same direction, but this was beaten off.

The night of 6/7 June saw the arrival of 6th Airlanding Brigade, which was by all accounts an awe-inspiring sight for those who witnessed it. At 2100 hours, the sky was filled with hundreds of tug aircraft towing 230 Horsa and thirty Hamilcar gliders. Casting off at an altitude of 800 feet, the gliders turned and swooped down on to their allotted LZs.

Down on to LZ 'N' went Brigade Headquarters and the 1st Battalion The Royal Ulster Rifles, while the 2nd Battalion The Oxfordshire & Buckinghamshire Light Infantry, less its coup-de-main force of six platoons holding the bridges, flew into LZ 'W' along with A Company of the 12th Battalion The Devonshire Regiment, 6th Airborne Armoured Reconnaissance Regiment, 211th Airlanding Light Battery RA, 249th Field Company RE and two sections of 195th Airlanding Field Ambulance.

Major Napier Crookenden was the Brigade Major. He later recalled the flight and subsequent landing in Normandy:

> Brigade Headquarters and the Royal Ulster Rifles took off from Brize Norton on time. An hour before take-off, the battered and dirty figure of Bill Collingwood, the Brigade Major of 3rd Parachute Brigade, appeared in the Officers' Mess, where we were eating bacon and eggs, and asked for a lift. He had got stuck and injured on jumping from his Albemarle aircraft early that morning and had been forced to land back in England. We fixed him up with a spare glider for his stick and he was able to rejoin his brigade that night.
>
> The flight itself was smooth and uneventful. In my glider was the DAAG from divisional headquarters, my batman/driver, two signallers, a jeep and trailer, and a No. 22 radio set. Shortly before 2100 hours, we sighted the French coast and could soon pick out the mouth of the River Orne and Ouistreham. Spread out to our right we could see the invasion fleet, and the muzzle flashes from the guns of the bombarding ships were clearly visible. Over the land were masses of smoke and haze. Our tug and glider stream ran in down the line of the Orne, turned through 180 degrees and landed on LZs 'N' and 'W'. There was a little light flak coming up and I could see one of the tug aircraft ahead of us going down on fire. LZ 'N' was already covered in gliders and parachutes, and one glider on the ground was burning with a column of black smoke.

Our glider pilot released from the tug at about 800 feet and made a steep diving turn towards the LZ. We were all strapped in by now and we put our arms around each other's shoulders and lifted our legs off the floor, ready for the landing. In a few seconds we were down, bumped twice, broke off a wing on an anti-landing pole and stopped. We got the tail off without difficulty, unloaded the jeep and were moving off to our RV in Le Bas de Ranville a few minutes after landing. Our first impressions were how like our briefing models and photographs the countryside was, and how like an exercise the whole thing seemed.

The enemy reaction to the landing was swift, with Ranville coming under mortar fire and Divisional Headquarters suffering several casualties. The LZs came under mortar and small-arms fire but casualties were light. A 6-pounder anti-tank gun and its jeep were hit while being driven off LZ 'N', but The Royal Ulster Rifles only sustained one casualty. On LZ 'W', one glider, carrying men of the 2nd Battalion The Oxfordshire & Buckinghamshire Light Infantry, was hit by anti-aircraft fire and broke up over the LZ; only three of its passengers survived, all of whom were badly injured. An hour and a half later, however, the Battalion was heading for its assembly point north of Benouville.

The 6th Airborne Armoured Reconnaissance Regiment encountered problems on landing and disembarking. Two of its Tetrarch light tanks were destroyed when their Hamilcar gliders collided on landing, while the remainder became immobilized when their bogies and sprocket wheels became entangled in the rigging lines and canopies of parachutes lying on the LZs. It took their crews some time to disentangle them before they could move off the LZ and head for the Regiment's harbour area that had been reconnoitred the night before by a harbour party dropped with the pathfinders, but which subsequently lost its commander and a complete stick through enemy action.

Brigadier Hugh Kindersley established his headquarters in an orchard in Le Bas de Ranville and held his first orders group at 2230 hours, only an hour and a half after the first gliders had landed. He tasked the 1st Battalion The Royal Ulster Rifles, commanded by Lieutenant Colonel Jack Carson, with capturing the villages of Longueval and Sainte Honorine the following morning, while Lieutenant Colonel Michael Roberts, commanding the 2nd Battalion The Oxfordshire & Buckinghamshire Light Infantry, was given the task of taking Escoville.

By midnight on 6 June, 6th Airborne Division was deployed in Normandy and had undergone its baptism of fire. 3rd Parachute Brigade was deployed on a 4-mile-wide front with 9th Parachute Battalion at Le Plein in the north, 1st Canadian Parachute Battalion and James Hill's headquarters at Le Mesnil in the centre, and 8th Parachute Battalion in the southern part of the Bois de Bavent and Bures. 5th Parachute Brigade was holding Le Bas de Ranville and Ranville with 12th and 13th Parachute Battalions, with 7th Parachute Battalion in reserve on the western edge of DZ 'N'. 6th Airlanding Brigade had two of its battalions deployed and ready to begin operations to extend the Division's bridgehead the following morning. 1st Special Service Brigade, still under command of the Division, was holding the villages of Hauger, Le Plein and Amfreville, situated to the north and north-east of DZ 'N'.

All that remained to arrive by sea the following day were the 12th Battalion The Devonshire Regiment (less one company), 53rd Airlanding Light Regiment RA (less one battery), 3rd Airlanding Anti-Tank Battery RA (less one troop), 2nd Airlanding Light Anti-Aircraft Battery RA, 195th Airlanding Field Ambulance (less two sections) and other divisional troops.

Chapter 10

On the morning of 7 June, 9th Parachute Battalion left its location in the grounds of the Château d'Amfreville at Hauger to rejoin the Brigade south of Breville. Its new positions would be in the area of the Château St Côme, extending across the road between Breville and Le Mesnil, inclusive of a villa called the Bois de Mont. The planned route for the move had been cross-country, bypassing Breville to the west, but those in the lead somehow made an error and the Battalion found itself marching through Breville itself. By 1330 hours it had reached its new location and started digging in, although shortly afterwards the Germans reoccupied Breville.

Following a discussion concerning the weak strength of the Battalion, James Hill decided that it should hold the Bois de Mont and endeavour to deny the area of the Château St Côme by patrolling. Lieutenant Colonel Otway thus altered his positions so that they centred on the villa, which was situated in a clearing surrounded by trees. Almost opposite its gates was the entrance to the 300-yard-long drive leading to the small château, which was a stud farm; beyond the château itself were stables and outbuildings. Opposite the gates to the château was a narrow lane, lined by trees and deep ditches on either side, which ran along the northern edge of the Bois de Mont towards the west.

Brigade Headquarters and 1st Canadian Parachute Battalion were located 1,000 yards away to the south at Le Mesnil, while 8th Parachute Battalion was in the Bois de Bavent, holding the southern edge of the ridge. 5th Parachute Brigade was holding Ranville and the two bridges over the Orne and Caen Canal, while 6th Airlanding Brigade was covering the southern approaches from Herouvillette and Le Bas de Ranville. 1st Special Service Brigade meanwhile was holding Le Plein and Amfreville.

Within 9th Parachute Battalion, A Company was in positions along both sides of the château, while B Company was located along the sunken lane along the northern edge of the Bois de Mont. C Company held the southern and western sides of the position and was the Battalion's counter-attack force. The Vickers guns of the Machine Gun Platoon were positioned in a ditch near the château gates, covering both ways along the Breville-Le Mesnil road. Battalion Headquarters and Regimental Aid Post were located in the Bois de Mont villa itself.

The following day, 8 June, a patrol led by Lieutenant Dennis Slade reconnoitred the Château St Côme, which was found to be unoccupied. A search of the building, however, uncovered a German payroll amounting to the equivalent of £500 and this was promptly appropriated for the Battalion funds. Other signs of recent occupation by the enemy were evident in the form of discarded items of uniform and equipment strewn about.

At around midday, a German patrol approached A Company's positions but was beaten off. Later that afternoon, a series of attacks were mounted against B Company by troops of the 857th Grenadier Regiment but these were driven off without any difficulty. The Regimental Sergeant Major, WO1 Cunningham, played a key role in these actions by leading his own small counter-attack force of a Vickers medium machine gun (MMG) detachment, a Bren light machine gun (LMG) group and some members of the Anti-Tank Platoon, whom he moved swiftly to areas in the Battalion's perimeter under threat.

That night, 9th Parachute Battalion received two 3-inch mortars, three Vickers MMGs and a resupply of ammunition. All the Battalion's mortars had gone astray during the drop and thereafter had been sorely missed, as had the members of the Mortar Platoon who were nearly all still missing. Within a very short space of time, however, a number of replacements had been trained to a very creditable standard by Sergeant Hennessy of the Mortar Platoon. Likewise, a new Machine Gun Platoon had been formed by Sergeant McGeever, who mounted one of the Vickers MMGs on a jeep for use as a mobile fire support vehicle.

This period saw 3rd Parachute Brigade involved in some very heavy fighting as James Hill later summed up:

> The fighting on our ridge became particularly fierce. Alastair Pearson and 8th Parachute Battalion were separated from us by some 2 miles, denying the enemy the approaches to the ridge from the south. Their success was a remarkable feat and vital of course to our success. 9th Parachute Battalion, whose strength fluctuated from ninety to between 190 and 270, held the wooded area and road adjoining the Château St Côme. 1st Canadian Parachute Battalion held the Le Mesnil crossroads area immediately to the south. My headquarters and the thirty-strong defence platoon, numbering some

150 in all, and the Canadians with about 300 men, were concentrated over a front of about a mile, astride the Breville-Troarn road running north to south along the top of the ridge.

Enemy probing attacks initially concentrated on the Canadians at Le Mesnil then switched to 9th Parachute Battalion following the reoccupation of Breville by the Germans on 8th June. It was only then that I realised we were up against a first-class German infantry formation, the 346th Grenadier Division, which was supported by tanks and self-propelled guns. During this period, some six attacks were launched against 9th Parachute Battalion from Breville and the east, three of which were coordinated with attacks on 1st Canadian Parachute Battalion at Le Mesnil.

Dawn on 9 June found 9th Parachute Battalion under heavy mortar fire, this being followed by a strong attack by enemy infantry against A Company and part of B Company on either side of the road. Both companies waited until the enemy were 50 yards away before opening fire. Heavy small-arms fire, together with a hail of 2-inch and 3-inch high-explosive bombs, wreaked havoc among the German infantry who broke and fled into the woods near the château. A second attack, which followed about an hour later, met the same fate.

Later that morning, the Battalion received a report that Brigade Headquarters was under threat. Lieutenant Colonel Otway gathered a force of some thirty men from his battalion headquarters and C Company, under Lieutenant Christie, together with a fire support group of two LMG groups, equipped with captured MG-42 machine guns, under Major George Smith. Leading them swiftly through the wood to the south-east, Otway was able to trap the enemy between his own force and the Brigade Headquarters Defence Platoon. Nineteen enemy were killed and one was taken prisoner, but unfortunately the GSO 3 Intelligence, Captain Wilkinson, was killed during this action.

It was following this action that James Hill narrowly escaped injury or worse as he later recalled:

I was taking tea with Terence Otway which his batman served on a silver tray from the house while we sat on the side of a slit trench. The chaps loved this! Unfortunately, just then a mortar bomb burst in the tree immediately above our trench. The rumour quite erroneously went round that we never spilt our tea. Unfortunately, I was never able to hear properly in my right ear thereafter.

During the afternoon, A Company came under threat again when two platoons of infantry began infiltrating through the wood to the east and south of the Company's positions. A platoon of C Company, under Major Eddie Charlton, the Battalion's Second-in-Command, and Lieutenant John Parfitt, carried out a counter-attack. Unfortunately, however, they encountered two enemy machine guns and Charlton, Parfitt and five others were killed, their bodies being recovered that night by a patrol.

That afternoon witnessed some enemy air activity in the form of Focke-Wulf 190 fighter-bombers which were engaged by the 40mm Bofors guns and 20mm Hispano-Suiza cannons of 2nd Airlanding Light Anti-Aircraft Battery RA. Later, RAF Stirling bombers dropped supplies and 6-pounder anti-tank guns to the north of Ranville.

In the early hours of 10 June, an eight-man patrol led by Sergeants Frith and Woodcraft was despatched to the Château St Côme. Having divided the patrol in half, Sergeant Frith and his three men headed off to search the stables while Sergeant Woodcraft and the remainder entered the château. On entering the building, they searched the ground floor before heading upstairs to search the bedrooms. Shortly afterwards, Sergeant Frith and his men came under fire from enemy in the area of the stables and withdrew to the château where they rejoined the rest of the patrol as Sergeant Woodcraft later recounted:

> By now our Bren gunner was in action and Lance Corporal Jack Watkins was sent out to stoke up some more fire while we got the signaller out. We did this by telling him to go to the far side of the room and to run like hell. By the time he got to the door he was flat out and away he went down the drive; we could see the sparks as bullets hit the cobbles just behind him. We now had to get out but it was impossible to use the door as the Germans were concentrating their fire on it. The woodwork was rapidly being reduced to splinters and pieces of brickwork were flying about. We shouted to Watkins to get back down the drive and we would go out through the French windows on the other side of the room. When we reached these we found they were locked but by running at them together we went out on to the lawn among pieces of window frame and broken glass.
>
> We picked ourselves up and ran for the wood on the other side of the house, and just as we reached it I looked back and saw a small party of Germans come round the far end of the château in hot pursuit. Instead of running straight through and into the orchard, we turned left and found ourselves in a vehicle park.

We took up a position behind one of the vehicles and as the Germans passed some 20 yards in front of us, we both opened up with our Stens and then, without waiting to see the result, turned and galloped down through the wood yelling 'Olly! Olly!' the rallying call of A Company.

Just after dawn on 10 June, Captain Robert Gordon-Brown appeared, accompanied by about thirty men. These new arrivals increased 9th Parachute Battalion's strength to 270 all ranks, which was still a low figure. Despite the fact that everyone was extremely tired, morale in the Battalion was very high. Rations were adequate and the only items in short supply were 3-inch mortar bombs.

The rest of the day witnessed the Battalion experiencing plenty of action, a half-hearted attack on A Company at 1100 hours being easily beaten off. Shortly afterwards, after a platoon of A Company had been redeployed forward about 50 yards into a ditch north-east of the château gates, about fifty enemy infantry began digging in along the ditch beside the Breville road in full view of two of the Battalion's medium machine guns. At a range of 500 yards, they were in perfect enfilade. Joined by two Bren LMG groups from B Company, the machine-gunners had a field day and virtually wiped out the entire enemy force. Shortly afterwards, the recently forward-deployed platoon ambushed a German patrol at a range of 10 yards, virtually annihilating it.

During the morning, the Germans had reoccupied the château and by early afternoon were there in force. A company of infantry advanced down the drive, supported by two self-propelled guns that opened fire on A and B Companies. Due to stocks of 3-inch mortar ammunition running very low, the Anti-Tank Platoon's PIATs were being used as makeshift mortars that proved very effective in breaking up the enemy infantry. At that point, Sergeant McGeever's jeep-mounted Vickers MMG engaged one of the self-propelled guns which had suddenly appeared to the north of the château; to the amazement of all those watching, it suddenly exploded and stopped in its tracks. Shortly afterwards, two companies of enemy attacked B Company from the north. It was a strong attack and was only repulsed by the Battalion's mortars, which had now been resupplied, and B Company's Bren LMGs.

At this juncture, Lieutenant Colonel Otway called for supporting fire from HMS *Arethusa* via the Royal Navy forward observers who should have been located at Brigade Headquarters. Unfortunately, however, this was no longer the case and James Hill had to resort to improvisation as he later recalled:

> The two sailors who were to direct the guns of the *Arethusa* had been killed in the early bombing raid. We did have one No. 22 radio set and one bedraggled naval rating who didn't know anything about firing guns but could work the set. I now had to find someone who could direct the *Arethusa*'s guns and so went across to Lieutenant Colonel Bradbrooke's Canadians and saw their very smart Regimental Sergeant Major, WO1 Clark. I thought, 'By God, he's the one to fire the guns of the *Arethusa*!' Unbelievably, in a short space of time, RSM Clark was bringing down the shells within 400 yards of our front line and we had restored contact. It was marvellous! An RSM who had never heard of the *Arethusa*, and a wet sailor with no training! That just shows what initiative can do. Sad to tell, however, within forty-eight hours RSM Clark was dead.

It took only fifteen minutes from Lieutenant Colonel Otway requesting fire support for the first salvoes of 6-inch shells to crash down 400 yards from 9th Parachute Battalion's positions. Standing in full view of the enemy, Captain Paul Greenway called out corrections to Otway who transmitted them by radio to Brigade Headquarters. Despite suffering heavy casualties from the shelling, the leading enemy troops still succeeded in reaching B Company's positions, where they received a further mauling which few survived. Those taken prisoner, including the Commanding Officer of the 2nd Battalion 857th Grenadier Regiment, revealed that their battalion had suffered heavy losses and that the Regiment had met a similar fate during the fighting in Ranville and Amfreville.

Late that night, Major Ian Dyer led C Company forward to occupy the château. Following some skirmishing with small groups of enemy, he and his men succeeded in doing so. Throughout the rest of the night, enemy patrols probed the company's position and kept it busy while the rest of the Battalion was left undisturbed.

1st Canadian Parachute Battalion had received a resupply on 7 June, including sorely-needed 3-inch mortars, to replace those lost in the drop, and a large quantity of ammunition. This proved particularly fortuitous as the mortars proved to be a decisive factor the following day when a strong attack was launched on the Battalion's positions at the Le Mesnil crossroads by enemy infantry of the 857th and 858th Grenadier Regiments, which were supported by tanks and self-propelled guns. These had formed up in a column along the road leading to Le Mesnil in the apparent belief that the Battalion possessed no mortars; before the enemy were in a position to assault, however, the Canadian mortars opened fire and caused heavy casualties.

The enemy, however, were determined and pressed home an attack on B and C Companies, supported by a single Mk IV tank which advanced between them, causing heavy casualties until driven off by PIATs. As it withdrew, the enemy infantry accompanying it came under heavy fire and fled when B Company counter-attacked with a bayonet charge, withdrawing to a fortified farmhouse some 200 yards down the road. Surrounded by a low wall, this was heavily defended and from it the Germans could threaten the crossroads.

At 0900 hours on 8 June, B Company was ordered to attack and clear the enemy from the farmhouse. Two platoons, under the command of Captain Peter Griffin and reinforced by members of Headquarter Company, were detailed for the task. While Griffin and one and a half platoons mounted a frontal assault through the orchard, taking the enemy by surprise and forcing them to withdraw to the farmhouse itself, the remainder took up a position to protect their flank. As Lieutenant Norman Toseland led a bayonet charge on an enemy position in a hedgerow, he and his men came under heavy fire which killed four of their number and wounded two. On their left flank, meanwhile, three men were killed and two more were hit by machine-gun fire from the hedgerow, which was cleared by Captain Griffin's group as it attacked the farmhouse.

A further assault on some outbuildings ground to a halt when Griffin and his men encountered a large number of enemy and some armoured vehicles in the farmyard. At the same time, German mortars opened fire on the farmhouse and an enemy counter-attack ensued with a tank in support. As Griffin and his men withdrew, his flank protection group opened fire on the counter-attack force which was caught in the crossfire and suffered heavy casualties.

Due to the strength of the enemy, B Company was forced to withdraw. The engagement had cost it dear: eight men killed and thirteen wounded. The farmhouse, however, was subsequently abandoned and thereafter the enemy confined themselves to sniping from the hedgerows, although several snipers were eliminated by patrols.

By this time, 6th Airborne Division had adopted the strategy of 'static offensive', which comprised heavy patrolling by day and night, and harassing the enemy whenever the opportunity arose. This ensured that the enemy was kept off balance as much as possible, not knowing when or where a threat would arise and thus being forced to deploy large numbers of troops who had to be constantly on their guard; on a number of occasions patrols encountered enemy patrols and some fierce actions ensued. This strategy also had the beneficial effect of maintaining an aggressive spirit and high morale throughout the Division.

One such patrol was carried out on 9 June in broad daylight by 1st Canadian Parachute Battalion. A platoon of C Company, commanded by Lieutenant Sam McGowan, moved out through B Company's positions and headed for the village of Bavent with the mission of determining enemy strength in the village and the surrounding area, and to pinpoint the number and positions of guns sited in the village itself. The platoon was to attack the village in such a way as to force the enemy to retaliate with all their weapons. One member of the patrol was Corporal Hartigan, who later described what happened:

It was a bright sunny morning as we slithered along hedgerows parallel to the Le Mesnil-Varaville road and passed beneath the rough planked bridge over a shallow brook or anti-tank ditch with a foot or two of water in it. We turned right towards Bavent once we were beyond our own B Company positions and followed this shallow waterway towards the village. Thick hedges arched over the water so it gave us good cover, provided the enemy didn't have machine guns posted to fire straight down its length. It turned out the route was clear; as we neared the village, we became over-confident because of the lack of activity by the enemy, and came up out of the waterway into the fields a little way from its hedges. All was still quiet. Now we became totally over-confident and, shouldering our arms, prepared to walk right into what we now thought to be an unoccupied village.

The enemy waited until they could see the whites of our eyes – maybe 75 feet out from the hummock or low stone wall which surrounded our side of Bavent before an MG-42 machine gun blasted away at us from point-blank range.

Its crew, however, didn't have the right stuff and missed us completely. Just ahead was a huge crater, put there by one of the RAF's blockbusters. Our section, Sergeant Morgan's, was in the lead and we ended up in this crater with all of us going in head first, feet first, upside down and sideways – all tangled up. It took a moment or two to regain some form of composure; for we all knew we had been spared from a literally bloody and sudden death by a bungling enemy. Sergeant Morgan, though, remained alert and was definitely made of the right stuff. The forward edge of the crater, where he had positioned himself, was only about 30 to 40 feet from where the machine gun had fired. He threw a couple of phosphorous grenades, followed by a Gammon bomb, then ordered us forward.

Private Morrison and I tore up a slight rise on the right edge of the village, with his Bren LMG and my 2-inch mortar and rifle, to give covering fire from the rear right flank, while Sergeant Morgan took the remaining six men of our section right into the houses after the enemy. The village, far from being undefended, was crawling with enemy troops, with machine-gun and rifle fire coming from everywhere. One surprising thing was that the enemy, well within range of Morrison's and my weapons, and positioned on upper floors and balconies, were obviously afraid to withdraw by way of the streets and could be seen scrambling over the rooftops. These became our best targets and, for a fleeting moment or two, we made the most of the opportunities offered.

As Sergeant Morgan led the rest of the section up the main street towards the first enemy-occupied house, Private Commeau was hit by machine-gun fire and died instantly on the road. Sergeant Morgan got the section into the houses, leaving one man by the door of each to warn of any impending trouble. At the first house he leaped through the entrance, followed by Private Mallon, and shot two enemy soldiers before they knew what was happening to them. On entering another house, however, he met his opposite number, a German sergeant, pointing a Schmeisser machine pistol at him; both men fired, the German falling and Sergeant Morgan being hit twice in the lower abdomen.

After Morrison had sprayed the rooftops with his Bren, harassing the retreating enemy scrambling over the rooftops, an enemy machine gun returned his fire. Since our cover was not particularly good, we had to back off to a less exposed position from which we used my 2-inch mortar.

Sergeant McPhee, our platoon sergeant, had found a German 2-inch mortar near the position from where the MG-42 had blasted away at us earlier. It was the regular infantry type with a heavy base plate and bipod, and there was a good supply of bombs for it in a dug-out nearby. Someone, however, had attempted to destroy the weapon by detonating a grenade in its barrel. We could only assume that it had been done by the enemy when Sergeant Morgan had thrown his grenades and Gammon bomb. The barrel of the mortar had a hole about 8 to 10 inches from the muzzle but Sergeant McPhee, cool as always, experimented with this weapon while under a considerable volume of fire. Although he found its range was severely limited, he proceeded to rain a heavy shower of bombs down on the village.

Our platoon commander, Lieutenant McGowan, decided that he was not going to let Jerry off the hook. He already had a pretty good idea of the number of enemy in Bavent, having judged it from the strength of the reaction to our attack. He called forward three men to draw the enemy's fire and sent them galloping across the open fields in front of the village to a copse which lay about 250 yards from the main enemy positions. The enemy took the bait and spewed out a torrent of fire across the fields. The worst of it was that the three men had to do the same thing to get back. Anyone who watched this spectacle never forgot it. All three did get back but we all knew that miracles were happening that day.

The following day, 10 June, the commander of I Corps, Lieutenant General Sir John Crocker, had decided to extend the bridgehead to the east of the River Orne. Accordingly, 51st Highland Division crossed the bridges to take over the southern half of the sector from 6th Airborne Division.

In his headquarters, James Hill had a good view of much that was happening in 6th Airborne Division's area at the time, as he later recalled:

My main task at this time was to endeavouring to enthuse everyone to hang on to their positions, some of them doing so by the skin of their teeth. My room was on the top of a barn with access only from the outside. When at my headquarters I sat on the top step with my left backside overhanging the steps, which was just as well as I smelt of gangrene poisoning – imagine my delight when I received a new pair of battledress trousers with accompanying underwear, on D+2.

I had a bird's eye view of the Germans' advance from Breville on D+4 and their attack on Peter Luard's battalion. The 13th held their fire until the last moment and then mowed them down. For the next two days, the enemy filtered back through the rear of our positions. I knew it was highly irregular to have Germans creeping about like that but we had neither the time nor resources to chase them.

It was about this time that we were strafed by our own Typhoons – it happened twice. Unfortunately, on one occasion the pregnant lady of the château, walking in the garden with her husband, was hit and died. Our doctors tried to save the baby but to no avail, and we buried them in a shroud in her garden with what dignity we could muster under such difficult circumstances. Soon after that, the husband and housekeeper left and my headquarters occupied the château.

That night of 10 June witnessed the arrival of the 5th Battalion The Black Watch at an assembly area a short distance south-west of 9th Parachute Battalion's position. Detached from 153rd Infantry Brigade and now under James Hill's command, the Highlanders had been given the task on the following day, 11 June, of attacking and capturing Breville, which was occupied by a strong force of infantry and self-propelled guns, from the south-west in order to dislodge the Germans from their vantage point on the ridge overlooking Ranville. The Château St Côme, held by C Company, was a vital element in any successful attack on Breville from the south as any assault from that direction would be vulnerable to counter-attack through the area to the north of the château.

The Commanding Officer of The Black Watch arrived at 9th Parachute Battalion's headquarters to plan his attack. His main assault would approach from the south-west after a heavy barrage of supporting fire from the guns of 51st Highland Division's artillery and the mortars of both battalions. Before dawn a company of The Black Watch took over the château from C Company, while Captain Hugh Smyth led a reconnaissance patrol along the road towards Breville to check the ground over which The Black Watch would advance.

When the attack went in, the leading companies of The Black Watch had to cross 250 yards of open ground. As they did so, the supporting artillery and mortar fire lifted and the Highlanders were immediately subjected to heavy machine-gun and mortar fire which caused several casualties. At the same time, the Germans laid down a heavy mortar bombardment on the area to the south-west through which The Black Watch reserve companies were moving. Heavy casualties were inflicted among them as well and the attack quickly ground to a halt. The Highlanders withdrew through 9th Parachute Battalion's positions to reorganize in the Bois de Mont before taking up positions around the château.

10 June also saw 1st Canadian Parachute Battalion posed with a serious threat when two enemy battalions moved onto the glider LZ north-west of the Le Mesnil crossroads. A combined force of the 2nd Battalion 857th Grenadier Regiment, 1st and 2nd Battalions 858th Grenadier Regiment and

several companies of the 744th Grenadier Regiment, supported by tanks and armoured cars, launched an attack at a point between 1st Canadian and 9th Parachute Battalions. This was broken up by heavy fire from artillery and machine guns, and the enemy were prevented from reaching the Canadians' positions.

At midday on 12 June, the entire front of 3rd Parachute Brigade was subjected to heavy artillery and mortar fire. This was followed at 1500 hours by an attack on 1st Canadian Parachute Battalion, as James Hill later recorded:

> At this juncture, the German divisional commander decided that our positions at St Côme and Le Mesnil must be liquidated once and for all, and on D+6 (12th June) launched a major attack on 9th Parachute Battalion, the Canadians and The Black Watch. This attack was in strength, preceded by a heavy bombardment lasting some three hours, and it went in at 1500 hours supported by tanks and self-propelled guns. The Black Watch were driven back and came back through 9th Parachute Battalion and my defence platoon positions.

Within a short space of time, all The Black Watch anti-tank guns had been knocked out and nine of the Battalion's Bren carriers put out of action. The centre of the fighting began to take place around the Château St Côme, the Germans desperately trying to seize it from The Black Watch who doggedly held on despite the heavy fire from tanks and self-propelled guns. Eventually, however, the pressure began to tell and gradually the enemy started to force the Highlanders back from other positions towards the Bois de Mont. At one point a platoon of The Black Watch, which was under heavy fire and had lost its commander and some of its NCOs, began to look as though it might lose its nerve. The situation was saved by Captain Hugh Smyth of A Company 9th Parachute Battalion, who left his trench and walked up the drive. Strolling around their positions, he talked to the Highlanders and restored their confidence before returning to his company.

The enemy then began switching their attention to 9th Parachute Battalion, A and B Companies coming under heavy fire from tanks and self-propelled guns. The Battalion's mortars were in constant action, dropping their bombs 300 yards away in the woods while enemy shell and mortar fire burst around them. More enemy infantry, supported by two tanks, now appeared opposite B Company. One tank received two hits from a PIAT but remained unscathed, responding by knocking out two of the Battalion's machine-gun positions astride the road leading to Breville, before a third hit from a PIAT forced it to withdraw. At that juncture the enemy infantry, who had managed to advance within very close range of A and B Companies, withdrew back into the woods around the château.

At that point in the battle Lieutenant Colonel Otway radioed James Hill that he would not be able to hold out for much longer, as the latter later described:

At 1600 hours, I received a radio message from Terence Otway saying that he was doubtful if he could hold out much longer. His position had already been penetrated on the previous day but the Germans had been driven out. Realizing that he would not have sent me this signal unless things were serious and that something must be done about it, I went immediately to Lieutenant Colonel Bradbrooke whose headquarters was 200 yards away at the end of our drive to ask him if he would let me have what reserves he had available at his headquarters. At that moment, however, he was hard pressed because for the first time in the operation in his sector, the Le Mesnil-Troarn road had been crossed by enemy tanks which were shooting up his right-hand company headquarters which was in a sawmill. However, he felt that they could cope with this situation and let me take what was left of his reserve company, forty men under Major John Hanson, an excellent commander. Together with any cooks and any spare men, we set off for the 9th Parachute Battalion.

Private Anderson, a young Red Indian aged 18, informed me that he would act as my bodyguard. We set off across the 400 yards that separated the brigade headquarters defence platoon from 9th Parachute Battalion. I remember seeing, as we entered the wood between the road and the château, a great tall figure which was Padre Nicol of The Black Watch who was calmly walking up and down, steadying his young soldiers who had fallen back across the road. I thought to myself, 'Here is a great man in anybody's army.' And so it was to be, for the Padre later became Moderator of the Church of Scotland.

I took the Canadians up through the wood to the north-east of 9th Parachute Battalion where a shambles reigned. It appeared to be occupied by Germans and Black Watch. At the far end of the wood, a Mark IV tank was cruising up and down at close range but my men had no means of dealing with it. At that stage Private Anderson was shot through the arm but refused to leave the field. I then handed over command to Major Hanson with orders for him to work his way on to the château. When he and his men got there, they found that a gallant section of The Black Watch was still holding out in one of the outhouses and drove out a large number of Germans who retreated. A great defensive victory had been won by 9th Parachute Battalion, the Canadians and The Black Watch.

One of those in 1st Canadian Parachute Battalion who took part in the counter-attack led by Hill was Private de Vries of C Company, who later recalled it clearly:

About 450 of us reported on call to the company headquarters. On arrival, we were told to double to brigade headquarters where we were met by the Brigadier who immediately set out with the order for us to follow him. We ran for the most part, until we came to a depressed cart track or lane up which we moved to the road ahead. We were now in the midst of bursting mortars, shells and machine-gun fire and moving forward somewhat cautiously, when I looked to my left and saw the Brigadier marching along in what must have been full view of the enemy, unperturbed and telling us to 'Move along lads, nothing to worry about.'

We crossed the road and hurried past burning jeeps, Bren gun carriers with exploding ammunition inside them and many dead lying about in a sort of laager, following the curve of trees at the edge of a field. We soon discovered most of the damage was being caused by a self-propelled gun that was sending over airbursts. We were ordered to repel an attack, firing at will. A Bren gunner and I had just taken up a position in a shallow trench we had scraped out when three Sherman tanks wheeled in front of us and were brewed up immediately. What happened from then on from my point of view is based on hearsay, but a runner and signaller told me later that the Brigadier had called on the Navy to shell the Germans preparing to attack. We heard the now familiar whistling sound of the heavy shells going over and the big crump of explosions. The airbursts stopped and the sound of machine guns diminished, and the battle was over. The Navy shells had caught the enemy in the open, taking the heart right out of them for further action. The airbursts had put almost half of our reinforcements out of action but fortunately the day had been saved.

That evening, however, saw further action, with 9th Parachute Battalion suffering more punishment, as described briefly by Hill:

James as a baby, aged three months, with his mother. (*Hill family collection*)

James at the age of three and a half, with his mother and three-month-old baby sister Bridget. (*Hill family collection*)

James at Scampton in 1916, stalking a rabbit. (*Hill family collection*)

James at the age of 18, after leaving Marlborough and just before entering The Royal Military College Sandhurst. (*Hill family collection*)

Second Lieutenant S.J.L. Hill in Royal Fusiliers full dress uniform in June 1932. (*Hill family collection*)

The Sword of Honour being presented by Field Marshal Sir George Milne to Senior Under Officer S.J.L. Hill on the passing-out parade at the RMC Sandhurst in July 1931. (*Hill family collection*)

Trainee parachutists at No. 1 Parachute Training School RAF. (*Airborne Assault Museum*)

C-47s of No. 64 Troop Carrier Group USAAF carrying 1st Parachute Battalion on the first-ever operational battalion drop by a British airborne unit on 16 November 1942. (*Airborne Assault Museum*)

R Company leading the march through Beja as part of the efforts by 1st Parachute Battalion to impress the French. (*Mr Doug Charlton*)

HQ, S and T Companies of 1st Parachute Battalion assemble at Beja prior to the move to reinforce Medjez-el-Bab in November 1942. (*Mr Doug Charlton*)

German machine-gunners taken prisoner by 1st Parachute Battalion following the battle for Gué Hill on 25 November 1942. (*Mr Doug Charlton*)

1st Parachute Battalion 3-inch mortar crew in action outside Medjez-el-Bab in November 1942. (*Mr Doug Charlton*)

James Hill (right) looks on as an officer of 3rd Parachute Squadron RE explains sapper equipment to HM King George VI, Queen Elizabeth and HRH Princess Elizabeth during a royal visit to 6th Airborne Division on 19 May 1944. (*Airborne Assault Museum*)

James Hill and HRH Princess Elizabeth observing the parachute drop during the royal visit to 6th Airborne Division on 19 May 1943. (*Airborne Assault Museum*)

James Hill with officers of 1st Canadian Parachute Battalion. In the centre background is Major Bill Collingwood, Brigade Major of 3rd Parachute Brigade. (*1st Canadian Parachute Battalion Association*)

James Hill (on right) looks on as General Sir Bernard Montgomery, Colonel Commandant The Parachute Regiment, shakes hands with WO1 Parsons, RSM of 8th Parachute Battalion, during a visit to 6th Airborne Division in May 1944. (*Airborne Assault Museum*)

Paratroops of 6th Airborne Division emplaning on the night of 5/6 June 1944. (*Airborne Assault Museum*)

C-47s dropping paratroops of 6th Airborne Division by night. (*1st Canadian Parachute Battalion Association*)

An aerial view of 6th Airborne Division's LZs on the morning of D-Day, 6th June 1944. (*Airborne Assault Museum*)

Field Marshal Sir Bernard Montgomery talks to senior officers of 6th Airborne Division during his visit to the division during operations in the Ardennes in December 1944. Left to right: Lt Gen Eric Bols (GOC 6th Abn Div), FM Montgomery, Brig Edward Flavell (Comd 6th AL Bde), Brig James Hill (Comd 3rd Para Bde), Brig Nigel Poett (Comd 5th Para Bde) and Lt Col Napier Crookenden (CO 9th Para Bn). (*Airborne Assault Museum*)

A patrol of 9th Parachute Battalion coming under mortar fire during operations in the Ardennes in December 1944.
(*Airborne Assault Museum*)

C-47s of IX Troop Carrier Command USAAF dropping 1st Canadian Parachute Battalion at the start of Operation Varsity on 24 March 1945.
(*1st Canadian Parachute Battalion Association*)

Paratroops of 6th Airborne Division en route for the Rhine. (*Airborne Assault Museum*)

The wreckage of the Horsa glider that brought in James Hill's jeep, signaller and batman on Operation Varsity. (*Hill family collection*)

James Hill with Major General Eric Bols in the latter's jeep during Operation Varsity. (*Airborne Assault Museum*)

Members of 1st Canadian Parachute Battalion aboard a Cromwell of the 4th Tank Battalion Grenadier Guards while advancing near Greven. (*1st Canadian Parachute Battalion Association*)

Members of 9th Parachute Battalion passing through an enemy roadblock on 6th Airborne Division's main axis of advance near Brelingen. (*Airborne Assault Museum*)

Troops of 6th Airborne Division on the main axis of advance near Osnabrück. (*Airborne Assault Museum*)

8th Parachute Battalion's Machine Gun Platoon on the road to Wismar. (*Airborne Assault Museum*)

The town square at Wismar, crowded with surrendered enemy troops. (*Airborne Assault Museum*)

James Hill is awarded the US Silver Star by Major General Matthew Ridgway, commander of XVIII Airborne Corps as in the background Field Marshal Sir Bernard Montgomery looks on. (*Hill family collection*)

James Hill receiving the 2nd bar to his DSO from Field Marshal Sir Bernard Montgomery in May 1945. (*Airborne Assault Museum*)

James Hill in later years with his wife Joan and daughter Gillian. (*Mrs Joan Hill*)

James and Joan Hill during one of the annual commemorative pilgrimages in Normandy. (*Mrs Joan Hill*)

(*Left*) James Hill with HRH The Prince of Wales during the official inauguration by the latter of the Pegasus Memorial Museum on 4 June 2000. (*Mrs Joan Hill*)

(*Right*) James Hill greets HRH The Prince of Wales on the occasion of the unveiling of the statue of himself on 5 June 2004. (*Mrs Joan Hill*)

The statue of Brigadier James Hill DSO** MC in its current location at the Pegasus Memorial Museum in Normandy.
(*Parachute Regimental Association*)

At 2100 hours a heavy concentration of shells fell on 9th Parachute Battalion's headquarters. Terence Otway was blown across the drive and stunned, while Captain Paul Greenway and Lieutenant Hugh Pond were knocked unconscious. Sadly, Lieutenant Christie was killed. This was a very sad end for brave men who had survived some eight days of concentrated fighting.

In the meantime 8th Parachute Battalion had been dominating with vigour its area of operations from its strong base in the Bois de Bavent. Despite being only at approximately half-strength, it had been very active in despatching reconnaissance and fighting patrols by day and night into Troarn, Bures, Bavent, Touffreville, Escoville and other villages in order to give the enemy the impression that it was a parachute brigade holding the area of La Grande Bruyère, and not just a sorely depleted battalion.

On 10 June, B Company occupied a brickworks at Sannerville, approximately a mile to the south of La Grande Bruyère. The following morning, a battalion of the 51st Highland Division arrived and took over the position. Two days later, however, the Germans launched an attack, driving the Highlanders out of the brickworks and forcing them to withdraw to La Grande Bruyère. 8th Parachute Battalion was in reserve by this time, albeit still continuing its vigorous programme of patrolling. On 14 June, it moved up the main road towards Le Mesnil to an area where the road from La Petite Bruyère and Bavent joined this road at a point opposite another brickworks. There it established a strong defensive position on the edge of the Bois de Bavent and in the area of the brickworks.

Movement was impossible through the forest except via the network of tracks running through it. The road running through the forest and from a point south of Le Mesnil through to Troarn was dominated by the Battalion. Visibility and fields of fire within the forest were very limited, being no more than a few yards. The road and tracks were under constant mortar fire from the enemy and the Battalion soon learned to avoid track junctions, which were death traps as the Commanding Officer, Lieutenant Colonel Alastair Pearson, discovered on one occasion in particular:

At 0400 hours on 16 June, the Germans launched quite a severe attack in which they used half-track vehicles with a 105mm gun. They also had a weapon called a *nebelwerfer* which fired lots of rockets. I got caught at the crossroads and heard these rockets coming, so I lay down in this ditch, which wasn't too deep, with my hands over my head. I thought, 'Oh Christ! I'm going to get it!' There was a hell of a crash in front of me and I felt I should be dead.

Always afterwards there is a deathly hush, and so I opened my eyes and there in front of me was one of those bloody rockets which hadn't gone off! I took off a bit fast. The Germans had advanced some way, but I'd anticipated where they would come in and brought up my reserve company and we did a flanking counter-attack at 1930 hours, which was successful. However, we did suffer considerable casualties from their 105 guns and mortars.

Pearson and his men became adept at leaping into their trenches at the sound of incoming mortar bombs. Initial casualties were inflicted by bombs exploding in the branches of trees above but overhead cover was soon constructed and this helped to reduce the risk of head wounds caused by flying steel fragments and wooden splinters. Conditions in the forest were grim because everything was permanently soaked with rain, the foliage of the trees being so thick that the sun could not penetrate it. Trenches soon became waterlogged and the mud slippery and slimy. To make matters worse, the forest was infested by large and voracious mosquitoes which plagued all members of the Battalion, their bites causing skin sores when scratched. Pearson himself was a sick man, suffering from a hand wound and covered in boils and sores. Despite these grim conditions, however, the Battalion's confidence was unshaken and its morale was as high as ever.

The following day, 17 June, the situation was quiet as the Battalion was relieved by 7th Parachute Battalion before marching to Herouvillette, where it went into reserve before moving three days later to a rest area at L'Ecarde, on the eastern bank of the Orne. Three days later, however, the Battalion found itself redeployed in support of units of 51st Highland Division mounting an attack on Ste Honorine la Chardonnerette. On 25 June, it returned to its old positions in the Bois de Bavent where it remained until 4 July when it was relieved. On returning to the rest area at L'Ecarde, it received ninety-seven men from infantry units as partial replacements for the twenty officers and 251 other ranks who had been killed, wounded or reported as missing in the four weeks since D-Day.

Chapter 11

While 3rd Parachute Brigade fought doggedly on, 5th Parachute Brigade was being heavily engaged in its area around Ranville.

On the morning of 7 June, A Company of 12th Parachute Battalion, which was holding the high ground south of Le Bas de Ranville, was attacked by seven tanks supported by a force of some 150 infantry. The crew of the Company's sole 6-pounder anti-tank gun was knocked out, as was a section of one of the platoons. The day was saved, however, by Private Hall who ran across to the gun and proceeded to knock out three of the tanks while putting the remainder to flight.

That same day, 13th Parachute Battalion came under attack from three self-propelled guns which attempted to break through A Company's positions, but were knocked out while doing so. The following day, the Battalion repelled another attack and destroyed six tanks.

Before dawn on 10 June, B Company of 13th Parachute Battalion detected a large force of enemy in the wooded areas south-east of Breville. A reconnaissance patrol from C Company was despatched, subsequently returning to report that the enemy were forming up for an attack. At 0900 hours, the latter began their advance, crossing DZ 'N' and heading for the two bridges. The Battalion waited until the enemy was at a very close range of no more than 50 yards before opening fire, inflicting heavy casualties on the Germans before C Company counter-attacked with a bayonet charge. The remaining enemy withdrew in confusion into three areas of woods at Le Mariquet, along the road between Ranville and Le Mesnil, suffering further casualties inflicted by 7th Parachute Battalion which opened fire with its mortars and machine guns. Total enemy losses in this engagement were over 400 killed and over 100 taken prisoner.

During the morning of 10 June, Divisional Headquarters received reports from both parachute brigades and 1st Special Service Brigade that they were all heavily engaged by enemy forces attacking from Breville in two directions: north-west against Lord Lovat and his commandos in and around Le Plein, and south-west across the LZ towards Le Mariquet, which was held by 13th Parachute Battalion.

Major General Gale had already requested armoured support from I Corps and this duly appeared during the early afternoon of 10 June in the form of Sherman tanks of B Squadron of the 13th/18th Royal Hussars which, having been placed under his command, was given the initial task of supporting 5th Parachute Brigade in a counter-attack to clear the enemy from the three woods into which they had been driven.

The proximity of 13th Parachute Battalion and 3rd Parachute Brigade units – the latter being positioned to the left of and beyond the three objectives – was such that the use of mortar or artillery fire support was out of the question. The task of clearing the woods was given to A and B Companies of 7th Parachute Battalion, preceded by a troop of four Shermans which would remain on the open ground of the DZ to the left of the companies' axis of advance. The tanks would provide covering fire into the woods for two minutes before signalling the companies to advance by firing smoke. A second troop would advance in reserve behind the leading troop, while the Squadron's reconnaissance troop of Stuart light tanks would move along the left flank, covering the Breville ridge.

During the attack, however, the tanks encountered problems. One of the reserve troop's vehicles was hit by enemy fire from the DZ and, as fire was being brought to bear on the second wood, the reconnaissance troop leader's tank became entangled in the rigging lines of parachutes lying on the DZ; completely immobilized, it was almost immediately knocked out by a self-propelled gun. Meanwhile, the leading troop leader's Sherman was hit and set ablaze while the rest of the troop also came under fire. At that point the Squadron Leader's tank was hit as well and burst into flames; the rest of the Squadron began to withdraw but two more tanks were hit while a third was immobilized after rigging lines became entangled in its tracks, and was knocked out almost immediately.

In the meantime, the two 7th Parachute Battalion companies had succeeded in clearing the woods of the enemy infantry, who were subsequently identified as being a battalion of the 857th Grenadier Regiment. B Company cleared the first two woods while A Company moved through and tackled the third.

By the end of the afternoon a further twenty enemy had been killed and 100 more prisoners taken, for the loss of ten members of 7th Parachute Battalion wounded. The Hussars had suffered more heavily, losing one officer and nine other ranks killed and one officer and four men wounded.

On the afternoon of 12 June, Major General Gale decided that the security of the Division's front depended on removing the enemy from Breville once and for all. By this time, 3rd Parachute Brigade was so exhausted and weak in numbers that he had no choice but to use his reserve to carry out the task: the desperately understrength 12th Parachute Battalion, which by this time numbered only 300 men, D Company of the 12th Devons and a squadron of the 13th/18th Royal Hussars. He added to this small force the 22nd Independent Parachute Company to deal with any enemy counter-attack. Artillery support, however, would be available from four field and one medium regiments.

Gale decided to mount an attack on Breville that evening in the hope of catching the enemy off-guard while still recovering from the day's fighting. It would begin at 2200 hours and would be mounted from a start line on the outer eastern edge of Amfreville, which would be secured by No. 6 Commando.

Due to the limited time available, the Commanding Officer of 12th Parachute Battalion, Lieutenant Colonel Johnny Johnson, had to make his plans rapidly: C Company was to seize the first objective – the Breville crossroads – following which D Company of the Devons would swing to the left on reaching the village; A Company would then pass through C Company and advance to secure the south-eastern part of Breville, with B Company following up behind as the Battalion's reserve.

The terrain between the start line and the edge of the village comprised 400 yards of open ground. In order to provide cover for the attacking companies as they advanced, one troop of the 13th/18th Royal Hussars would move down on their right flank and knock out an enemy strongpoint situated some 200 yards from the village.

Captain John Sim, who by this time was Second-in-Command of B Company, later recalled the events leading up to the battle:

A whole German battalion was concentrated behind Breville and all indications pointed to the possibility that it was going to attack at first light next morning and drive through the bridges. This had to be prevented at all costs. Breville was held at that time by at least two companies of the enemy, plentifully supplied with automatic weapons, mortars and self-propelled guns. Standing on high ground, it overlooked the bridges and was an ideal starting point for an attack. We had to get our attack in fast and time for reconnaissance was all too short.

At 2000 hours we were ordered to prepare for battle and the company commanders were whisked away for orders and a quick recce. At 2035 hours the battalion moved off, up the hill, towards Amfreville. To our surprise, on our arrival we filed into the church, a large solid building standing in the middle of the village green. The men sat in the pews talking in subdued whispers and sucking sweets, while others gazed at the gaily-painted effigies of saints and at the elaborate gilded cross on the altar. The time dragged by, then the platoon commanders were called for and some sergeants and corporals filed out. We continued to sit and wait. Soon there was a scurry and bustle. Quick orders were given and the battalion filed out of the church.

We lined up along the side of the road with the head of the column nearest to Breville. Our company commander had just sufficient time to brief us that we were going to attack Breville and hold it, that our artillery would fire on the village for twenty minutes, and that we were to be supported by a squadron of Sherman tanks. The advance was to be made in four waves in the order of C Company, A Company, a company of the Devons, and B Company. Headquarter Company was to arrive later.

With a crash, the show commenced and we moved off down the road to Breville. It was 2150 hours. Shells whistled over our heads and the noise was colossal. Trails of white smoke from smoke shells appeared overhead. Then we came under very heavy gun and mortar fire. We hurriedly took cover in the narrow ditches beside the road; many of us had to be content lying in the open hugging the walls of houses. It was not until 2210 hours that the fire slackened and we were able to move on to our start line.

On crossing the start line, C Company almost immediately lost all its remaining officers and its Company Sergeant Major. Nevertheless, it continued to advance under the command of Sergeant Warcup while still under fire from self-propelled guns, as well as a continual hail of mortar bombs and artillery shells which set the village ablaze. By the time the Company reached the village, only fifteen of its number remained on their feet.

A Company also suffered heavy casualties as it crossed the start line, its commander, Captain Paul Bernhard, falling wounded, and the whole of Lieutenant James Campbell's No. 2 Platoon being either killed or wounded. Company Sergeant Major Marwood assumed command but was killed as the Company entered the village. Captain Bernhard succeeded in getting to his feet and following slowly after his company, passing the commander of C Company, Major Steve Stephens, who was lying wounded in the road while urging his company on into Breville. On reaching the village square, he found the remnants of No. 3 Platoon whose commander, Lieutenant Brewer, was killed shortly afterwards. Command of the remaining nine members of the platoon thereafter devolved to Sergeant Nutley who led them forward to clear the Château de Breville, while the remnants of No. 1 Platoon, under Sergeant Murray, cleared the garden that was their objective.

As the supporting artillery began at 0950 hours, D Company of the Devons moved past the church in Le Plein under its Second-in-Command, Captain Warwick-Pengelly, on its way to the start line where it would rendezvous with its commander, Major John Bampfylde. At that moment, however, a shell exploded in the middle of the Company, wounding several men. The Company pushed on regardless, however, heading towards Amfreville along a narrow sunken lane where it encountered wounded members of 12th Parachute Battalion limping or crawling back from the direction of Breville.

On reaching Amfreville and the start line, D Company set off towards Breville. Shortly afterwards it was followed by Major Eddie Warren, whose Support Company was not involved in the battle but who had been asked by Major Bampfylde to assist in bringing forward D Company. Accompanied by a dozen men, Warren was moving up behind the Company when he came across a group of bodies, two of which he recognized as being those of Major Bampfylde and Lieutenant Colonel Johnny Johnson, the Commanding Officer of 12th Parachute Battalion. It transpired that as D Company had crossed the start line, a salvo of shells, reportedly fired by the supporting artillery of 51st Highland Division, had fallen short and exploded nearby in the centre of a group comprising Johnson and two other senior officers, Brigadiers Hugh Kindersley and Lord Lovat, who were badly wounded.

B Company of 12th Parachute Battalion was the last to cross the start line, as described by Captain John Sim:

As soon as we were in position, our company commander signalled us to advance. Between us and the burning, dust-hazed village was a large open field in which were four Sherman tanks blazing away with tracer at the houses. Steadily and in line we advanced up to the tanks and, as they were still firing, halted and waited for them to cease fire. Behind and to the left, a black pillar of smoke poured out of one of the Shermans. When the tanks switched their fire over to the left of the village and into the dark shadows of a wood (by this time it was getting dark), B Company advanced again.

Without any fuss or bother, we moved into Breville and took up defensive positions in an orchard. There were masses of trenches. Dead Germans lay around and the ground was littered with arms and ammunition. Our men quickly found themselves trenches, as they had been trained to do, so as to be ready for the counter-barrage. For about ten minutes it was hell in that orchard as shells and mortar bombs rained down. Then it ceased suddenly. While the church and some houses continued to blaze and with the eerie wails of an air-raid siren to cheer us up, we waited for the counter-attack, everyone now in the possession of a captured enemy automatic weapon. The Germans, however, had had enough.

As darkness fell, the few survivors of C Company under Sergeant Warcup secured the crossroads, with the remaining eighteen men of A Company, under Sergeants Nutley and Murray, holding the south-east corner of the village and the north-east corner occupied by the twenty survivors of the Devons' D Company.

By this time, B Company had been joined by Colonel Reggie Parker, the Deputy Commander of 6th Airlanding Brigade and the former Commanding Officer of 12th Parachute Battalion. He had been standing near Lieutenant Colonel Johnson when the latter had been killed; although wounded in the hand, he had come forward to take command of his old battalion. Parker set off along the road towards C Company's position, accompanied by Captain Hugh Ward, an FOO from 53rd Airlanding Light Regiment RA, and the latter's signaller. As he did so, he called for defensive fire to thwart any enemy counter-attack. In spite of the message to HQRA 51st Highland Division being clearly sent, however, there was a misunderstanding at the gun end and Breville was subjected to another heavy bombardment of artillery fire that caused even more casualties. Among these was Captain Ward who was killed, his signaller fortunately having the swift presence of mind to transmit the order to cease firing. Others included ten men of 12th Parachute Battalion, among them the commander of B Company, Major Harold Rogers, who died shortly afterwards, and Captain Paul Bernhard, the commander of A Company, who suffered further wounds to those he had already sustained.

At 0200 hours the following morning, a troop of the 13th/18th Royal Hussars moved into Breville, taking up positions alongside C Company at the crossroads. Later in the early morning, 22nd Independent Parachute Company appeared and was followed in due course by the 1st Battalion The Royal Ulster Rifles who arrived from Ranville to relieve 12th Parachute Battalion.

The cost of taking Breville had been very heavy: nine officers and 153 men of 12th Parachute Battalion and D Company of the 12th Battalion The Devonshire Regiment were killed during the battle. Enemy losses were far lighter, numbering seventy-seven killed.

Such were 12th Parachute Battalion's losses by this early stage in the Normandy campaign that out of the 550 officers and men who had jumped into Normandy on the night of 5/6 June, only Headquarter Company and an understrength composite rifle company numbering fifty-five men remained.

The following night, 12/13 June, witnessed 152nd Infantry Brigade crossing the Orne. At 0400 hours on 13 June, the 5th Battalion The Queen's Own Cameron Highlanders attacked and captured Longueval, but at 0915 hours the Germans counter-attacked and recaptured it. At 1800 hours that evening, the 7th Battalion The Argyll & Sutherland Highlanders arrived in Ranville, and that night 51st Highland Division assumed responsibility for the southern part of the bridgehead from 6th Airborne Division.

Chapter 12

By 14 June, 6th Airborne Division's front stretched 9,000 yards from a point in the Bois de Bavent due east of Escoville to the sea. To hold it, Major General Richard Gale now had only nine weak battalions and 1st Special Service Brigade, who had all been fighting continuously for eight days and nights, their total strength being less than 6,000 men. Consequently, and in order to be able to withdraw one brigade at a time for rest and provide him with some form of reserve, Gale was allotted 4th Special Service Brigade, commanded by Brigadier B.W. Leicester RM, which comprised Nos. 41, 46, 47 and 48 Commandos Royal Marines.

3rd Parachute Brigade was the first to be pulled out of the line because it was particularly tired and had suffered very heavy casualties. 1st and 4th Special Service Brigades covered from Breville to the coast while 5th Parachute Brigade took over the southern part of the front, up to and including Le Mesnil. 6th Airlanding Brigade was deployed along the rest of it to Breville.

On 18 July, 6th Airborne Division witnessed the launching of Operation GOODWOOD. At 0745 hours a large formation of British armour, comprising the 7th, 11th and Guards Armoured Divisions, advanced on a front of 1,000 yards behind a rolling artillery barrage along a corridor that had been subjected already to three days of concentrated bombing by Allied aircraft. Members of the Division watching from their positions looked on in awe as the tanks advanced and waves of bombers struck at targets further forward. The battle raged for two days, the three armoured divisions encountering increasingly stiff resistance, finally grinding to a halt on the afternoon of 20 July when bad weather and heavy rain turned the ground into a quagmire. During these two days, 6th Airborne Division was subjected to retaliatory fire from enemy mortars and artillery, although this did not inflict any serious casualties. During this period, the bridgehead was expanded and 49th Infantry Division moved up to take its place between 6th Airborne Division and 51st Highland Division.

Over the following two months, until 16 August, 6th Airborne Division was employed in static defence. 'Static' is perhaps a somewhat misleading term to describe the Division's operations during that period because they were far from being as such; from the very start of this new phase, the Division adopted a policy of aggressive patrolling, seeking out the enemy wherever it could and inflicting maximum damage on the enemy at every opportunity.

On 7 August, Major General Gale received orders from the Commander I Corps, Lieutenant General Sir John Crocker, to prepare for a withdrawal by the enemy and to plan for a follow-up. One major problem facing Gale was the woeful lack of transport in his division, making any swift pursuit of a retreating enemy difficult. Furthermore, 6th Airborne Division's own artillery was an odd assortment comprising its own airlanding light regiment, two field regiments and a heavy anti-aircraft regiment being used in the ground role as field artillery. These were augmented by a battery of 25-pounders from the 1st Belgian Brigade which, together with the Princess Irene of the Netherlands Brigade, was now under command of 6th Airborne Division. An additional problem was the shortage within the Division of bridging equipment, which would be a crucial element in any pursuit operation. Gale, however, was determined that all such difficulties should be overcome. He was well aware that two months of defensive operations had resulted in an abundance of pent-up energy among his troops, and he was determined to exploit it to the full.

The overall plan was for First Canadian Army to break out of the bridgehead and advance south-east from Caen towards Falaise before turning eastwards towards the River Seine. The main axis of I Corps' advance would be through Lisieux, which lay some 15 miles from the coast, with pressure being maintained constantly by 6th Airborne Division on the German right flank to assist the Canadians' advance.

The Division's final objective was the mouth of the River Seine, but a number of rivers would have to be crossed in order to reach it, the three main ones being the Dives, Touques and Risle. Due to the fact that the crossings would have to be carried out near their estuaries, the rivers at that point would be wide, deep and tidal. The Dives lay in a broad and marshy valley, its strength as an obstacle increased by the derelict Dives Canal running alongside it. In the middle of the valley was a large island, with the river on its western side and to its east the Dives Canal and large areas of swamp. To the east of the Dives valley was a line of hills dominating it. The Touques and Risle meanwhile lay in narrower valleys with marshy water meadows.

There were two routes to the Seine. The first led from Troarn through Dozulé, Pont L'Évêque and Beuzeville to Pont Audemer, the distance by road being approximately 45 miles. The second ran along the coast through Cabourg, Trouville and Honfleur. The terrain along both routes was similar: undulating ground with hills covered in woods and scrub, between which was pastureland divided by very thick hedges.

Gale opted for the inland route through Troarn and Pont Audemer, despite the fact that this would mean crossing an 8,000-yard-wide valley of marshes and streams as well as the double obstacle of the River Dives and Dives Canal. His decision to select this route was influenced by his lack of sappers and bridging equipment, which meant that only one route could be maintained. The route via Troarn and Pont Audemer would pose fewer bridging problems, being further away from the estuaries and the sea, and would also keep 6th Airborne Division's axis closer to that of 49th Infantry Division on its right.

In essence, Gale's plan was for the main body of the Division to advance on its main route via Troarn and Pont Audemer, while 6th Airlanding Brigade, with the Belgian and Dutch brigades under command, would mop up enemy positions along the coast, taking the area between Franceville Plage and Cabourg before crossing the Dives at Cabourg if possible. 3rd Parachute Brigade would push forward to Bures, crossing the Dives there before moving on to the island in the middle of the valley. 5th Parachute Brigade would then follow on to the island while 4th Special Service Brigade would remain at Troarn and hold the area to the south of the town, both brigades being prepared to exploit any gains made by 3rd Parachute Brigade and open up the main axis of advance. In the meantime, 1st Special Service Brigade would take Bavent and Robehomme where it would prepare to cross the Dives. It was Gale's intention that the impetus of the advance would be such that the Germans would have little or no time to establish defensive positions east of the Dives.

During the night of 17/18 August, the Germans, under observation from 6th Airborne Division patrols, began their withdrawal. At 0300 hours the following morning, 3rd Parachute Brigade commenced its advance and by 0600 hours the whole of the Division was on the move. An hour later, 8th and 9th Parachute Battalions had taken Bures without meeting any opposition, and at 0800 hours 1st Canadian Parachute Battalion began moving through the Bois de Bavent where it encountered mines and booby traps. In the meantime, 4th Special Service Brigade was advancing towards Troarn and St Pair, while 1st Special Service Brigade headed for Bavent and Robehomme.

6th Airlanding Brigade, now commanded by Brigadier Ted Flavell, who had replaced Brigadier Hugh Kindersley following the latter's evacuation as a result of the serious wounds he had sustained at Breville, began its advance on the morning of 17 August along two roads: on the left, on the Breville-Merville road, was the 12th Battalion The Devonshire Regiment supported by 210th Airlanding Light Battery RA, while the 2nd Battalion The Oxfordshire & Buckinghamshire Light Infantry advanced along the Le Mesnil-Varaville road with 212th Airlanding Light Battery RA in support. The 1st Battalion The Royal Ulster Rifles meanwhile followed up in reserve.

The Devons' first bound was on an axis heading towards Cabourg and they had almost reached the end of it when they came under heavy mortar and machine-gun fire from an enemy force astride the road north of the crossroads at Longuemare. Following a fierce fight, this resistance was overcome and The Royal Ulster Rifles moved through the Devons and The Oxfordshire & Buckinghamshire Light Infantry to take over the lead, while the Devons moved into reserve in the area of Breville.

The Oxfordshire & Buckinghamshire Light Infantry had orders to secure Varaville and then move north to cut off enemy units reportedly attempting to withdraw in the path of the Devons in the area of Breville. A number of machine-gun positions, obviously deployed as a delaying tactic, were encountered while enemy artillery and mortar fire came down on some of the crossroads along the Battalion's axis of advance. Enemy were encountered in Descanneville but withdrew as the Battalion was preparing to mount an attack.

The night of 17/18 August found the Battalion consolidated with A and B Companies at Descanneville, the remainder at Gonneville and Merville, and Battalion Headquarters in the Merville Battery itself. The Battalion remained in the Merville area until 20 August when it moved south to the brigade concentration area at Troarn.

Having taken the lead, The Royal Ulster Rifles continued the advance with a close pursuit force, comprising C Company, the Reconnaissance and Pioneer Platoons, and a section of 249th Field Company RE, deployed forward of the main body of the Battalion. As they pushed forward, the noise of enemy demolition charges could be heard ahead. On reaching Le Petit Homme the Reconnaissance Platoon was within 800 yards of the enemy when the road ahead was suddenly cratered. At this juncture, B Company was left in Le Petit Homme to interdict any enemy withdrawing from Franceville Plage where the Belgian Brigade was operating on the left of the Company.

Meanwhile, the rest of the Battalion advanced along the coast road. Due to the area being heavily mined and speed being essential, the companies remained on the road itself. Fortunately no resistance was encountered and progress was swift until the battalion reached the outskirts of Cabourg, where stiff opposition was encountered and all attempts to outflank the enemy failed due to the lack of space to manoeuvre. The Commanding Officer, Lieutenant Colonel Jack Carson, had been ordered to pursue the enemy but to avoid becoming heavily engaged. In view of the fact that dusk was approaching, he decided to concentrate the Battalion in the area of Le Homme and Les Panoramas.

The following day, 18 August, a patrol reconnoitred the area for a possible right-flanking attack but reported that this was not feasible due to minefields, enemy strongpoints and areas of flooded ground. Carson then decided to try to force an advance with the support of armour, but this failed after the leading tank was knocked out having hit a mine while bypassing a crater in the road. Shortly afterwards, however, he received orders from Brigadier Flavell that the Battalion was to remain in its location and maintain contact with the enemy while continuing to avoid becoming heavily engaged.

Little of note occurred the following day but on 20 August the situation changed dramatically when from early morning onwards the Battalion was subjected to increasingly heavy artillery fire. That afternoon the Battalion moved to Le Plein after being relieved by 1st Belgian Brigade, the relief operation itself being carried out under heavy fire; in the early morning of 21 August it was moved by transport to a brigade concentration area east of Troarn before eventually arriving at 2130 hours at a lying-up area at Lieu St Laurent.

The Devons crossed the start line at 1000 hours on 21 August and resumed the advance. No enemy were encountered until the early afternoon when D Company, which was in the lead, came under heavy mortar and machine-gun fire. Heavy fighting ensued in and around the hedgerows of A Company's area and casualties occurred. The two companies were too close for mortar and artillery support to be used and there was insufficient time for an attack to be mounted on the enemy positions before last light.

At 0300 hours the following morning, C Company carried out a flanking move to Branville to reconnoitre whether the enemy had withdrawn or were still occupying the village. On reaching it two and a half hours later, the Company discovered a number of enemy fast asleep in their positions, these being taken prisoner without any resistance. Later that morning, B Company arrived to join C Company in occupying Branville.

Meanwhile in 3rd Parachute Brigade, 8th Parachute Battalion had crossed its start line in the Bois de Bures at 0300 hours on 17 August. The night was dark and the terrain difficult as C Company led the way to Bures and the River Dives. On reaching the river, the Battalion consolidated in Bures while patrols went forward, crossing the river via the remnants of the railway bridge which had been blown by the enemy and was impassable to vehicles. These probed forward to Bassenville, Roucheville and Troarn, all of which were reported to be clear of enemy. C Company then crossed the river and secured the high ground in the area of Butte de Bois L'Abbé, after which the rest of the Battalion crossed the Dives at 1000 hours and headed for the Caen-Rouen road just to the east of St Sampson.

No enemy were encountered until B Company, which was in the lead, came under fire from some farm buildings on rising ground above St Richer. A fierce battle ensued with the Company attempting unsuccessfully to outflank the enemy who were some forty strong and equipped with four machine guns and light mortars. After several attempts, A Company eventually succeeded in dislodging the enemy, who withdrew; by that time, however, the Battalion had suffered three officers and one other rank killed, and one officer and nine men wounded.

Thereafter the Battalion continued its advance, pushing through the village of La Cholerie with A and B Companies in the lead, but experiencing difficulty in doing so due to the lack of its Vickers MMGs and 3-inch mortars which, along with the transport, had still not crossed the Dives. It was not until 1600 hours that the Battalion's Regimental Aid Post jeep arrived with a Vickers and a 3-inch mortar, and ammunition. Thereafter, following a bout of heavy shelling, C Company moved through to Goustranville where it reported the bridge had not been blown. On attempting to capture it intact, however, it came under heavy machine-gun and mortar fire.

8th Parachute Battalion established itself in defensive positions around Chille Ste Anne, covering the bridges, and at 2200 hours that night was subjected to very heavy artillery and mortar fire, which inflicted casualties. During this period, James Hill arrived at Battalion Headquarters and ordered patrols to be sent out at first light to discover whether the Germans had withdrawn. A patrol under Lieutenant Carden found the bridge to the south to be clear, but observed an enemy patrol withdrawing from some buildings in the vicinity, while another from C Company, under Sergeant MacIllargey, succeeded in capturing three Germans who revealed that there were two enemy battalions in the area.

The rest of 3rd Parachute Brigade's crossing of the Dives at Bures was delayed until the late afternoon of 18 August while the sappers of 3rd Parachute Squadron RE constructed a bridge. By dusk, the entire brigade was across the river, by which time 1st Canadian Parachute Battalion had encountered the enemy at Plain-Lugan.

The following day, 19 August, the Brigade advanced to Goustranville where it encountered stiff opposition and at the same time came under artillery fire from the heights of Putot. In view of the fact that the island was under constant observation, any attack could only be carried out under cover of darkness. Major General Gale thus decided on a leapfrog assault in which 3rd Parachute Brigade would advance and secure the railway line east of a canal which would be the start line for the second phase. 5th Parachute Brigade would then move through for the assault on the enemy positions on the heights of Putot.

At 2000 hours, the Brigade crossed its start line with 1st Canadian Parachute Battalion in the lead. Half an hour later, C Company had taken the northernmost railway bridge which was found to have been blown but was considered usable by infantry. The next two bridges to the south were found to have been blown and completely destroyed, but the fourth and southernmost was captured intact by A Company. By midnight, the Battalion had overrun two well-fortified positions manned by infantry of the 744th Grenadier Regiment and had taken 150 prisoners.

9th Parachute Battalion then moved through the Canadians on its way to the station at Dozulé, and by 0100 hours on 20 August had reached the outskirts of the town where it came under artillery fire, which inflicted fifty-four casualties and hit the Battalion's Regimental Aid Post.

5th Parachute Brigade crossed the canal at 0400 hours on 19 August and advanced on the village of Putot-en-Auge, 7th Parachute Battalion having been tasked with securing a spur immediately to the east before 12th Parachute Battalion began taking the village itself. The latter task would be a very difficult one as the enemy were well dug in and obviously prepared to put up strong resistance.

13th Parachute Battalion, which was to cross the canal and move up behind 9th Parachute Battalion to the brigade's start line, initially attempted to cross via the blown bridge but by the time it arrived there the water level was such that a crossing was impossible. The Battalion then headed for a small footbridge, which had been discovered earlier by a patrol of 1st Canadian Parachute Battalion, where it took cover and waited in reserve.

7th Parachute Battalion meanwhile had experienced difficulties with the impenetrable hedges for which the bocage country of Normandy is famous and which either held up the advance or forced the Battalion to make detours. Furthermore, the enemy were alert and using sustained-fire machine guns firing on fixed lines, albeit their use of tracer enabling the Battalion to pinpoint these and avoid them.

The Battalion's start line was the area between the canal and the railway, but this had not been completely cleared. Consequently, several enemy positions and anti-tank guns were encountered and had to be dealt with; at one point, fifty enemy were spotted and successfully ambushed with heavy losses inflicted. By the time it crossed the start line, however, the Battalion was an hour late and dawn was approaching.

B Company was in the lead and advancing up a hedgerow when it became pinned down by machine-gun fire. At this point A and C Companies were still crossing the start line and there was a risk of the Battalion becoming dangerously concentrated in a small area. The problem was resolved, however, by a section despatched to deal with the machine gun, which was captured along with its crew.

At that point, infantry were observed advancing in extended line across an open field towards the Battalion. Initially it was assumed that these were members of 13th Parachute Battalion, which was due to move through, but as they drew nearer were identified as enemy. The Battalion swiftly took up positions in the hedgerow, which concealed it completely from the advancing line, while a Bren LMG group was deployed to cover the enemy from a flank. The Commanding Officer, Lieutenant Colonel Geoffrey Pine-Coffin, decided to try to take the advancing troops prisoner and thus, when they were at a distance of no more than 25 yards, the Intelligence Officer, Lieutenant Bertie Mills, who spoke fluent German, called out and ordered them to halt and lay down their arms.

Such was the astonishment of the Germans that they stood motionless. One of their number, however, reacted swiftly by dropping to the ground and opening fire with a machine gun. The Battalion retaliated by returning fire, inflicting devastating casualties at such close range. Fifteen minutes later the surviving Germans surrendered, although during the firing three of their number had escaped. Thereafter, the Battalion continued its advance and took its objective, the spur east of the village, while 12th Parachute Battalion occupied Putot-en-Auge itself.

In the meantime, 13th Parachute Battalion was advancing on its objective, a prominent feature known as Hill 13, situated just beyond Putot-en-Auge. After a pause of three hours in the open, while under constant fire, the Battalion now had to cross 1,000 yards of open terrain. The Commanding

Officer, Lieutenant Colonel Peter Luard, later gave an account of the events that ensued:

> Obviously, speed was the only way to cross the open space and I called my company commanders and issued my orders. B Company, commanded by Major Reggie Tarrant, was to lead, followed by Battalion Headquarters, then Major John Cramphorn's A Company and finally C Company which was commanded by Major Nobby Clark. I said that it was my opinion that the Germans would not expect us to do anything so mad, and that by the time we had started and they had given the necessary orders to engage, we had a fool's chance, and a good one, of getting away with it. In any case, we had no real alternative as there was no cover.
>
> So off we went. The distance was about three-quarters of a mile, of which the middle 200 yards was the most hazardous. We were all very fit young men and there is no doubt that everyone knew that the speed they made was likely to save their lives. And they moved. The whole Battalion was across, except for the last four men, before the Germans realized the danger and opened fire. There were a couple of casualties, neither serious, and I lost my water bottle but had not the slightest intention of looking for it!
>
> Major Reggie Tarrant and his company went straight up the hill with A Company, under Major John Cramphorn, supporting them. I remember so well seeing them storming into the Germans, using the bayonet and getting right to the top of the hill. Then – suddenly – they were counter-attacked and a well-sited machine gun opened up, seriously wounding Major Tarrant and killing Lieutenant Bibby, who was leading his men with the utmost gallantry, and killing many others. The leading platoons were almost all killed or wounded and the supporting platoons fell back to join us on the intermediate ridge. What had happened was that a fresh German battalion had arrived to reinforce the hill position and it had caused the damage. Had we been just a little earlier, and been able to have organized ourselves on the hilltop, it would have been more difficult for them. But it was not so.
>
> The Germans counter-attacked very well and I remember lying with the men of A Company in the grass on the reverse slope of the ridge and hearing the bullets singing through the grass all around us. There was no fear; we just felt that as the enemy came into view, they would be very welcome to everything we had.

At that moment I heard a voice, coming from a Bren carrier, saying: 'We must have immediate fire! We are being counter-attacked!' It was Colonel Mitchell of the Gunners talking to his regiment. He had crossed the open ground and there he was, cool and calm. His support was marvellous! The fire from his guns was so accurate that it stopped the Germans about 100 yards from him.

Realising that the initiative might now be with us again, I told C Company to make a flanking attack to the right. Off they went with Major Clark leading them, but the re-entrant up which they had to go was well covered by the enemy and they could make no progress. On reporting to brigade headquarters, I was told to hold where we were. This was no difficulty as on the intermediate ridge we were in a commanding position, and in any case the enemy counter-attack had failed. B Company had lost many men and casualties had been suffered by the other companies. The Battalion had been on the move and in action for forty-eight hours, almost without let-up, and was very tired.

So we stayed where we were. I had a company commanders' meeting and in the middle of it I was so tired that I went to sleep as I was actually talking. They left me sleeping, and left word I was not to be disturbed. I woke up two hours later and the rest of the meeting was resumed with my apologies.

Despite the mauling received by 13th Parachute Battalion, the attack on Putot-en-Auge was a great success with the enemy being driven back from all except one of a number of well-prepared positions, while suffering considerable losses in the form of 160 men taken prisoner and two 75mm guns, four 20mm mortars and a considerable number of machine guns captured.

The following morning of 21 August found 3rd Parachute Brigade beginning its advance towards Pont L'Évêque. It encountered stiff resistance on the way, in particular at the village of Annebault where enemy infantry was supported by armour. 8th Parachute Battalion was tasked with clearing the village and advanced with C Company in the lead under covering fire from the Battalion's mortars. The company soon came under fire from a number of buildings, which were cleared and occupied but soon the Battalion was being held up again by heavy fire. At this juncture Lieutenant Colonel Alastair Pearson took personal command of the situation, leading C Company in a left-flanking attack. While he was doing so, Battalion Headquarters came under fire from a *nebelwerfer* which scored a hit, killing the Battalion's Signals Officer, the Intelligence Sergeant and four signallers, and wounding six other men.

Throughout the battle, radio communications were very bad and it proved difficult for contact to be maintained with each of the companies. Furthermore, the close country prevented the further use of mortars or artillery support. Eventually, however, after further very heavy fighting, 8th Parachute Battalion succeeded in taking Annebault and clearing it of the enemy. Losses suffered during the battle totalled one officer and ten other ranks killed, twenty-one wounded and two missing. By dusk, it had established a defensive position and that night 5th Parachute Brigade moved through 3rd Parachute Brigade and continued to advance until it reached Pont L'Évêque at 1200 hours the following day, 22 August.

The town of Pont L'Évêque is situated on both banks of the River Touques which flows through it via two channels spaced some 200 yards apart. Alongside the eastern channel is a railway line running along an embankment, while on either side of the valley are wooded hills dominating the town.

13th Parachute Battalion was allotted the task of infiltrating into the town and securing a bridgehead across both channels. In the meantime, 12th Parachute Battalion was to carry out a crossing of the river south of the town and secure both the railway embankment and the feature of St Julien which dominated the approach from the south. The Battalion was by now commanded by Lieutenant Colonel Nigel Stockwell, who had replaced Lieutenant Colonel William 'Bill' Harris who was wounded shortly after taking over command on the death of Lieutenant Colonel Johnny Johnson at Breville.

At 1500 hours, A Company, commanded by Captain J.A.S. Baker, advanced under cover of smoke laid down by the supporting artillery across open ground towards two fords, over which it would cross the river. Initially, all went well but after the Company had advanced some 400 yards, it came under fire. As soon as it appeared that A Company had reached the fords, Major E.J.O'B. 'Rip' Croker's B Company set off after it. Unfortunately, however, A Company had missed the fords but was unable to report this because Major Croker's radio set had been hit and rendered useless. While the remainder of the Company took cover in ditches on the west bank, Captain Baker and nine men swam the river and succeeded in dislodging the enemy from the railway embankment, albeit they soon found themselves running short of ammunition.

Meanwhile, B Company was pinned down by artillery and machine-gun fire from the St Julien feature to the south and from the high ground to the east of the river, one of its platoon commanders, Lieutenant Bercot, being killed just before reaching the river. More smoke was laid down on St Julien, the railway embankment and station, enabling the Company to push further forward to some dykes but soon it was pinned down again. At this point, with A Company unable to cross the river to join them, Captain Baker and his small group withdrew to the west bank as they had run out of ammunition and thus their position was becoming increasingly precarious.

At this juncture Brigadier Nigel Poett realized, with 12th Parachute Battalion's leading companies pinned down and the enemy still in possession of the railway embankment which dominated all approaches, that there was no chance of the attack being successful in daylight and thus decided to break it off. It was only after last light that the two companies were able to withdraw, having lost sixteen killed and some fifty wounded.

In the meantime, 13th Parachute Battalion had succeeded in entering the town and crossing the western channel. It had been unable, however, to clear the main street leading to the bridge spanning the eastern channel due to stiff resistance from enemy in well-prepared positions. Furthermore, the Germans had set several houses ablaze, the majority being of wooden construction, and this hampered the Battalion's advance. At this point, a troop of A Squadron 6th Airborne Armoured Reconnaissance Regiment came forward in support, its four Cromwell tanks providing covering fire and knocking out a strongpoint. Shortly afterwards, however, one of the tanks was knocked out by an anti-tank gun and the troop was forced to withdraw.

That evening, the Battalion consolidated its positions in the town. During the night, it was decided that 12th Parachute Battalion would withdraw from its positions south of Pont L'Évêque into reserve, while 7th Parachute Battalion took over responsibility for the western and southern approaches to the town.

By the following morning of 23 August, a patrol had succeeded in crossing the eastern channel, without encountering any opposition, via the remaining intact girder of one of the two bridges blown by the enemy the previous day. Realizing that there was now a better chance of establishing a bridgehead, Brigadier Poett ordered Lieutenant Colonel Luard to carry out a crossing as soon as possible.

B Company was soon across the channel but shortly afterwards encountered stiff opposition. A Company moved up to support B Company while C Company remained in reserve at the eastern end of the crossing point. Thereafter a vicious close-quarter battle ensued in the streets of the town in which the Battalion had to fight hard for every yard gained from an enemy in well-sited positions and determined to give a good account of themselves. Brigadier Poett soon realized, however, that the bridgehead was too weak for the attack to be successful and thus ordered 13th Parachute Battalion to withdraw back across the river through a firm base established by 7th Parachute Battalion.

At dawn the following day, patrols from 7th Parachute Battalion found that the enemy had withdrawn from the town during the night and so 13th Parachute Battalion was ordered to follow up immediately, using the Pont Audemer road as its axis of advance. Meanwhile 7th Parachute Battalion pushed on with all speed across the river and on to the high ground to the east of Pont L'Évêque, soon being followed by 12th Parachute Battalion.

Thereafter, 5th Parachute Brigade continued its advance until it reached a point east of the railway line at Bourg where it encountered some opposition. This was soon overcome, however, and the high ground at Bourg was taken and secured. Shortly afterwards, Brigadier Poett was ordered by Major General Gale to limit any further action by his brigade to patrolling while 1st Special Service Brigade moved through.

Meanwhile, on 22 August, 6th Airlanding Brigade had succeeded in taking Vauville and Deauville. The following day a reconnaissance patrol of The Royal Ulster Rifles succeeded in crossing the River Touques in an assault boat and discovered enemy positions on the far side. Deciding any crossing would thus have to take place further upriver, Lieutenant Colonel Carson withdrew the Battalion from Deauville and moved it to La Poterie from where a patrol crossed the river and made its way to Bonneville sur Touques. There it came under heavy fire from the area of a railway line, forcing it to withdraw. On subsequently learning that a strong enemy force of between 1,000 and 2,000 was deployed along the railway line, Carson realized that a crossing at that location would be impossible and thus withdrew the Battalion to an area between Glatigny and La Poterie.

The following morning, 24 August, he received the news that The Oxfordshire & Buckinghamshire Light Infantry had crossed the river the day before and 1st Belgian Brigade had occupied Trouville. Shortly afterwards, he was ordered to cross the river as quickly as possible and occupy Bonneville-sur-Touques and St Philibert.

The crossing by The Oxfordshire & Buckinghamshire Light Infantry had been led by Major John Howard's D Company, which had swum the

Touques and established a small bridgehead on the far bank. Efforts by the Reconnaissance Platoon to find a suitable crossing point for the rest of the Battalion and its vehicles had been unsuccessful because the river was some 30 feet in width, 10 feet in depth and fast-flowing; to make matters worse, its banks were steep and slippery. The problem had been solved by D Company which discovered a boat that was pressed into service as a ferry, the Battalion's vehicles subsequently being ferried across on improvised rafts constructed by the Pioneer Platoon.

The following day found the Battalion advancing again at the head of the Brigade, pushing on through St Philibert, La Correspondence and Petreville, and heading for Malhortie. At 1130 hours, however, a report was received that the Germans were holding the bridge at Malhortie and the high ground to the east near the village of Manneville La Raoult.

The Commanding Officer, Lieutenant Colonel Michael Roberts, was ordered to capture the bridge as quickly as possible. The task was allotted to B Company, commanded by Major 'Flaps' Edmunds, which attacked and seized the bridge intact but came under fire from further enemy positions to the east. C Company, under Major Johnny Granville, meanwhile had been carrying out a right-flanking attack to link up with B Company and then to advance round Manneville La Raoult up to the line of a road running north-south to the east of the village. Due to the difficult terrain, this took longer than expected and it was not until 1600 hours that the link-up took place. When C Company advanced in the direction of Manneville La Raoult, they came under fire some 300 yards from the village. This problem was soon dealt with, the enemy being forced to withdraw, and the Company took its objective soon afterwards, establishing itself in defensive positions by last light.

Major Granville was unable to inform the Commanding Officer of his success, however, as all his radio sets were out of action. Unable to communicate with C Company but hearing the sounds of action, Lieutenant Colonel Roberts despatched A and D Companies to attack Manneville La Raoult. A fierce battle ensued during which the enemy brought down artillery and mortar fire on the village, inflicting casualties on both sides. Nevertheless D Company succeeded in taking and clearing the village by dusk, taking a number of enemy prisoner and capturing some transport.

6th Airborne Division was now advancing on a 10-mile-wide front. On its left were 6th Airlanding Brigade and 1st Belgian Brigade moving on a twin axis towards the towns of Honfleur and Foulbec, while the remainder of the

Division advanced along the road towards Pont Audemer. It was not until its leading elements reached the large town of Beuzeville that the Division once again encountered strong opposition from the enemy on the southern axis of its advance. Situated in rolling countryside and cider apple orchards, the town lay at the junction of five roads: one approaching from the north, one from Pont L'Évêque to the west, one from Pont Audemer to the east and two from the south.

On 23 August, 3rd Parachute Brigade received a warning order to mount an airborne operation. Such were the casualties in the Brigade by this stage in the campaign, however, that the numbers of qualified parachutists in its three battalions were sorely depleted: in 8th Parachute Battalion, these numbered only fourteen officers and 260 other ranks, including a reinforcement of three officers and twenty-three men who had arrived three days earlier from England. The Brigade immediately began preparing for the drop and stood by to move at half an hour's notice, but in the early hours of the following day the operation was cancelled.

On the morning of 25 August, 1st Special Service Brigade was held up short of Beuzeville. 3rd Parachute Brigade and 4th Special Service Brigade were tasked with moving through and clearing the enemy from the town. Initially, some heavy losses were sustained when some troops came under heavy mortar fire while advancing from the south along a sunken lane towards the town as part of a flanking move. At midday, 8th Parachute Battalion encountered enemy troops at the crossroads in Beuzeville but these were soon cleared by B Company. C Company then moved through with the task of securing a second crossroads but soon encountered strong resistance from enemy positioned in a number of buildings. A Company was initially tasked with clearing and securing the town's railway station but was subsequently withdrawn and tasked with securing a third crossroads. During the afternoon, the Battalion despatched a patrol into the town but it came under fire from a machine gun and suffered casualties. Under covering fire from the Cromwell tanks of a troop of A Squadron 6th Airborne Armoured Reconnaissance Regiment, the wounded were recovered and the patrol withdrew. That night, the Battalion consolidated its positions. The day's fighting had cost it one officer and fourteen other ranks killed, one officer and sixteen wounded, and three men missing.

That evening, Major General Gale received orders from Headquarters I Corps with regard to operations on the following day. These laid down the boundaries for 6th Airborne Division's advance and excluded Pont Audemer, which would be on the axis of 49th Infantry Division. Gale, however, was convinced that his division was nearer to Pont Audemer and thus in a better position to reach the town swiftly and seize the bridge over the Risle, which was a major obstacle, before the Germans could blow it.

Gale gave the task of leading the race to the bridge to the Dutchmen of the Princess Irene of The Netherlands Brigade, which was placed under command of 5th Parachute Brigade. On the morning of 26th August, mounted on the tanks of A Squadron 6th Airborne Armoured Reconnaissance Regiment, the Dutchmen raced for Pont Audemer but unfortunately arrived too late as the Germans had blown the bridge twenty minutes beforehand. Shortly afterwards, 7th Parachute Battalion arrived and occupied the town while the Dutchmen took up positions overlooking the river.

In the meantime, 6th Airlanding Brigade had been advancing rapidly on the town of Berville-sur-Mer beyond Honfleur. By 0800 hours on 26 August, it had become apparent that the enemy had withdrawn and the advance developed into a race between 1st Belgian Brigade and the 12th Battalion The Devonshire Regiment. The Belgians overtook the Devons only to discover that The Royal Ulster Rifles had arrived before them.

On 27 August, 6th Airborne Division was ordered to concentrate in the area between Honfleur and Pont Audemer. The Division's task in the Normandy campaign was complete and it was to return home during the early days of September. It had been fighting continuously for almost three months and had suffered 4,457 casualties: 821 killed, 2,709 wounded and 927 missing. In the ten days of fighting since 17 August, it had liberated 400 square miles of enemy-occupied territory and taken over 1,000 prisoners.

On the day before the Division's entry into Pont Audemer, Major General Richard Gale had received, via Lieutenant General Sir John Crocker, the following signal from the commander of First Canadian Army, Lieutenant General Harry Crerar, under whose command I Corps had operated since the Canadians had assumed responsibility for the sector east of the Orne at the end of June:

> Desire you inform Gale of my appreciation of the immense contribution 6th Airborne Division and all Allied contingents under his command have made during recent fighting advance. The determination and speed with which his troops have pressed on in spite of all enemy efforts to the contrary have been impressive and of the greatest assistance to the Army as a whole.

Chapter 13

Following 6th Airborne Division's withdrawal from Normandy in early September, 3rd Parachute Brigade returned to its bases in Wiltshire. After seven days of well-deserved leave, James Hill set about retraining and re-equipping his brigade and filling the gaps in its sorely depleted ranks. During operations in Normandy it had suffered grievously: of its 650 all ranks who jumped on the night of 5/6 June, 8th Parachute Battalion had suffered some 127 officers and other ranks killed, 236 wounded and fifty reported as missing or taken prisoner; while 1st Canadian Parachute Battalion had lost twenty-four of its twenty-seven officers and 343 men of its total strength of 516, losing 117 on D-Day itself. 9th Parachute Battalion had also suffered grievously.

During this period Hill encountered a problem with the Canadians, as he later recalled:

> Retraining obviously played an important part of our lives during this period, as did the reimposition of discipline with heroes and crooked berets being knocked on the head. The Canadians, however, resented the very firm line taken by their new Commanding Officer, Lieutenant Colonel Jeff Nicklin, and decided to go on hunger strike. I was standing in for the divisional commander, who fortunately was away, when one day the *Daily Express* rang up and said that they had heard there was a battalion on hunger strike in the Division and asked if it would be possible to come down and investigate. I replied that they were quite right, but there was a war on. I asked if they could give me a couple of days to solve the problem; if it had not been resolved by then, they would be welcome. They agreed.
>
> On Sunday at 2.00 pm, I summoned the whole of 1st Canadian Parachute Battalion to the gymnasium and ordered all officers and warrant officers, with the exception of the RSM, to leave. I listened to what one or two of the men had to say and then told them in no uncertain terms what I thought of them and the damage they were doing, before ordering them to go and eat their Sunday lunch. After

the RSM had called them all to attention, I stalked out with all the dignity I could muster and then spent an anxious half-hour at my headquarters waiting for the result: they all ate their lunches. On the following morning, at 9.00 am, my Brigade Major came in and said that six Canadians wanted to see me: they were the six ringleaders of the hunger strike and had come of their own volition to apologize to me personally.

I had one further Monday morning incident with the Canadians. The Brigade Major announced a very irate station master from Salisbury who complained that the Canadians had sabotaged our brigade leave train, which ran between Bulford and Andover at weekends after much hard negotiation on my part. It came to the Canadians' turn to have the train and two of their number, having boarded the train at Andover after a very good weekend in London, climbed along the roof of the train in pitch darkness and dropped two grenades down the engine's funnel. In those days, engines were very difficult to replace and irate station masters to placate.

Hill impressed the urgency of the situation on the officers and men of the Brigade with the words, 'Gentlemen, time is short!' There was no definite information as to where and when 6th Airborne Division would be committed next but indications were that it could well be involved in a crossing of the River Maas in Holland or the Rhine, followed by a push into Germany. Training thus was intensive, the emphasis being on assault river crossings and street-fighting, this culminating in November in a divisional exercise, code-named Eve, in which the Thames represented the Rhine.

It was at this time that Hill was awarded a well-deserved bar to his DSO, the citation stating that the award was for 'conspicuous gallantry and devotion to duty from D-day until 1st September 1944'.

By December 1944, 6th Airborne Division was fully retrained, re-equipped and its losses replaced. In the meantime there were a number of changes in command appointments, with Major General Eric Bols replacing Major General Richard Gale as Divisional Commander on 19 December. The three brigade commanders retained their posts but among the battalion Commanding Officers there were also a number of changes: in 3rd Parachute Brigade, 8th Parachute Battalion was now commanded by Lieutenant Colonel George Hewetson, who replaced Lieutenant Colonel Alastair Pearson after the latter had been forced to hand over his command because of ill health; 9th Parachute Battalion was under the command of Lieutenant Colonel Napier Crookenden, who previously had been the

Brigade Major of 6th Airlanding Brigade; while Lieutenant Colonel Jeff Nicklin had assumed command of 1st Canadian Parachute Battalion following the departure of Lieutenant Colonel George Bradbrooke who moved to a staff appointment.

Suddenly, the situation changed very rapidly. On 16 December, the Germans launched a series of powerful counter-attacks against General Omar Bradley's 12th US Army Group with the objective of seizing Antwerp; under cover of the noise of salvoes of V1s roaring low overhead towards Liege and Antwerp, fourteen German infantry divisions surged through the Eiffel forests before dawn, their intention being to strike towards Namur and Liege, cross the River Meuse and advance northwards to Antwerp. Facing them on a sector of 100 miles width were a mere four divisions of the US VIII Corps comprising the 4th, 28th and 106th Infantry Divisions, and the 9th Armoured Division.

The enemy plan was to prevent an invasion of Germany by disrupting the build-up of Allied reserves of troops and equipment. At the same time, it was designed to provide a breathing space that would permit the regrouping and re-equipping of forces for the defence of Germany.

The offensive involved the use of three armies comprising a total of no less than seventeen infantry, parachute and panzer grenadier divisions to be committed behind a spearhead of Wehrmacht and SS armoured divisions. These armies consisted of the following: Sixth SS Panzer Army in the north, with the objectives of capturing Monschau and Butgenbach and subsequently opening up the road leading north-west to Eupen and Verviers; Fifth Panzer Army, tasked with capturing the key cities of St Vith and Bastogne, and subsequently advancing westwards to the River Meuse and Namur; and Seventh Army in the south where it was to advance over the river into the Ardennes between Vianden and Echternach, and subsequently provide a flank guard north of Luxembourg and Arlon.

At 0530 hours, 2,000 enemy artillery pieces opened fire, bringing down a heavy barrage on American positions between Monschau and Echternach. At the same time, infantry supported by five panzer divisions began to advance.

The Americans were caught totally unawares. The 28th Infantry Division, in the River Our sector, was overwhelmed, while two regiments of the 106th Infantry Division in the Schnee Eifel found themselves outflanked and surrounded by the following morning, 17 December, by elements of Fifth Panzer Army which had advanced west across the Our. On the southern flank, however, 4th Infantry Division stood its ground while in the north the US V Corps put up stiff opposition against Sixth SS Panzer Army and halted the enemy advance at Monschau. In the meantime, however, 1st SS Panzer Division launched an attack on the junction between the US V and VIII Corps, overrunning the armoured unit holding that area and penetrating to a depth of approximately 6 miles by the evening of 16 December.

Fighting back hard, the US VIII Corps was outnumbered. Nevertheless, the Germans did not achieve all their objectives on the first day. At the higher levels of the US command element, the full extent and scale of the German onslaught was not appreciated, the situation being aggravated by the lack of accurate and sound intelligence from the front. Consequently, reactions were slow and it was not until the late afternoon of 16 December that the 7th and 10th Armoured Divisions were despatched to the Ardennes as reinforcements. Moreover the 82nd and 101st Airborne Divisions, in reserve under direct command of the Supreme Allied Commander, General Dwight Eisenhower, were not even alerted for possible deployment from their locations outside Rheims until the evening of 17 December.

On 20 December, General Eisenhower placed Field Marshal Montgomery in command of all Allied forces north of the German breakthrough, as later related by James Hill:

On being given overall command by Eisenhower, Monty summoned seven liaison officers and detailed each of them to proceed to each American headquarters down to divisional and, in some cases, brigade level and find out the exact location of all their units. They were to report back to him at 0600 hours on the following morning. He then summoned all the American commanders involved, ordering them to report to him at 1000 hours. The blinds of his caravan were then drawn and he went to sleep.

Despite the fact that the night was foggy and freezing cold, and the countryside iced up, snow-bound and the Germans possibly anywhere, every single one of those liaison officers turned up on time, having completed his task. At 1000 hours, the American commanders arrived, tired and bleary-eyed after an awful drive, and to their astonishment were told by Monty exactly where all their units were – something which some of them did not know themselves. He then told them how he was going to fight the battle and exactly where they would be for the next six weeks. They were astonished – heartened – morale rose and Monty had ensured they

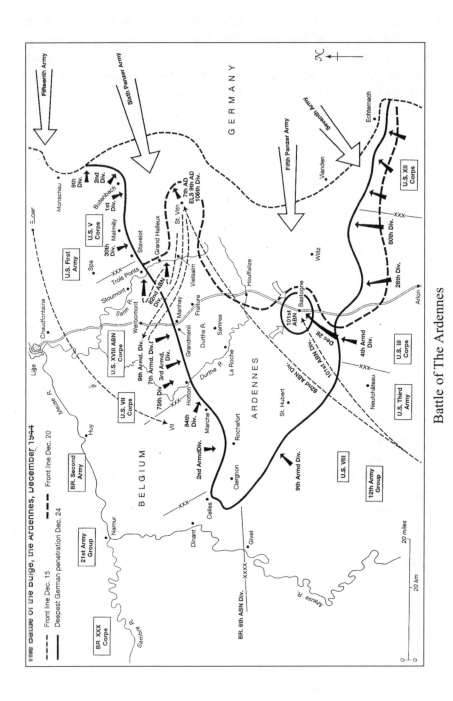

Battle of The Ardennes

had full confidence in him. He then visited our Division, sending for all lieutenant colonels and above, and repeated the process.

By this time First US Army was conducting a series of individual delaying actions, with divisions moving up as reinforcements and being committed to battle as soon as they arrived rather than being deployed as part of an overall plan. On taking command Montgomery, who had familiarized himself thoroughly with the situation, laid his plans to push the Germans away from their planned axis of advance and force them to head south-west instead.

On 20 December, 6th Airborne Division, which was Montgomery's strategic reserve, received orders to move to Belgium and the following day advance parties left for Tilbury docks. The majority of personnel were on Christmas leave at the time but within forty-eight hours all had reported back to their units. Along with the rest of the Division, 3rd Parachute Brigade was ordered to move by rail, boat and road with the best possible speed to the Ardennes where it would fight in the infantry role. Entraining at Amesbury in the early hours of Christmas Eve, it arrived at Dover and that night embarked on the *Ben Machrie*, an Isle of Man steam packet boat, which ferried it across the Channel. Disembarking at Calais at 0845 hours on Christmas Day, the Brigade travelled by road in a large convoy which transported it via Saint Omer, Menin and Ypres to Tournai where it arrived that evening.

On Boxing Day, the Division concentrated in an area between Dinant and Namur; by this time, the Germans' advance had been halted and the Allies had gone over to the offensive. On 29 December, the Division was ordered to prepare for an advance against the very tip of the German salient, with 3rd Parachute Brigade occupying the area of Rochefort.

On 1 January 1945, the Brigade pushed forward with the task of destroying enemy formations east of Rochefort. The weather was bitterly cold, with heavy snow and some 30 degrees of frost by night, and there was the threat of frostbite; in some units this was countered by every man taking off his boots and socks each morning and running barefoot in the snow, following which feet were towelled briskly to restore the circulation.

The terrain was hilly and heavily wooded, intersected with fast-flowing streams in torrent. All buildings had been destroyed and the area was littered with the detritus of war, including dozens of knocked-out Tiger and Panther tanks. These, along with numerous destroyed anti-tank guns and the bodies of dead American troops, which were buried by the Brigade, pointed to the ferocity of the fighting that had taken place earlier.

Meanwhile 5th Parachute Brigade advanced on the right of the Division towards Grupont. During the ensuing two weeks none of the Brigade's three battalions were involved in little more than skirmishes with the enemy until 7th Parachute Battalion was tasked with mounting an attack on the small village of Wavreille, supported by tanks, which proved successful. The Battalion remained there before pushing on through Jemelle to another village called On. Gradually, the Germans were pushed out of the area bounded by the towns and villages of Humain, Marche, Roy and Bande.

Enemy resistance grew stiffer, however, and 13th Parachute Battalion was ordered to mount an attack on the village of Bure. The Commanding Officer, Lieutenant Colonel Peter Luard, allotted the task of assaulting the village itself to Major Jack Watson's A Company as the latter subsequently recalled:

> This was the furthest point that the enemy's armour had reached during their offensive. It was the battalion's task to drive them out of Bure.
>
> We were the left assault company with B Company, under Major Bill Grantham, on our right and C Company in reserve. We were to attack Bure itself while B Company secured the high ground. We formed up and were ready for H-Hour at 1300 hours. It was bloody cold and it was snowing heavily. Moving up to the start line was very difficult because of the very deep snow but we reached it and looked down on the village, which was silent.
>
> The enemy knew we were there, however, and were waiting for us; as soon as we broke cover we came under heavy fire – I looked up and saw the branches of the tree above me being shattered by machine-gun fire and mortar bomb splinters. The enemy had set up sustained-fire machine guns on fixed lines and these pinned us down before we had even left the start line. This was the first time that I had led a company attack and after a few minutes I had lost about a third of my men. We were held up for about a quarter of an hour because of the dead and wounded among us but we had to get going.
>
> We were some 400 yards from the village and so, as quickly as I could, I got a grip of my company and gave the order to advance. Whatever happened, we had to get into the village as quickly as possible. On the way we suffered more casualties, including my batman. One of my men was hit by a bullet, which ignited the

phosphorous grenades he was carrying. He was screaming at me to shoot him. He died later.

We reached the village and took the first few houses, installing my company headquarters in one of them. At this stage, I was unaware that B Company was also suffering badly in its attempt to take the high ground, having come under fire from tanks and artillery. Major Bill Grantham had been killed on the start line along with one of his platoon commanders, Lieutenant Tim Winser, and Company Sergeant Major Moss. His company second-in-command and one of the other two platoon commanders had been wounded and so it was the only surviving platoon commander, Lieutenant Alf Largeren, who led the remainder of B Company to their objective. Unfortunately he was killed later in the day while clearing a house in which there was an enemy machine gun.

Once we were in the village it was very difficult to find out exactly what was happening. I instructed my platoon commanders to ensure that their platoons were secure and to give them orders for moving forward to start clearing the rest of the village. It was a most peculiar battle because we would be in one house, with my company headquarters and me on the ground floor when my radio operator would suddenly tell me that there were enemy upstairs; in other instances we were upstairs and the enemy downstairs!

We were suffering heavy casualties as we advanced, clearing each house in turn. Eventually we reached the crossroads in the middle of the village by the old church. I had kept the Commanding Officer informed as to our progress and he decided to move C Company up to support us. However, by that time the enemy had decided to send in some of their Tiger tanks and they were now firing at us, demolishing some of the houses in the process. I moved from one side of the road to the other, drawing their fire. One of the tanks opened fire on me and the next thing I knew was that the wall behind me was collapsing. At that point one of my PIAT teams came running up and opened fire on the tank, destroying its tracks. They were extremely brave.

The battle continued in the same vein all day. The enemy counter-attacked but Watson and his men succeeded in beating them off. The fighting continued during the night during which armoured support appeared in the form of Sherman tanks of C Squadron of the Fife & Forfar Yeomanry. A troop approached the village, but its leading tank hit a mine. The Squadron then approached from a different direction and succeeded in reaching the village, but lost another tank. Three tanks remained with A Company throughout the night but all had been knocked out by the following morning.

Further reinforcements for A Company arrived from 6th Airlanding Brigade when C Company 2nd Battalion The Oxfordshire & Buckinghamshire Light Infantry, commanded by Major Johnny Granville, appeared. The battle continued throughout 4 January and into the following day when the Germans launched five counter-attacks supported by armour. By that time, however, 13th Parachute Battalion had artillery support from a field regiment and a medium battery that proceeded to bring down heavy fire. The enemy, however, continued to fight hard as Major Jack Watson recalled:

The Germans responded to our shelling by trying to blast us out of Bure with their own artillery. Luckily, however, most of my men had experienced heavy shelling in Normandy and thus knew what to expect.

I instructed Major Johnny Granville to move his men forward beyond my own positions in order to find out what was happening. As his company advanced, the enemy counter-attacked again with two Tiger tanks in support. However, we beat them off and then everything went quiet. At that point, I decided that it was now high time that we secured the other half of the village along with C Company and Major Granville's company, and cleared the enemy out of all the houses. This we did, with much hand-to-hand and close-quarter fighting going on all day.

By 2100 hours that night 13th Parachute Battalion had finally taken the whole of Bure, with A Company overcoming the last enemy position. That same night, however, the Battalion received orders to withdraw. It was later discovered that 7th Parachute Battalion, which had advanced on a different axis, had taken Grupont and thus there was no requirement for 13th Parachute Battalion to advance any further. The Battalion had suffered heavy casualties during the attack on Bure, totalling seven officers and 182 other ranks. Of the sixty-eight men killed, about half were from A Company.

The sub-zero temperature and terrain covered with deep snow continued to make operations, particularly patrolling, somewhat hazardous. An illustration of the problems encountered is the account of a patrol of 22nd Independent Parachute Company that was sent out on a reconnaissance task to locate the enemy in the area of a wood near the town of Marloie, situated between Namur and the border with Luxembourg. The leading man was wounded after treading on an anti-personnel mine. The patrol commander, a corporal, attempted to rescue the injured man but also trod on a mine and was wounded. Help arrived in the form of five medical orderlies, of whom two were promptly wounded after treading on mines. Eventually, a medical officer appeared; after ordering everyone else to remain where they were until the arrival of more men with mine detectors, he entered the minefield, made his way to the nearest wounded man and stopped the bleeding. He then went to each of the other wounded in turn, rendering first aid.

Shortly afterwards, a sergeant from 22nd Independent Parachute Company appeared with mine detectors and a party of stretcher-bearers. Having cleared a path through the minefield, they made their way to the medical officer who was by then supporting one of the wounded in a sitting position. On sweeping the area around the two men, the rescue party located a mine where the sitting man's shoulders would have been if he had laid down, and two more by the medical officer's feet.

The wintry conditions also made life extremely difficult for those operating the Division's radio and line networks. Linesmen found themselves going out to repair the same lines twenty times in a day, while despatch riders were forced to abandon their motorcycles and take to their feet to deliver signals. Radio technicians frequently had to work in the open, repairing equipment with frozen fingers. Most of the Division's radio equipment was mounted in jeeps or open trailers and thus was susceptible to the freezing temperatures.

Life in the Ardennes, however, did have its lighter moments as was illustrated by this account from an officer in one of the brigade signals sections:

> We had arrived in Namur after a difficult drive through cold, fog and snow and then had moved to the high ground above the Meuse, just to the east of Dinant. Conditions were very bad with snow and ice. On New Year's Eve the Brigade Major and I decided to celebrate the New Year. We went to the Château Royal d'Ardennes, a sort of luxury country hotel. We arrived and, to our astonishment, were greeted by a receptionist and a head waiter in a tail coat. Having organized a bath and a bottle of wine, we enquired as to how long

ago the Germans had left and were told, 'They went through the garden ten minutes ago.'

By the end of January 1945, 6th Airborne Division had been withdrawn to Holland and deployed near the River Maas, in the area of Venlo and Roermond. A vigorous programme of patrolling was conducted, this being particularly hazardous because of the requirement for patrols to cross the Maas, which was very wide and in full flood. Small assault craft had to be used and these were swept along by the strong current, making it extremely difficult to land at any predetermined spot on the far bank.

3rd Parachute Brigade was initially transported to the area of Hour and Houvain, but then, after a few days, was moved again by night north through Liège up into Holland where it took up defensive positions on the west bank of the Maas opposite Roermond. There it conducted a programme of aggressive patrolling with patrols crossing the river into enemy-held territory each night. A composite unit, called the Birmingham Highlanders, was formed from elements of 8th Parachute Battalion, members of 3rd Airlanding Anti-Tank Battery RA and some commandos; this crossed the Maas south of Roermond and established a firm base from which it patrolled.

The enemy, in the form of the 7th Parachute Division, were also very active and had sown mines thickly on the banks on their side of the river. Their positions comprised an extensive system of trenches and defences extending along a low ridge overlooking the valley from Venlo in the north to Roermond in the south. In addition, the Germans had opened a dam on the upper River Roer, releasing a large quantity of water that in turn raised the water levels in the low-lying area between the Roer and Maas. Boats were the only practical means of deploying patrols for both sides; on one occasion a 3rd Parachute Brigade patrol passed another boat heading in the opposite direction, whispered passwords in English and German swiftly resulting in an explosion of oaths and a furious exchange of fire. On another occasion an enemy boat capsized in front of 1st Canadian Parachute Battalion's positions and one of its occupants, a *fallschirmjäger* warrant officer, was taken prisoner by a forward platoon of C Company 8th Parachute Battalion.

On 29 January, two members of 1st Canadian Parachute Battalion, Lieutenant Don Proulx and Sergeant MacLean, escorted an artillery forward observation party across the Maas with the mission of leading it behind enemy lines to a location where it was to establish an observation post (OP) from which it would direct artillery fire on targets on the main road and railway line running parallel to the river. The forward observers were equipped for the task with a new type of radio that could not be detected by enemy radio direction-finding equipment.

The patrol left 1st Canadian Parachute Battalion's lines after last light and successfully crossed the river in an assault boat. Disembarking on the far bank, it waded up a small stream for some 100 yards before reaching high ground where it crawled past an enemy-occupied house. Shortly afterwards, however, two German soldiers were encountered in a trench and both had to be despatched silently by Proulx and MacLean with fighting knives before the patrol could continue on its way to the OP location which was some 2 miles away.

Dawn found the forward observers in their OP and the radio set up and functioning perfectly, Proulx and MacLean having installed themselves nearby in an abandoned gun pit. The position of the OP afforded a clear view of the main road and railway line, while affording good cover for the forward observers. Throughout the day, a series of effective artillery barrages was brought down on enemy troops and transport despite the bad weather conditions.

As dusk was approaching, the commander of the forward observer party decided to withdraw. The move back to the RV with the assault boat was slow and without incident, the patrol making a wide detour to avoid the enemy-occupied house. On reaching the riverbank, however, the patrol came under fire. Taking cover in the stream, it crawled down to the river to the RV point about 100 yards away. Once clear of the area, the patrol waited until all was quiet before sending the signal for the boat to cross. Half an hour later, the patrol was picked up and returned safely to 1st Canadian Parachute Battalion's lines.

By the middle of February, the flood conditions were making patrolling conditions ever more hazardous for both sides, the level of the Maas rising even further. Conditions on the front became relatively quiet, the main battle being to the north. First Canadian Army had already crossed the Maas and, having cleared the forest areas of the Reichswald by 13 February, was only one day's march from the town of Emmerich on the banks of the Rhine.

Nevertheless, patrolling continued throughout 6th Airborne Division's area. During the latter part of February, a reconnaissance patrol of C Company 1st Canadian Parachute Battalion was sent across the Maas to a small village situated on the far bank of the river. The patrol commander,

Lieutenant Eric Burdon, Sergeant Saunders and other members of the patrol established a firm base while two more members of the patrol entered the village to discover the strength of the enemy. This task having been carried out successfully, Burdon studied the movements of the enemy and noticed that a number of them regularly left a house at the edge of the village and moved a short distance along a destroyed stretch of railway line to another house, returning later. On his return, Burdon reported this information to his company commander, Major John Hanson, who tasked him with returning to the same area on the following night with the mission of taking a prisoner.

The following evening, Burdon and his patrol crossed the river and made their way to a large draining ditch which had previously been spanned by a small railway bridge destroyed by shellfire but was now crossed by a plank of wood; from his study of enemy movements the previous day, Burdon knew that each time a German soldier left the village and crossed the ditch to the lone house, another would return via the same route a few minutes later.

It was a dark night due to an overcast sky and the absence of a moon. As soon as an enemy soldier had crossed the ditch, the patrol removed the plank and waited. Sure enough, a few minutes later they heard the sound of approaching footsteps from the direction of the lone house and shortly afterwards a very startled German found himself tumbling into the ditch and into the arms of a group of Canadian paratroopers. He was immediately subdued and swiftly bundled back down the ditch to the river and the waiting boat, which ferried the patrol and its prisoner back to the other side of the Maas.

The Germans meanwhile were equally aggressive in their operations in 3rd Parachute Brigade's sector. On one occasion a forward position of C Company 9th Parachute Battalion was subjected to heavy artillery and mortar fire, following which a twenty-strong patrol of enemy *fallschirmjäger* appeared at a range of 15 yards in front of a building housing a Bren LMG. The gunner opened fire but suffered a stoppage, whereupon the enemy rushed the building and blew their way into it with a pole charge. A small number entered but were driven back by fire at close range. Four members of C Company were wounded in this encounter, which was followed shortly afterwards by another heavy barrage of mortar fire.

During the third week of February, 6th Airborne Division was relieved by American troops of the 75th Infantry Division and withdrawn to England to prepare for its coming role in a major airborne operation that would take place in the latter half of the following month: Operation VARSITY – the crossing of the Rhine. While the Division's logistical 'tail' remained in Belgium, the intention being that it would rejoin the Division once it had landed, the three brigades, together with those divisional troops taking part in the operation, returned to their bases in Wiltshire to begin preparations for the airborne assault on Germany.

Chapter 14

By the end of January 1945, with the routing of their forces in the Ardennes, the Germans' gamble in attempting to prevent an Allied invasion of the Fatherland had failed. Their losses were huge, amounting to some 40,000 killed or wounded and over 50,000 taken prisoner by the time their forces withdrew over the Rhine.

Despite their own heavy losses, Allied forces in North-West Europe, on the other hand, were now at full strength, amounting to almost 4 million men under arms with very high levels of effectiveness and morale.

The commander of 21st Army Group, Field Marshal Sir Bernard Montgomery, had drawn up plans for a crossing of the Rhine north of the Ruhr, between Wesel and Emmerich, and the establishment of a bridgehead from which his formations subsequently would advance into northern Germany. Two armies, General Hood Simpson's Ninth US Army and Lieutenant General Sir Miles Dempsey's Second British Army, would carry out the crossing. Montgomery later summarized his plan as follows:

> My intention was to secure a bridgehead prior to developing operations to isolate the Ruhr and to thrust into the northern plains of Germany.
>
> In outline, my plan was to cross the Rhine on a front of two armies between Rheinberg and Rees, using the Ninth American Army on the right and the Second British Army on the left. The principal initial objective was the important communications centre at Wesel. I intended that the bridgehead should extend to the south sufficiently far to cover Wesel from enemy ground action, and to the north to include bridge sites at Emmerich: the depth of the bridgehead was to be made sufficient to provide room to form up major forces for the drive to the east and north-east.

The code name allotted to the operation was PLUNDER and the date set for it was 24 March. The forces available consisted of the XIII, XVI and XIX Corps of the Ninth US Army, and the VIII, XII and XXX Corps of the

US XVII Airborne Corps area of operations, the Rhine, March 1945

Rhine Crossing

Second British Army. In addition, II Canadian Corps and XVIII Airborne Corps were allotted to Second British Army.

XVIII Airborne Corps, commanded by Major General Matthew B. Ridgway, comprised 17th US Airborne Division, under Major General William 'Bud' Miley, and 6th Airborne Division commanded by Major General Eric Bols. Both formations were to be dropped and landed by day to the east of the Rhine after the main crossings had begun, and would be supported by a heavy concentration of artillery on the western side of the river. The code name for the airborne operation was VARSITY.

On the opposing bank of the Rhine, the enemy forces defending the area selected for the crossing comprised First Parachute Army under Generaloberst Alfred Schlemm, a *fallschirmjäger* and veteran of German operations in Crete, the Eastern Front, Italy and the bitter fighting in the Reichswald. First Parachute Army consisted of II Parachute Corps, LXXXVI Infantry Corps, LXIII Corps and XLVII Panzer Corps, the latter providing Schlemm's reserve. II Parachute Corps comprised the 6th, 7th and 8th Parachute Divisions, each numbering 3,000 to 4,000 men but still effective as fighting formations. LXXXVI Infantry Corps consisted mainly of the 84th Infantry Division, a very weak formation whose strength was only just over 1,500 men, while XLVII Panzer Corps comprised the 116th Panzer and 15th Panzer Grenadier Divisions.

The amount of armour allotted to 1st Parachute Army was in the region of 100–150 vehicles: 116th Panzer Division was reported as having up to seventy tanks, with 15th Panzer Grenadier Division having fifteen tanks and twenty to thirty self-propelled guns. A heavy anti-tank battalion was also reported as possibly having arrived in the area.

German artillery located in the area chosen for the airborne landings was estimated at only fifty field or medium guns, but anti-aircraft artillery was reported as comprising 153 light and 103 heavy guns. By the first week of March, however, these figures had been revised upwards to 712 light and 114 heavy weapons, indicating that the enemy were anticipating an airborne assault to be launched against them.

The terrain on which XVIII Airborne Corps would land was flat and almost featureless, forming part of the Rhine flood plain. Its sole dominating feature was the Diersfordterwald, an area of high, heavily wooded ground overlooking the area where Second British Army's XII Corps would cross the river. The main road linking Wesel to Rees and Emmerich ran through the Diersfordterwald, the terrain to the east being open and flat, consisting of fields bounded by wire fences and small ditches. Running along the east of XVIII Airborne Corps' area was the

River Issel, which varied between 30 and 50 feet in width and thus formed an obstacle to armour. Also running along the eastern edge of the area was an unfinished *autobahn*, while all the other roads entering it converged on the town of Hamminkeln.

The tasks allotted to XVIII Airborne Corps were firstly the seizing and holding of the Diersfordterwald and the area north of Wesel up to the Issel, and secondly the defence of the bridgehead against counter-attacks. The lessons of Normandy and Arnhem had been heeded because the entire corps would be flown in a single lift, both its divisions being dropped or landed in daylight on top of their objectives, within range of the supporting guns on the west bank of the Rhine, in order that artillery support would be immediately available when the landings had taken place. In addition, the planned link-up with ground forces would take place on the first day of the operation.

6th Airborne Division would drop and land on the northern part of the area at 1000 hours on 24 March. Its tasks were to seize the high ground east of Bergen, Hamminkeln itself and a number of bridges over the Issel, while also protecting the northern flank of XVIII Airborne Corps. Having carried these out, the Division was then to establish contact with 17th US Airborne Division on its right and with XII Corps, which would cross the Rhine and then move up to its rear and on its left.

In the meantime, 17th US Airborne Division would land on the southern part of the VARSITY area, seizing the high ground to the east of the Diersfordterwald and the remaining bridges over the Issel. It was also to protect XVIII Airborne Corps' southern flank while establishing contact with 6th Airborne Division on its left and with 1st Commando Brigade on its right, the latter having seized Wesel the night before. It was also to link up with XII Corps, which would be to its rear and on its right after crossing the Rhine.

An early link-up and provision of armoured support would be the responsibility of 6th Guards Tank Brigade, whose leading element, a squadron of the 3rd Tank Battalion Scots Guards, would cross the Rhine on D+1 to link up with 6th Airborne Division. The remainder of the Battalion, plus the 4th Tank Battalion Grenadier Guards and the 4th Tank Battalion Coldstream Guards, both of which would be in support of 17th US Airborne Division, would cross as soon as the situation permitted.

On receipt of orders from Headquarters XVIII Airborne Corps on 25 February, Major General Eric Bols and his staff set to work and on 2 March he issued his provisional plan which was followed on 12 March by the divisional operation order.

Bols's plan was for 3rd Parachute Brigade to drop on to DZ 'A' at the north-west corner of the Diersfordterwald and seize a feature known as the Schneppenberg, before clearing and holding the western side of the forest and the road junction at Bergen. Thereafter it was to patrol out to, and if necessary hold, the area of the railway line running through the north-east of the forest.

It was also to establish contact as soon as possible with 5th Parachute Brigade which would drop on DZ 'B' north-west of Hamminkeln and secure an area on either side of the main road leading from the DZ to the town. It was then to patrol westwards and hold the area immediately east of the railway line, while linking up with 3rd Parachute Brigade.

6th Airlanding Brigade meanwhile would land in company groups as close as possible to their individual objectives. Brigade Headquarters and the 12th Battalion The Devonshire Regiment would land south-west of Hamminkeln on LZ 'R', while the 2nd Battalion The Oxfordshire & Buckinghamshire Light Infantry would land on LZ 'O' to the north of the town, with the task of seizing and securing the road and rail bridges over the Issel between Hamminkeln and Ringenberg. The 1st Battalion The Royal Ulster Rifles meanwhile would touch down on LZ 'U' south of Hamminkeln, and would capture and hold the bridge over the Issel on the main road leading to Brunen.

Divisional Headquarters, along with two batteries of 53rd Airlanding Light Regiment RA, 6th Airborne Armoured Reconnaissance Regiment and certain other supporting arm elements would land on LZ 'P' north-east of the Diersfordterwald near Kopenhof.

A massive amount of artillery support had been allotted to 6th Airborne Division. Three field regiments and two medium regiments would be in direct support with two more medium regiments being on call. In addition, a battery of American long-range artillery would be available for harassing fire tasks. Artillery support for 3rd Parachute Brigade would be provided by the three field regiments, while the two other brigades would each be supported by a medium regiment and 53rd Airlanding Light Regiment RA. 2nd Forward Observation Unit RA, which had been newly formed for this role, would provide all the forward observation parties and fire control for all the supporting artillery, as well as fire liaison parties at the gun end of each supporting battery.

In order to eliminate the risk to aircraft transporting the two airborne divisions, however, a limitation had to be placed on the preliminary bombardment of German positions. Provided by nine field regiments, eleven medium regiments, one heavy regiment, four heavy batteries, one heavy anti-aircraft regiment, one super-heavy battery and three American 155mm batteries, this would begin one hour and 40 minutes before the time of the drop (P-100) and cease forty minutes beforehand (P-40).

An anti-flak bombardment, to neutralize the enemy anti-aircraft defences, would begin thirty minutes before the drop (P-30) up to the time of the drop itself (P-Hour), the guns ceasing fire as the leading aircraft flew over the line of the gun areas. Despite the risk that this would afford the enemy a chance to recover while the drop was taking place, all firing would cease on commencement of the fly-in in order to avoid any risk of aircraft being hit.

3rd and 5th Parachute Brigades would be flown in by aircraft of the IX US Troop Carrier Command USAAF, while Nos 38 and 46 Groups RAF would provide the tug aircraft for the gliders transporting 6th Airlanding Brigade, Headquarters 6th Airborne Division and divisional troops. The total number of aircraft and gliders required to lift the two airborne divisions was 2,740.

Early in March, two full-scale divisional exercises were held in Suffolk, in the area of Bury St Edmunds, to exercise 6th Airborne Division in operations behind a major enemy defensive line. On 19 and 20 March, all units of the Division moved into secure transit camps where the Commanding Officers issued orders to their battalions, as Lieutenant Colonel Napier Crookenden, commanding 9th Parachute Battalion, later described:

> We set up our models and air photographs in a specially guarded room, and I gave out my orders to the company commanders. We were to drop last on Drop Zone 'A' after the 8th and 1st Canadian Parachute Battalions and, while they secured the landing area, we were to move southwards to attack and capture the highest part of the Diersfordterwald and the Schneppenberg, destroying several batteries of German guns on the way.

> Then the whole Battalion crowded into the same room, all 600 of them, and I explained to them our drop and our tasks in some detail. It was both an exhilarating and sobering experience, talking to so many men of such quality and realizing how intently each of them was following my words and their tasks, as the plan unfolded. I must

have spoken for twenty minutes or more with hardly a sound, cough or movement from the men. Afterwards, each company and each platoon took its turn in the briefing room and each man had to confirm, on the model in front of his platoon, his rendezvous, his task and the objectives of his company and those of the battalion.

One particular briefing that was undoubtedly designed to be a morale booster was that given by James Hill to 1st Canadian Parachute Battalion and other units in his brigade, which ended with the following exhortation:

Gentlemen, the artillery and air support is fantastic! And if you are worried about the kind of reception you'll get, just put yourself in the place of the enemy. Beaten and demoralised, pounded by our artillery and bombers, what would you think if you saw a horde of ferocious, bloodthirsty paratroopers, bristling with weapons, cascading down upon you from the skies? And you needn't think, just because you hear a few stray bullets flying about, that some miserable Hun is shooting at you. That is merely a form of egotism. But if by any chance you should happen to meet any one of these Huns in person, you will treat him, Gentlemen, with extreme disfavour!

On the night of 23 March, 3,500 Allied guns opened fire against German positions on the east bank of the Rhine in the area where the crossing would take place. The enemy had already been pounded by heavy bombing that had commenced on 21 February with 3,471 bombers dropping 8,500 tons of bombs on roads, railways and airfields, while another 2,090 unleashed a further 6,600 tons on enemy barracks and defensive positions. In addition, Allied fighter aircraft conducted sweeps over the area east of the Rhine, attacking convoys, anti-aircraft batteries and, on one occasion, the headquarters of First Parachute Army when Generaloberst Schlemm was severely wounded.

At 2100 hours on 23 March, units of 1st Commando Brigade crossed the Rhine in assault craft, while RAF Lancasters attacked Wesel. At 2200 hours, XII Corps began crossing near Xanten and an hour later XXX Corps crossed the river further north. By 0400 hours on 24 March, the Ninth US Army had started crossing south of Wesel and by dawn 21st Army Group had established a number of bridgeheads on the east bank.

Meanwhile, in England, 6th Airborne Division was preparing to emplane and by 0530 hours each stick of paratroops or airlanding infantry was waiting beside its aircraft or glider. Dawn broke bright and clear and at

0730 hours the first aircraft began taking off. Soon the entire vast armada of aircraft was airborne and heading for Germany; for many members of the Division, it would be their first jump or landing into action and their first encounter with the enemy. As the aircraft crossed the Ruhr, they met heavy bombers heading back after softening up targets on the ground. Some of them were limping along, trailing black smoke from damaged engines.

Over Belgium, they turned north-east and joined another column carrying 17th US Airborne Division. The two streams of aircraft, each nine wide, flew on side-by-side as they headed towards the Rhine.

3rd Parachute Brigade's drop went according to plan, albeit nine minutes early. 8th Parachute Battalion led the way, followed by Brigade Headquarters and 1st Canadian Parachute Battalion, with 9th Parachute Battalion, a troop of 3rd Parachute Squadron RE and 224th Parachute Field Ambulance bringing up the rear. Anti-aircraft fire was only light when the leading C-47 transports arrived over the DZ, but intensified as the drop continued and the enemy recovered from the artillery bombardment.

James Hill later described the events that took place before and during the drop:

As the great battle for the Rhine Crossing approached, everyone felt it would mark the beginning of the end. I myself looked with amazement at the progress that had been made in airborne warfare since the days when I had led 1st Parachute Battalion in its drop in North Africa in October 1942 from thirty-two American Dakota aircraft whose crews had never dropped parachutists before and which were not equipped with radio communications equipment. On that occasion, I had sat in the cockpit with the American commander. The Dakotas were flying in line astern and, aided by a quarter-inch to the mile French motoring map, the navigators located our DZs in Tunisia some 400 miles away. On seeing the leading aircraft disgorge its load, the remainder followed suit.

Two and a half years later the airborne armada, in which 3rd Parachute Brigade and the rest of 6th Airborne Division were travelling, comprised some 540 Dakotas flying low in tight formation, followed by 1,300 gliders and their tug aircraft in which 6th Airlanding Brigade and the divisional troops were riding into battle – some 2,740 aircraft, all communicating with each other by radio.

By this time, lessons from previous operations had been learned and I had the choice of dropping 3rd Parachute Brigade on a small DZ, measuring some 1,000 yards by 800 yards, which was located in a clearing in a wood among enemy positions manned by German parachute troops. The alternative was a far more ideal DZ some 3 miles away, but with the prospect of having to fight all the way to our objective. The choice for me was simple: land on top of the objective and take the risks of a bad drop, which in the event did not occur as the American pilots performed brilliantly, although they dropped us some nine minutes later.

Regrettably, one of the few soldiers to be dropped into the surrounding trees was Lieutenant Colonel Jeff Nicklin, Commanding Officer of 1st Canadian Parachute Battalion, who was immediately shot and killed before he could get down from where he was hung up.

Apart from the loss of a splendid battalion commander, I recall two other incidents: the first took place near my command post on the edge of the DZ where there was a small belt of trees. At the end of this was a spinney, which was held by some Germans who immediately engaged our troops as they landed. I saw Major John Kippen of 8th Parachute Battalion, one of the best company commanders in my brigade, and told him to collect some men and eliminate the enemy position, which he proceeded to do with considerable gallantry.

The second incident occurred when I was watching the approach of a Horsa that was obviously going to crash into the wood on the edge of which I was standing. It banked steeply and flew along the side of the wood until it caught its port wingtip in the trees 12 feet above the ground. To my amazement, I discovered that it contained, among other things, my batman, jeep, and wireless operator as well as a motorcycle. Regrettably, the pilot broke his legs but the other men in the aircraft survived.

No sooner had they landed than Hill's three battalions set about carrying out their respective tasks. 8th Parachute Battalion initially had to clear and secure the DZ, and in particular the enemy dug-in around it. The Battalion's objectives were the triangular and hatchet-shaped woods extending from the main area of woodland to the south of the DZ, and two small copses dominating the DZ itself. The time allotted to carry out these tasks was only four minutes and thus each company went into action against its allotted objective immediately on landing.

A Company, commanded by Major Bob Flood, advanced on a small wood in the north-east corner of the DZ, taking it by 1030 hours without any difficulty and taking several prisoners. C Company, under Major John Shappee, together with Battalion Headquarters and the Mortar Platoon, seized the triangular wood in the south-east corner of the DZ, occupying a number of well-sited enemy trenches as they did so.

B Company and the Machine Gun Platoon, however, were having a rough time. Their objective was the hatchet-shaped wood on the southern side of the DZ, but it was occupied by two platoons of *fallschirmjäger*. Unfortunately, the Company was disorganized on landing and thus began assembling in groups of two or three at the objective, which was also the RV location. Men crossing the DZ from the north found themselves under fire and eventually the company commander, Major John Kippen, formed a platoon-sized force of his men and led them in an attack from the south through the narrow part of the woods. This was beaten off, however, with Major Kippen and one of his platoon commanders being killed.

While B Company was struggling to take its objective, the rest of the Battalion was still arriving. The Commanding Officer, Lieutenant Colonel George Hewetson, later described the events that took place:

In the meantime, men were still coming in from the DZ. The stick of the Anti-Tank Platoon accompanying the platoon commander had jumped to the east of the DZ owing to a failure in the light signals in the aircraft. Returning to the DZ, they had a short sharp engagement in a house and captured an officer and fifteen men of a German signals unit together with their 3-ton lorry. This vehicle was invaluable later when the DZ had to be cleared.

The gliders began to arrive at 1100 hours. One of the first down, a 9th Parachute Battalion glider, overshot the LZ but although it was badly damaged, there were no casualties. My Second-in-Command, Major John Tilley, had gone off to see Brigade Headquarters and B Company. I was standing on the edge of the wood, briefing my Intelligence Officer to keep in touch with Brigade Headquarters on the wireless, while I went down to see how B Company was faring and to see if it would be necessary to put in an attack with C Company. Two sergeants, one from 9th Parachute Battalion, were standing a few yards away.

Suddenly, with a terrific crash, a glider came through the trees and I found myself lying under the wheel of a jeep. I managed to crawl out from the wreckage to find the glider, one of the medical Horsas of 9th Parachute Battalion, completely written off. The crew had been killed along with my Intelligence Officer and the two sergeants.

At about this time, my Second-in-Command reported back from B Company. The wood had been taken by a platoon attacking from the north-east using Nos 36 and 77 grenades, and under covering fire from the platoon that earlier had attempted an attack from the south. The last phase of the attack was a hand-to-hand fight down a trench, led by the platoon commander. A considerable number of the enemy had been killed, and one officer and twenty-six soldiers taken prisoner.

At 1115 hours, the Battalion's Hamilcar glider arrived, bringing in a very welcome load of a Bren carrier, spare 3-inch mortars, Vickers MMGs and some radio sets. Shortly afterwards, the enemy began bringing down mortar and shellfire on the DZ. The Battalion, however, continued to clear it of equipment and containers, almost completing the task by 1200 hours, at which time it was ordered into brigade reserve. It subsequently moved off from the DZ, leaving one platoon from C Company to finish clearing up and to guard the equipment dump. En route to its new position, the Battalion encountered two 88mm guns, one of which was firing into the trees and causing casualties from shrapnel bursts. Both guns, however, were attacked and knocked out. Later in the day, at 1830 hours, 8th Parachute Battalion was ordered to move again to a position covering the rear of Divisional Headquarters at Kopenhof.

1st Canadian Parachute Battalion came under machine-gun fire as it jumped, several men being hit in mid-air or when they landed in trees. Among them was the Commanding Officer, Lieutenant Colonel Jeff Nicklin who landed in a tree; as previously mentioned, he was killed as he hung helpless in his harness.

C Company jumped from its C-47 transports while 8th Parachute Battalion was in the process of clearing the enemy from the DZ, and encountered heavy machine-gun fire on landing. The Company Commander, Major John Hanson, suffered a mishap by breaking his collarbone on landing. The Second-in-Command, Captain John Clancy, had a narrow escape when his aircraft was hit by flak over the DZ; he and two others, Lieutenant Ken Spicer and Private Cerniuk, succeeded in jumping clear as the aircrew battled to keep the blazing aircraft airborne. Clancy was captured on landing but Spicer landed safely. As he descended, Private Cerniuk, who was the Company Headquarters signaller, came under heavy machine-gun fire that cut the cord by which the container holding his radio set was suspended below him. Landing safely, he later linked up with a unit of 15th (Scottish) Division.

The absence of the company commander and second-in-command resulted in command of the Company being assumed temporarily by Sergeants Saunders and Murray, who swiftly regrouped those who had landed nearby before mounting an attack which resulted in the Company's objective being taken and cleared, several enemy gun crews being overrun in the process. As the day continued, C Company came under heavy mortar and shellfire. The enemy advanced in force into some woods near the Company's positions, forestalling any attempts to reach the gliders on the DZ.

A Company, meanwhile, had landed at the eastern end of the DZ and within thirty minutes over two-thirds of its number had appeared at the RV. Major Peter Griffin thus decided to mount an immediate attack on a group of buildings. Fierce resistance was encountered, however, and at one point the attack faltered, but Company Sergeant Major Green swiftly organized covering fire before leading an assault group into the first house, which was cleared after some fierce close-quarter fighting. The other buildings were then cleared of the enemy in a similar fashion until the entire objective had been captured. Later in the day, the enemy launched a counter-attack, but this was beaten off. A heavy mortar concentration on A Company's position ensued, followed by an attack by a large enemy patrol. This was also repulsed, with several enemy being taken prisoner.

Meanwhile B Company, under Captain Sam McGowan, was also in the thick of the fighting. Having assembled at its RV, it immediately mounted an attack on a group of farm buildings and a wooded area, the latter being one of the Company's objectives from which the enemy was already bringing fire to bear. Under covering fire from its own Bren LMGs the Company swept forward, swiftly overrunning the enemy positions and clearing bunkers and trenches with grenades; at the same time, Company Sergeant Major Kemp mounted an attack on the farmhouse under very heavy fire. In less than thirty minutes, the company had taken its objective, capturing a number of enemy. Shortly afterwards, a patrol under Sergeant Page reconnoitred the woods in the area of the Company's positions, returning in due course with almost 100 more prisoners.

Thereafter B Company consolidated its positions, bringing fire to bear on numbers of enemy troops moving around its area. During the afternoon there came news that No. 5 Platoon had suffered very heavy losses on the DZ; its commander, Lieutenant Jack Brunnette, was among those killed.

As the day wore on, the intensity of the fighting slackened but the DZ, which was littered with wrecked gliders and equipment, still continued to be an area of danger. A number of casualties were incurred and it was here that Corporal George Topham, a medical orderly in 1st Canadian Parachute Battalion, performed the action that would in due course result in his being awarded the Victoria Cross, the only VC to be won by a member of 6th Airborne Division. A wounded man was lying out in the open and two members of 224th Parachute Field Ambulance went forward to rescue him but were killed as they did so. Corporal Topham's citation described what ensued:

> Without hesitation and on his own initiative, Corporal Topham went forward through intense fire to replace the orderlies who had been killed before his eyes. As he worked on the wounded man, he himself was shot through the nose. In spite of severe bleeding and intense pain, he never faltered in his task. Having completed first aid, he carried the wounded man steadily and slowly back through continuous fire to the shelter of a wood.
>
> During the next two hours, Corporal Topham refused all offers of medical help for his own wound. He worked most devotedly throughout this period to bring wounded in, showing complete disregard for the accurate and heavy enemy fire. It was only when all casualties had been cleared that he consented to his own wound being treated.
>
> His immediate evacuation was ordered but he interceded so earnestly on his own behalf that he was eventually allowed to return to duty.
>
> On his way back to his company, he came across a carrier that had received a direct hit. Enemy mortar bombs were still dropping around, the carrier itself was still burning fiercely and its own mortar ammunition was exploding. An experienced officer on the spot had warned all not to approach the carrier.
>
> Corporal Topham, however, immediately went out alone in spite of the blasting ammunition and enemy fire and rescued the three occupants of the carrier. He brought these three men back across the open, and although one died almost immediately afterwards, he

arranged for the evacuation of the other two who undoubtedly owe their lives to him. This NCO showed gallantry of the highest order. For six hours, most of the time in great pain, he performed a series of acts of outstanding bravery, and his magnificent and selfless courage inspired all those who witnessed it.

9th Parachute Battalion was the last element of 3rd Parachute Brigade to jump. Lieutenant Colonel Napier Crookenden later described the scene in his aircraft as it neared the DZ, and during the ensuing drop:

There had been some singing in the early part of our three-hour flight but most men had gone to sleep or relapsed into the usual state of semi-conscious suspended animation. The yell of 'Twenty minutes to go!' from the crew chief woke us up and sent the adrenalin pumping through our veins.

We were over the battle-scarred wilderness of the Reichswald and the terrible ruins of Goch when the order 'Stand up! Hook up!' brought us to our feet. Each man fastened the snap-hook on the end of his parachute strop to the overhead cable, fixed the safety pin and turned aft, holding the strop of the man in front in his left hand and steadying himself with his right arm on the overhead cable. The stick commander, Sergeant Matheson, checked each man's snap-hook. We all checked the man in front and, beginning with the last man of the stick, shouted out in turn, 'Number Sixteen okay – Number Fifteen okay!' and so on down to myself at Number One.

Just aft of the door stood the crew chief in his flying helmet and overalls, listening on the intercom for our pilot's orders. I was watching the red and green lights above the door and I am sure that the rest of the stick were too. The red light glowed, the crew chief yelled 'Red on! Stand to the door!' and I moved forward, left foot first, until I was in the door with both hands holding the door edges, left foot on the sill and slipstream blasting my face. Then the great, curving river was below me and seconds later a blow on the back from the crew chief and 'Green on! Go!' in my left ear sent me out into the sunlight.

Once the tumbling and jerking were over and my parachute had developed, I had a wonderful view of the drop zone right below me. I could see the double line of trees along the road to the west and the square wood in the middle of the DZ. The ground was already covered with the parachutes of the 8th and 1st Canadian Parachute Battalions and I could see them running towards their objectives.

There was a continuous rattle of machine-gun fire and the occasional thump of a mortar or grenade, and during my peaceful minute of descent I heard the crack and thump of two near misses. It was clearly a most accurate and concentrated drop, and I felt a surge of confidence and delight.

By 1300 hours, 9th Parachute Battalion was in position on its final objective with A Company on the Schneppenberg, B Company astride the main road to the south-east and C Company in the wood to the south of the road. At 1530 hours, B Company despatched a patrol that made contact with the leading elements of the 1st Battalion The Royal Scots.

Unlike 3rd Parachute Brigade, which suffered relatively light casualties during its drop, 5th Parachute Brigade encountered a much rougher reception on DZ 'B'. Leading the drop was Brigade Headquarters which was followed by 13th, 12th and 7th Parachute Battalions, together with the rest of the brigade group comprising 4th Airlanding Anti-Tank Battery RA, a detachment of 2nd Forward Observation Unit RA, a troop of 591st Parachute Squadron RE and 225th Parachute Field Ambulance.

As the aircraft carrying the Brigade approached the DZ, they encountered heavy anti-aircraft fire and two C-47s were hit. Having completed the drop, the formation swung away for the flight home but met further heavy anti-aircraft fire in the area of Mehr to the west of the DZ. Ten aircraft were shot down almost immediately, crashing on the east bank of the Rhine. A further seven were also brought down but these succeeded in crash-landing west of the river, and a further seventy transports were also damaged.

Brigadier Nigel Poett followed his usual custom of jumping with the leading element of his brigade. Together with the other members of his brigade headquarters forming his stick, he was in one of the leading C-47s as it neared the battle raging on the far side of the river ahead:

As we approached the Rhine, we could see ahead of us the battlefield covered by haze and the dust from the bombardment. At 1,000 feet, we passed over the administrative units and the supporting arms, and then the crossing places themselves.

However, there was no time to interest ourselves in the troops on the ground, or in the craft upon the river, because the red light was on and, almost before we realized it, we were over enemy territory. We were being shot at and the aircraft bumped and shook. Then we were over the DZ, the green light was on and we were out.

As we dangled from our parachutes we tried, in the very short time available, to pick up the landmarks. These had seemed so very clear and simple on the sand models and in the air photographs, but now they appeared somewhat different as we came down rapidly amongst the firing and into the dust and smoke caused by the artillery bombardment that had finished more than ten minutes previously. Although this had been heavy, ten minutes was ample time for those enemy not knocked out to recover sufficiently to be a considerable threat to our parachutists as they swung in the air or disentangled themselves from their parachutes and got their bearings.

We felt very naked but this was where the battle experience of the brigade became evident. All three of my battalion commanders had taken part in the landings in Normandy. Together with our gunners, sappers and field ambulance, we had fought with the division in France, Belgium and Normandy. Our officers and men all knew one another well and this was to prove an enormous advantage in this operation that was going to require a high standard of leadership right down to junior NCO level.

Assembly at RVs was always a tricky business and a landing in broad daylight, in an area covered by fire by enemy troops who were fully alert, meant that very rapid rallying and high standards of leadership on the DZ were essential. Moreover, the concentrated drop meant that the different sub-units of the battalions were inevitably mixed up. They had been shot at on their way down from the aircraft to the ground and they were under considerable harassing fire as they struggled out of their parachute harnesses, unfastened their kitbags, extracted their weapons and got their bearings.

Although all three battalions were dropped accurately, individual officers and men experienced trouble in working out their exact positions. This period on the DZ was where most of our casualties occurred. Once enemy positions had been located and action taken to deal with them, the troops in them generally surrendered without putting up a serious fight. However, until they were spotted, they were extremely troublesome.

Just as our chaps were reaching their RVs, the gliderborne element of the brigade group began to approach its landing zone. To the south, the gliders of 6th Airlanding Brigade also began to come in. This caused a considerable diversion of enemy artillery fire and provided a most welcome relief for us. It was, however, a most tragic sight to see gliders picked off in the air and on the ground. Their losses were very heavy and thus only a comparatively small proportion of our anti-tank guns and vehicles carrying the machine guns, mortars and ammunition reached the battalions at their RVs. There is no doubt that, had a strong enemy counter-attack developed later, we would have been seriously embarrassed by these losses of anti-tank guns and ammunition reserves.

It was about one hour after the drop that our battalions were sufficiently complete in their RVs to be able to report that they were ready to start on the second phase of the plan: the securing and consolidating of the brigade objective. Considering the circumstances of the landing, our casualties had not been unduly heavy. Our losses were approximately 20 per cent of those who had jumped. I lost my Brigade Major, Major Mike Brennan, and my Signals Officer, Lieutenant Crawford, on the DZ. My DAA & QMG, Major Ted Lough, was in a glider and also became a casualty when he was very badly wounded. As a result, my brigade headquarters had to be considerably reconstructed when we reached our RV.

One lesson I learned in Normandy was that of wireless communications. On the night of D-Day, I had lost the wireless team that jumped with me and I was without any proper communications throughout the whole night. This time, therefore, all my battalion commanders and I carried our own American walkie-talkie sets strapped inside our parachute harnesses. These radios were intended only to maintain control until proper communications had been set up in the RV or on the final objectives but they proved to be a huge success.

First to land was 13th Parachute Battalion, which found the entire area of the DZ covered in smoke, dust and haze that made identification of landmarks, and thus orientation, very difficult. Major Jack Watson, commanding A Company, later recalled vividly the scene below as he waited in the open doorway of the C-47 carrying him and his stick:

I was standing in the door over the Rhine and christened it by throwing an orange down. The next thing I noticed was the American despatcher putting on his flak suit, which was slightly worrying. Then I didn't see any more of him. As we got to the drop zone I could see where we were going. The thing that struck me most at the time was the amount of flak that was hitting the aircraft – the Germans really were pumping a lot of it into the Dakotas but that did not deter me.

Red on! Green on! Go! My batman, Private Henry Gospel, was behind me shouting 'I am right behind you, Sir!' and out we went!

It did not seem very long before I was on the ground and out of my harness. I threw away my helmet, put on my red beret and grabbed my Sten gun. The Commanding Officer had told us to put on our berets as soon as we had landed in order to 'put the fear of God' into the Germans. As I moved off, I found myself with a platoon of Americans who had dropped on the wrong DZ and they now joined my company as we started to move off the drop zone towards the farm which was our objective. The most amazing thing was watching the whole battalion in the air in one go – in fact, the whole brigade. The entire division, including the gliders, was on the ground within forty-five minutes in what one would call a saturation drop.

Once we were on the ground we were immediately faced with the enemy. One of my platoons to my left captured a machine-gun position and we started taking prisoners – the Germans were giving themselves up all over the place. Although there was a lot of firing going on, even 88mm guns being used in the ground target role, one seemed to be oblivious to what was happening because once one had landed, one was in action straight away. There was the objective and that is what we went for – wearing our red berets and shouting our heads off.

Like the Commanding Officer and all the company commanders in the battalion, I had a hunting horn. We each had our different calls to muster our men. I blew mine, calling my company as we went for the objective. My batman was still with me, saying 'Right behind you, Sir!' as we took the farm with no problems. We then secured all our objectives, and it was all over. Whilst we were at the farm the Commanding Officer, Lieutenant Colonel Peter Luard, and the divisional commander joined us. We invited them for breakfast and my batman cooked us all bacon and eggs.

The ground was covered in mist and haze, which had been created by the bombardment from our guns, and it was very difficult to see. This caused a lot of problems for our gliders. I think that the saddest thing I saw was when we were moving towards our battalion objective, in the direction of Hamminkeln. There were glider pilots still sitting in their cockpits, having been roasted alive after their gliders had caught fire. One pilot and co-pilot were still sitting there with their hands on their control columns. A lot of people were lost like that. Although we lost quite a lot of casualties in the air, it was nowhere near those of the gliderborne troops.

One of the major problems, as far as we were concerned, was that 3rd Parachute Brigade was the first to go in and it had been dropped about ten minutes too early. Consequently, the artillery bombardment had to be lifted so that, by the time 5th Parachute Brigade and the remainder of the division arrived, the enemy were able to recover and organize themselves. That is why there was such an awful lot of flak on my aircraft. However, it was all over and it was then a question of rooting the enemy out of all the buildings. They put up resistance for the first few hours but once they could see it was the 'Red Devils', as they called us, they started to give up.

Like the other two battalions in the brigade, 12th Parachute Battalion was well aware that speed and surprise were essential to the success of the operation. The Commanding Officer, Lieutenant Colonel Ken Darling, described how he ensured that the Battalion went straight into the attack as soon as possible after landing:

We were dropping in broad daylight on top of the enemy positions and also onto our objective. The essence of the plan was rapid action, taking risks early, and rushing our objectives before the enemy could recover from the preliminary bombardment and the surprise of a mass landing of parachutists.

We were flown in by thirty-three Dakotas of the US IX Troop Carrier Command whose practice was to fly in tight formation of Vs, or Vics, which produced a tight concentration of parachutists on the ground. During the short time that we had for training and rehearsals in England before the operation, we paid great attention to parachuting techniques and especially the handling of kitbags. As a result, there were very few losses of equipment on the drop.

In addition, we took drastic steps to cut down weight on the man and this was an important factor in respect of movement and success. Entrenching tools and No. 75 Grenades were not carried; one man in two carried a toggle rope; no spare clothing, except socks, was taken and the time-honoured custom of every man being equipped with two No. 36 Grenades was abandoned.

Finally, because of the tight flight formation of the aircraft, the positioning of a platoon and its jumping order was determined by where we wanted the men on the drop zone rather than in the air. Thus a platoon could be allotted to, say, the last ten places in each of three aircraft (a Vic) with the platoon commander travelling in the middle Dakota, another platoon occupying the remainder of the same three aircraft.

All of these measures enabled the battalion to act with speed, and they paid off handsomely.

Such was the poor visibility caused by smoke and the very thick haze that the majority of the Battalion assembled at its RV point only to discover it was in the wrong place and thus had to move across the DZ to the correct location. As it did so, however, it came under heavy fire and suffered a number of casualties. On arrival at the RV location, it found itself again under fire, this time at close range from a troop of 88mm guns that were attacked and knocked out by a platoon of A Company, commanded by Lieutenant Phil Burkinshaw, while the rest of the company under Major Gerald Ritchie secured its objective.

In the meantime, the two other rifle companies were carrying out their respective tasks. C Company, under Major Steve Stephens, secured its objective without any problems, but B Company, commanded by Major E.J.O'B. 'Rip' Croker, encountered fierce resistance on attacking a number of farm buildings held by a strong force of enemy; by the time it had secured the objective, several casualties had been incurred among the company's officers and senior NCOs.

7th Parachute Battalion was the last to jump, encountering the stiffest opposition as it did so. The Commanding Officer, Lieutenant Colonel Geoffrey Pine-Coffin, later gave an account of his Battalion's landing and the events that ensued:

The drop was at 1010 hours and was from rather higher than we liked for an operational one; it must have been from nearly 1,000 feet. This would normally have been an advantage, as it seems that one is in the air for longer than one expects and thus gets a good chance of spotting a landmark as one comes down, but in this case everyone was getting pretty anxious to get down quickly because it was far from healthy in the air. The German flak gunners weren't getting much success in shooting down the Dakotas, so a lot of them switched and burst their shells amongst the parachutists instead; this was most unpleasant and we suffered a number of casualties before we even reached the ground. There was mortar bombing and shelling on the ground but it was a great relief to get there just the same.

The suddenness of the drop had the desired effect and we found the Germans slow to react. The battalion was in this position for five hours and during that time there was no really serious attack put in on us. There were various attacks on B Company's position by parties of about platoon strength or slightly more and, at one point, C Company took on a company that was working its way round towards them. However, it was A Company who came in for the worst time: they had arrived late and found their area was a very nasty spot. Their casualties were high and so were those of the mortars and machine guns who were with them.

The trouble came from a small wood 700 yards away. There was a troop of 88mm guns located there, commanded by an officer whom one could not help but admire. When the drop took place, it appears that the gun crews panicked and ran away, but this officer managed to turn enough of them back to man one of the guns. He was, of course, in a hopeless position but he kept that gun firing and did an immense amount of damage before he was rounded up. Although A Company suffered badly, 12th Parachute Battalion and Brigade Headquarters got it worse. It was 12th Parachute Battalion that sent out the party who rounded him up; A Company, of course, should have done it but they were late in getting in and it had to be done quickly. We got our share of it in Battalion Headquarters and had quite a few casualties, as well I know because I got a splinter in the face myself.

Following behind the two parachute brigades was 6th Airlanding Brigade, commanded by Brigadier Hugh Bellamy. The flight to Germany had been peaceful and uneventful, but as the fleet of gliders and tug aircraft transporting the Brigade neared the Rhine, a huge pall of smoke could be seen in the distance, rising from the battle raging below. Among the pilots flying the gliders carrying the 1st Battalion The Royal Ulster Rifles was Lieutenant Desmond Turner of The Glider Pilot Regiment, who later described the scene as he approached the landing zones:

We were flying at roughly 2,900 feet to avoid slipstream. Three checkpoints were marked on our maps: Points A, B and C which were all five minutes flying apart, and with Point C being the release point. Point A was easily seen but from then on nothing could be distinguished on the ground. The flak was extremely heavy and concentrated, and flying in position behind the tug became harder as the surrounding air was more than a little bumpy. As we could not see our own LZ or anybody else's, we remained on tow.

Suddenly we saw the *autobahn* below us and, as a result of previous careful study of air photographs, we knew where we were. We released and did a tight 270 degree turn to port and saw the church spire of Hamminkeln in front of us. Owing to the immediate vicinity being rather crowded with gliders, we applied full flap and went down on to the LZ as briefed. Our passengers were none the worse after this unorthodox approach and proceeded to unload.

Others were not so fortunate, being unable to pick up their bearings because of the haze and smoke. Several gliders landed in the wrong locations, while others were hit by flak and destroyed in mid-air or crashed on landing, some being set ablaze.

Despite the scenes of chaos on the landing zones, a high proportion of the coup de main parties, tasked with capturing the bridges over the Issel, were delivered close to their objectives. The Brigade did, however, meet stiffer opposition than had been expected, finding that the enemy had converted many of the farm buildings into strongpoints, and encountering a number of armoured vehicles. The Commanding Officer of the 12th Battalion The Devonshire Regiment, Lieutenant Colonel Paul Gleadell, later described the scene after landing on LZ 'R':

> The sound of shellfire and machine guns, coming from all sides, was deafening and every now and then we came upon a glider blazing furiously, one or two with their crews trapped within and one could do little to extricate them. One glider, or what was left of it, had wrapped itself around a massive tree. The whole situation seemed chaotic and I wondered if we should ever get it unravelled. Every farmhouse appeared to contain a defended post and isolated battles were being fought all over the LZ and beyond.
>
> The enemy were in greater confusion than we were. A number managed to concentrate in Hamminkeln, particularly on the north-east side. They consisted mainly of flak gunners, Luftwaffe Regiment, Volksturm and parachutists. Three self-propelled guns, some tanks, armoured cars and half-tracks were cruising about the LZ and engaging troops who were deplaning.
>
> We concentrated in the area of a road junction. After meeting

some resistance, we eventually reached the northern edge of Hamminkeln. Contact was established by wireless with Battalion Headquarters and B Company, and so I gave the order for Phase Two to start at 1135 hours. The companies duly assaulted and the objective was taken by midday. Consolidation and mopping-up were vigorously carried out in anticipation of the expected counter-attack and to eliminate the remaining flak positions. A German strongpoint of some forty men in a windmill was accounted for by one NCO.

The 2nd Battalion The Oxfordshire & Buckinghamshire Light Infantry landed on LZ 'O'. During the landing, which lasted only ten minutes, the Battalion lost almost half its strength. Gliders approached the LZ through thick smoke and heavy anti-aircraft fire, some colliding as they touched down while others fell blazing from the sky. The pilot and co-pilot of the Horsa carrying the Quartermaster, Lieutenant Bill Aldworth, were both killed but the situation was saved by Aldworth who, despite having no flying experience, took over the controls and landed the aircraft safely. The glider carrying the Commanding Officer, Lieutenant Colonel Mark Darell-Brown, came under fire from a 20mm anti-aircraft battery near Hamminkeln. The pilot, Squadron Leader V.H. Reynolds, put the aircraft into a dive while the co-pilot opened fire through the front of the cockpit windshield. The glider landed beside the battery and Lieutenant Colonel Darell-Brown and his men deplaned at speed, attacking the enemy gunners and overpowering them.

All was confusion throughout the Battalion's area, with individual actions taking place on and around each of the companies' objectives, while in the background the continual noise of ammunition exploding in burning gliders added to the din of battle. As the Battalion stormed the anti-aircraft batteries, it came under mortar and machine-gun fire and shortly afterwards three enemy tanks appeared while apparently withdrawing to the east. These also opened fire, causing further casualties, before one was knocked out and the other two made good their escape. By 1100 hours, however, the Battalion had secured all its objectives, albeit it at a heavy cost as by then its strength had been reduced to 226 all ranks.

Meanwhile the 1st Battalion The Royal Ulster Rifles had also taken severe punishment, being met by heavy anti-aircraft fire as it approached LZ 'U', and engaged by enemy armoured vehicles as it landed. The glider carrying the Commanding Officer, Lieutenant Colonel Jack Carson, broke in half on landing and he was seriously injured. His adjutant, Captain Robin Rigby, found himself being landed about 80 yards from enemy positions in some houses. The glider was badly smashed up and Rigby and his men were unable to unload their jeep and equipment. He later recalled the events that ensued:

> I got everybody out of the glider into a ditch on the side of the road. Between ourselves and the houses a C Company glider was burning, the ammunition inside it exploding. About two minutes later, half a platoon of C Company came across the open ground towards us from the direction of the houses. On questioning these men, I was told that they had crash-landed and that their glider had caught fire almost immediately. About two-thirds of their platoon had got out alive and had moved towards the houses but had met considerable opposition and had been forced to withdraw. Very shortly after this, another platoon of C Company and one from B Company arrived with twelve prisoners from the houses on the west side of the road. One or two men from B Company's headquarters were also with them but Major Ken Donnelly had been killed.
>
> As this appeared to be the total sum of the battalion which had landed so far on this LZ, I decided to leave a small fire group in the ditch and to move around to the right and attack through the orchard. However, as I was just about to move, I saw Lieutenant Colin O'Hara Murray's platoon of B Company starting to advance through the orchard. I therefore had some 2-inch mortar smoke put down and put in an assault on the houses from where we were, going in at right angles to O'Hara Murray's line of attack.
>
> Fire was spasmodic and a very half-hearted defence was put up, most of the Germans throwing their weapons away when we got to within 40 or 50 yards of them. Quite a lot of Germans were killed by grenades and Stens in and around the houses and barns, and in about fifteen to twenty minutes they had all been rooted out. The whole area appeared to be fairly clear so I sent B and C Companies to the position laid down in the original plan.

By early afternoon The Royal Ulster Rifles had secured all their objectives and were in firm control of their area. They had, however, suffered heavy casualties totalling sixteen officers and 243 other ranks.

Losses were also significant elsewhere in 6th Airborne Division. 53rd Airlanding Light Regiment RA found itself with only about half of its twenty-four pack howitzers in action after landing; nevertheless, 211th and 212th Airlanding Light Batteries RA were in action ten minutes after landing at 1050 hours. Likewise, only half of the anti-tank guns of 2nd Airlanding Anti-Tank Regiment RA were brought into action, 3rd and 4th Airlanding Anti-Tank Batteries RA having suffered severe casualties: of the thirty-two anti-tank guns flown in, only three were in action an hour after landing, this figure increasing to twelve after six hours.

Eight Locust light tanks of 6th Airborne Armoured Reconnaissance Regiment were flown in to provide initial armoured support, but only four reached the regimental RV; of these only two were fully fit for action. Throughout the rest of the day, these two vehicles were involved in several encounters with the enemy; along with a number of glider pilots and a platoon of the 12th Devons, they formed a strongpoint on the edge of the woods to the west of Divisional Headquarters.

By 1100 hours Major General Eric Bols, who had been landed within 100 yards of the intended location for his headquarters, had established himself in a farm at Kopenhof. Ten minutes later, he was in radio contact with all three of his brigades and communications had been established on the artillery net. In the meantime, however, Rear Divisional Headquarters, located about half a mile away in a farm west of the railway, was being subjected to sniping and mortar attacks. That evening, it moved to join the main headquarters due to lack of manpower and resources to defend both locations.

During the night of 24/25 March, the commander of XVIII Airborne Corps, Major General Matthew Ridgway, accompanied by Major General Bud Miley, commanding 17th US Airborne Division, visited Major General Bols. The latter was informed that 6th Airborne Division was to remain in its positions during the next day, with the exception of 6th Airlanding Brigade which would be relieved by 157th Infantry Brigade of 52nd (Lowland) Division the following night. Bols was also ordered to be ready to advance eastwards at dawn on 26 March.

That night and in the early hours of 25 March, there was a considerable amount of activity in the area held by The Oxfordshire & Buckinghamshire Light Infantry. The bridge held by B Company had been blown at 0230 hours to deny its use to the enemy, who launched an attack which petered out half an hour later. At 0400 hours, enemy infantry succeeded in infiltrating between A and C Companies and three-quarters of an hour later attacked A Company. Artillery support was called down and A Company launched a counter-attack while a company of the 12th Devons moved up in support. The enemy withdrew in the face of the counter-attack and the Battalion's perimeter was restored. At 0530 hours, enemy armour was spotted moving towards Ringenberg. Air support was duly summoned and at 0700 hours two flights of RAF Typhoon fighter-bombers appeared and knocked out several tanks. One heavy tank, situated in a hull-down position, avoided destruction and continued to cause trouble throughout the rest of the day.

Shortly after first light in 3rd Parachute Brigade's area, an attack was launched against 1st Canadian Parachute Battalion by infantry supported by tanks, but this was beaten off.

At 0730 hours two Panther tanks, with infantry riding on them and approaching at high speed, attempted to recapture one of the two bridges over the Issel, held by The Royal Ulster Rifles. However, the leading tank was quickly knocked out and the other seriously damaged by anti-tank guns sited near the bridge. Later that morning, the Battalion was reinforced by a battery of self-propelled guns and a squadron of tanks to provide further protection for both bridges.

That afternoon and evening, The Oxfordshire & Buckinghamshire Light Infantry saw further action when two of its companies cleared enemy from a number of buildings to the north and north-west. At midnight, the Battalion was relieved by a battalion of The Cameronians (Scottish Rifles) and in the early hours of 26 March withdrew to a concentration area on the western edge of Hamminkeln.

In the meantime, the rest of 6th Airborne Division experienced a relatively quiet day as it made preparations for the break-out and the next phase of operations: the advance to the Baltic.

Chapter 15

The morning of 26 March witnessed 6th Airborne Division on the move, with 3rd Parachute Brigade moving south into 17th US Airborne Division's area as corps reserve, while 5th Parachute Brigade remained in its positions. 6th Airlanding Brigade meanwhile was tasked with attacking the high ground to the north-west of Brunen.

That afternoon, 3rd Parachute Brigade was released from corps reserve; in the meantime, patrols from the Brigade had moved forward to the Issel where they found the east bank of the river had been abandoned by the enemy. James Hill thus decided to seize the bridgehead and was given permission to exploit forward as far as his objective for the next day. The divisional objective was the town of Lembeck and the Brigade was tasked with taking and securing the area of the small village of Klosterlutherheim and the high ground to the south-east of Lembeck. Having crossed the Issel that evening, the Brigade pushed on during the night with the 3rd Tank Battalion Scots Guards under command.

The night of 26/27 March saw 1st Canadian Parachute Battalion spending the night in a farm in the area of the Upper Issel until the early morning, when at 0530 hours it advanced on its initial objective, the village of Burch. Weather conditions were poor with heavy rain falling as B Company led the way, taking the village and encountering only light resistance before pushing on towards its second objective, an area of wooded terrain overlooking another village.

At this point, the rain stopped but visibility was poor due to a heavy mist. Suddenly, a Tiger heavy tank appeared on the narrow lane along which a platoon of B Company was leading the Battalion, opening fire but withdrawing swiftly as a PIAT team responded. The Battalion followed up and on reaching its objective began to dig in, but as it did so came under fire from a number of tanks and self-propelled guns positioned in a small wood approximately a quarter of a mile away; a number of casualties were inflicted on B Company.

Faced with no alternative, Lieutenant Colonel Fraser Eadie decided to launch an attack on the enemy armour despite this having to take the form of a frontal assault over open ground; to make matters worse, there was no artillery support available.

The Battalion was preparing to attack when two armed jeeps of an eighteen-strong troop of 2nd Special Air Service Regiment, operating under command of 21 Liaison Group, made an unexpected appearance. Tasked with carrying out forward reconnaissance for 3rd Parachute Brigade, the troop was under the command of Lieutenant Doug Charlton who previously had served under James Hill in 1st Parachute Battalion in North Africa. Both vehicles were equipped with .50 calibre heavy machine guns and their crews thus offered to provide support for the assault, thereafter directing a heavy volume of covering fire into the wood as the Battalion attacked across the open ground with B Company once more leading the way; on reaching the wood, however, it was discovered that the enemy had withdrawn in haste. On pushing through to the village beyond, the Canadians found it deserted with several houses ablaze.

In the meantime, 9th Parachute Battalion had attacked Klosterlutherheim in the early hours of the morning. This had resulted in a short sharp battle in which twelve enemy were killed and 180 taken prisoner.

At midnight on 27/28 March 6th Airborne Division came under command of VIII Corps which was to advance in the direction of the Baltic, its axis being intersected by two major rivers, the Weser and Elbe. The Division's initial objective, as laid down in the orders from the Corps Commander, Lieutenant General Sir Evelyn Barker, was the town of Coesfeld situated some 35 miles to the north-east of Erle. The Division was to take the town while 11th Armoured Division advanced on a parallel axis to the north-east with the task of dominating the town from the north.

The advance began at 1200 hours. 3rd Parachute Brigade, having spent the night in the area of Brunen before moving to an assembly area west of Erle, led the way with elements of 6th Airborne Armoured Reconnaissance Regiment as its spearhead. Following it was 6th Airlanding Brigade.

Opposition was encountered approximately 2,000 yards east of Erle but this was easily overcome. Heavier resistance was encountered between Rhade and Lembeck, but this was cleared by 8th Parachute Battalion before pushing on towards Lembeck which lay some 6,000 yards away. It soon became obvious that the Germans would not permit the town to be taken

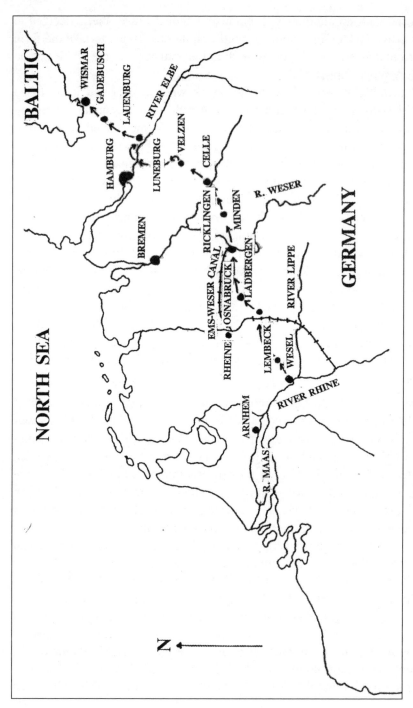

Advance to the Baltic

without a fight, so Hill ordered 9th Parachute Battalion to carry out a left-flanking move and approach the town from the rear, thus cutting it off from the east.

In the meantime, 8th Parachute Battalion continued its advance. Immediately to the west of the town, however, its leading company was pinned down by heavy fire from 20mm guns. 1st Canadian Parachute Battalion, which was in reserve, moved up to hold the main axis, while 8th Parachute Battalion mounted a right-flanking attack on the town supported by the tanks and 4.2-inch mortar troop of 6th Airborne Armoured Reconnaissance Regiment.

The battle for Lembeck lasted until dusk. At that point Hill decided to limit 8th Parachute Battalion's attack, ordering Lieutenant Colonel George Hewetson to take and hold the high ground south of the town. At one point, the leading company found itself separated from the rest of the Battalion while engaged in a fierce encounter with two companies of a panzer grenadier training battalion. By midnight, however, the Battalion had gained the upper hand, killing or capturing all of the enemy facing it, by which time the separated company had fought its way into the western suburbs of the town where it was joined in due course by 1st Canadian Parachute Battalion.

In the meantime, 9th Parachute Battalion had completed its flanking move to cut the enemy off from the rear. While moving over some high ground to the north of the town, however, it came under fire from a battery of four 20mm guns. These were engaged by A Company which laid down a heavy volume of fire, pinning down the gun crews while a patrol worked its way to a position within 300 yards from the battery before launching an attack, which resulted in several of the enemy gunners being killed and over twenty taken prisoner. The Battalion then continued to its blocking position from which it effectively cut off any movement into and out of Lembeck to the east.

The following morning, 30 March, found 3rd Parachute Brigade moving through 6th Airlanding Brigade and continuing its advance towards its next objective some 35 miles away: the town of Greven and the bridge there spanning the River Ems.

1st Canadian Parachute Battalion led the way, travelling in trucks and supported by Churchill tanks of Nos 1 and 3 Squadrons of 4th Tank Battalion Grenadier Guards. After some distance, however, A Company was transferred to the backs of the tanks. Not long afterwards, an enemy roadblock was encountered, but this was dealt with swiftly by A Company and the advance resumed. Further pockets of resistance were met en route, consisting mainly of small groups who attempted to ambush the tanks with *panzerfausts* and small arms; in each case, however, A Company dismounted and conducted a sweep along each side of the road while the tanks opened fire on likely enemy positions.

That night, as dusk was falling, 1st Canadian Parachute Battalion halted and dismounted at a point some 3 miles short of Greven. Thereafter, it advanced on foot while the Grenadiers' tanks moved forward to a line along the river. The bridge was taken within minutes of the Battalion reaching the town and shortly afterwards the Canadians were joined by 9th Parachute Battalion, whose Commanding Officer, Lieutenant Colonel Napier Crookenden, accompanied by his reconnaissance group, then advanced down the main street of Greven. As he arrived at the river he spotted another bridge and so, accompanied by one of his company commanders, went forward to reconnoitre it. As he did so, however, it was destroyed by the enemy who promptly withdrew. It was then discovered that the maps were inaccurate, showing only one bridge, and that 1st Canadian Parachute Battalion had taken the wrong bridge that led to an island in the middle of the river. There was thus no alternative but to await the arrival of sappers and bridging equipment.

9th Parachute Battalion withdrew and moved south-east along the river. In the early hours of the following morning, a footbridge crossing the river was found and two patrols from A Company were despatched across it, only to come under fire; in the ensuing action one of the patrol commanders was killed. An hour later, however, the enemy positions had been overrun and by 0730 hours Greven had been taken.

1st Canadian Parachute Battalion meanwhile had been kept busy during the night: an enemy troop train arrived at the town's station, whereupon all of its passengers were taken prisoner, and in the early hours of 31 March, on the far side of the river, the enemy blew up an ammunition dump, this resulting in a series of explosions that continued for some time. In the meantime, the Battalion's positions along the river were under almost constant fire.

That morning, sappers from VIII Corps having constructed a Bailey bridge across the river and strengthened another outside the town, 3rd Parachute Brigade continued its advance, with 8th Parachute Battalion leading the way, for a further 10 miles until it reached the west bank of the Dortmund-Ems Canal, where it was discovered that the main canal bridge and another smaller one half a mile to the south had both been blown by the enemy.

The following morning, 1 April, bridging of the canal began. At 1030 hours, two companies of 8th Parachute Battalion succeeded in crossing it and advancing about a mile. In the meantime the bridging site came under heavy fire from a number of self-propelled guns some distance away, this continuing until midday.

3 April found 3rd Parachute Brigade, mounted on the backs of tanks or travelling in half-tracks and armoured troop carriers, advancing on Wissingen which was situated some 6 miles to the east of Osnabrück. 9th Parachute Battalion led the way, followed by 8th and 1st Canadian Parachute Battalions. Wissingen was reached late that afternoon, being taken by 9th Parachute Battalion after some heavy fighting.

The advance continued the following morning with 1st Canadian Parachute Battalion leading the way to the town of Lübeck, the final objective for that day being the city of Minden on the River Weser. The pace was swift, the column of vehicles thundering through a succession of small villages. En route, the Brigade encountered large numbers of enemy troops who were surrendering, but there was no time to take them prisoner; instead they were merely disarmed and sent back down the road to be dealt with by other VIII Corps formations following behind.

Reaching Lübeck, the Brigade pressed on to the outskirts of Minden where the advance halted. Just after last light 8th Parachute Battalion, which had led the way from Lübeck, came under heavy fire and was pinned down. Following a reconnaissance patrol report that the enemy were not in strength, Hill decided to mount a night attack.

At 2345 hours the attack began with the Grenadier Guards' tanks surging through the enemy positions into the city, with 1st Canadian Parachute Battalion following close behind. Fierce fighting ensued, lasting throughout the night as the three parachute battalions cleared the enemy from the streets. By 0230 hours on 5 April, all opposition had ceased and the city had fallen.

3rd Parachute Brigade had achieved a remarkable feat in advancing 36 miles from Greven to Minden in seventy hours. The latter had been an objective of the Ninth US Army and was to have been the target of a mass bombing raid, but the Brigade had beaten the Americans to it and thus had saved the city from destruction. On the afternoon of 5 April, units of Ninth US Army arrived to take over and 3rd Parachute Brigade moved to the village of Kutenhausen, some 3 miles to the north.

Meanwhile, the rest of 6th Airborne Division was also advancing eastwards. 6th Airlanding Brigade passed through 3rd Parachute Brigade on the night of 31 March/1 April and crossed the Dortmund-Ems Canal via the remains of the destroyed bridge the following night. Its next objective was the town of Lengerich, which it approached on the morning of 2 April. There had been conflicting reports as to the strength of the enemy holding the town, so it was subjected to ten minutes of artillery and mortar fire before an attack was launched, this encountering a certain amount of opposition. A fierce battle ensued between A Company of 1st Battalion The Royal Ulster Rifles and members of a German NCOs' training school at Hanover, this lasting until midday when the town was captured. Outside the town, however, other units of the Brigade met equally strong resistance from pockets of enemy, among them a battalion of officer cadets. It was not until late in the day that all resistance was overcome, the Brigade taking up defensive positions in the area of Lengerich.

On 3 April, 5th Parachute Brigade, which had arrived at Greven on 31 March, began its advance with 12th Parachute Battalion leading the way, supported by No. 3 Squadron of 4th Tank Battalion Grenadier Guards. Having crossed the Dortmund-Ems Canal, the Brigade headed for Lengerich and passed through, reaching the forward positions of The Royal Ulster Rifles. In the early hours of the following morning, having earlier mounted a successful company attack on some enemy positions on the outskirts of a village, 12th Parachute Battalion continued the advance towards Osnabrück but soon encountered opposition in the area of a village called Hasbergen. This resulted in a battalion attack that was successful, 13th Parachute Battalion subsequently moving through to take over the lead.

5 April found 6th Airlanding Brigade advancing on the River Weser over which it was to establish crossing points at Petershagen and Todtenhausen. The terrain approaching the river was flat and low-lying, intersected by dykes and small canals. The early stages of the advance saw little resistance, but on reaching Kutenhausen the Brigade encountered stiff opposition from enemy units well armed with anti-tank weapons which knocked out two of the Grenadiers' tanks. At the same time, it came under artillery fire which inflicted casualties. During the afternoon, however, elements of the 2nd Battalion The Oxfordshire & Buckinghamshire Light Infantry succeeded in crossing the Weser and attacking the villages of Wietersheim and Frille, where they encountered stiff resistance that was finally overcome by about 2000 hours that evening.

The following day, 7 April, saw the east bank of the Weser being cleared of enemy between Petershagen and Dohren, the latter situated 8 miles to the north, to enable 11th Armoured Division to bridge the river south of Dohren. That afternoon, enemy infantry and armour were observed forming up further to the east; on being subjected to artillery and mortar fire, however, they withdrew to the north. Dawn on 8 April witnessed The Oxfordshire & Buckinghamshire Light Infantry mounting an attack on two hamlets, Frillerbank and Heinrichsteich, some 2,000 yards to the east of Frille, both of which were taken and occupied without any enemy being encountered.

Meanwhile the 12th Battalion The Devonshire Regiment had advanced on 5 April to the western edge of the Heisterholz Forest, through which it moved to the west bank of the Weser, crossing the river during the night. The following day, an attack was launched on the villages of Masloh and Quetzen to secure the bridgehead, both being taken without any opposition.

5th Parachute Brigade meanwhile had concentrated at Fried Walde as Osnabrück had been rendered uninhabitable by Allied bombing. It had been intended that 15th (Scottish) Division should pass through 6th Airborne Division and take the lead during the advance to the Baltic, but it was unable to move up in time and so 6th Airborne Division remained the spearhead of VIII Corps.

On the morning of 8 April, 5th Parachute Brigade resumed the advance, tasked with establishing two bridgeheads over the River Leine 3 miles apart at Neustadt and Bordenau, some 35 miles away. The axis of advance would be via Petershagen, on the Weser, where bridgeheads had been secured by 6th Airlanding Brigade, and then via Roisenhagen, Bergkirchen and Altenhagen to an area of high ground north of Wunstorf and 2 miles from the River Leine. From there the Brigade would take the bridges at Bordenau and Neustadt, 12th and 7th Parachute Battalions being given these two tasks respectively.

Having crossed the Weser, the Brigade first encountered the enemy at Roisenhagen, but these were dealt with swiftly and the advance continued. An account of what ensued was later given by the Commanding Officer of 12th Parachute Battalion, Lieutenant Colonel Ken Darling:

> As we neared Wunstorf, C Company and the Grenadier squadron reached the village of Altenhagen. Shock tactics were again employed and after a few 17-pounder shells had been sent bouncing down the street by our troop from 4th Airlanding Anti-Tank Battery, the enemy fled.

> The vanguard was now 5 miles short of the River Leine and the decision had to be taken as to which of two routes, which led to the

objective, should be taken. The one to the north ran through a series of small villages and then on to some high ground north of an airfield at Wunstorf.

Major Ivor Crosthwaite, the Grenadier squadron leader, and I discussed the choice open to us. I had developed a very close liaison with him since the start of the advance after the breakout. I travelled behind his squadron, sitting on the scout car of his liaison officer, Major Bill Agar. Ivor Crosthwaite and I considered which route to take and how we should proceed. We both felt that there was a good chance of 'bouncing' the bridge if we went via the route to the south through open country.

At this point Brigadier Nigel Poett, our brigade commander, and Major General Eric Bols, arrived. They were frequently well up in the line of advance and this was a great help to me as the vanguard commander. They both confirmed the decision that Ivor Crosthwaite and I had taken.

We therefore instructed the vanguard to bash on towards the bridge on the southerly route. All went well for 3 miles but after C Company and the Grenadiers had passed through Wunstorf, resistance was met on the edge of the airfield. C Company dealt with the problem very quickly and without much trouble. The enemy were a motley collection of soldiers, some of them with wooden legs which amused our men enormously.

The fighting at the airfield was creating a delay and so I instructed the reconnaissance regiment to watch the enemy, whilst the vanguard bypassed the airfield and moved to Bordenau by an alternative route. The bridge was now just 2 miles away and C Company and the Grenadiers bashed on towards it.

This now had the makings of an interesting race as by now the enemy must have realized that trouble was brewing and they might have time to blow the bridge. The Grenadiers had very definite ideas on the subject and covered those 2 miles at record speed. As the leading tank rounded the last bend, the bridge could be seen intact but on it was a German lorry and a couple of men moving about and obviously up to no good.

As the column roared towards the bridge, parallel to the river for about 1,000 yards, a hail of fire from every weapon – Besas, Stens, rifles and Brens – was quickly brought to bear on the lorry. This had the desired effect and the Hun decamped at speed. In a twinkling of an eye the Grenadiers' tanks were on and over the bridge.

This brought to a close a very successful day's work. The battalion had covered 49 miles between 0400 and 1700 hours, and had captured a Class 40 bridge intact. Success was due to the fine cooperation between C Company and the Grenadiers. The latter's bold handling and the tactics of outflanking and getting behind enemy positions crushed all resistance with very few casualties to ourselves, these numbering precisely two.

In the meantime, 7th and 13th Parachute Battalions had cleared the airfield at Wunstorf, following which 7th Parachute Battalion pushed on to Neustadt where it found the bridge intact. As B Company began to cross, however, a sapper noticed that the bridge had been prepared for demolition. Tragically, his shouted warning went unheard and seconds later the enemy blew the bridge just as the leading platoon was halfway across, killing twenty-two men and wounding several others. Nevertheless, a bridgehead was established by a small group of four men, under Captain E.G. Woodman, who had been the first to run across.

By the evening of 7 April, 5th Parachute Brigade had advanced the furthest into Germany of any elements of 21st Army Group.

On 11 April, 15th (Scottish) Division assumed the role of spearhead of VIII Corps while 6th Airborne Division took on the task of clearing up the axis of advance, moving north-eastwards through the large town of Celle on the Lüneberg Heath. On 16 and 17 April, the Division took and held several villages to the east of Uelzen to prevent any withdrawal by the Germans when the town was attacked by 15th (Scottish) Division on the 18th. Opposition in the town was the stiffest that the Division had encountered east of the Rhine and the enemy artillery, comprising mainly self-propelled guns, proved particularly troublesome. This was not overcome until units of 15th (Scottish) Division had fought their way into Uelzen and 6th Airborne Division had bypassed the town and advanced eastwards to Rosche, which was attacked and taken that night. Thereafter the Division concentrated east of Uelzen, reconnoitring the roads leading to Lüchow and Dannenberg.

By the morning of 23 April, the whole of VIII Corps had reached the Elbe where it deployed on a 38-mile-wide front. The river was a major obstacle, being over 300 yards wide; on its west bank, the terrain comprised marshland offering no cover and dominated by enemy positions located on the far side in a steep wooded escarpment.

The Elbe was to be crossed in an operation comprising five phases. During the first, 15th (Scottish) Division, with 1st Commando Brigade under command, would carry out an assault river crossing at Lauenburg and establish a bridgehead. Thereafter, it was also to attempt to seize the bridges over the Elbe-Trave Canal to the east of the town. The second and third phases would then see the Division extending the bridgehead to Kruzen, situated 2 miles north of Lauenburg, and subsequently out to a number of villages 7 or 8 miles to the north and north-west of the town.

The fourth phase of the operation would see 15th (Scottish) Division regrouping and handing over the eastern sector of the bridgehead to 6th Airborne Division, the latter thereafter extending it eastwards to include two villages 5 miles from Lauenberg. In the fifth and final phase, 6th Airborne Division would secure the final limit of the bridgehead by deploying 15th Infantry Brigade of 5th Infantry Division to secure the area west of the Elbe-Trave Canal and capture two bridges spanning the canal some 8 miles to the north of Lauenburg. Having crossed the canal, 6th Airborne Division would revert to being under command of XVIII Airborne Corps.

Initially, Major General Eric Bols had intended to mount an airborne operation that would see 5th Parachute Brigade dropping on an airfield at Lauenburg, on the far side of the river, ahead of 15th (Scottish) Division and 1st Commando Brigade. In the event, however, it was discovered that the enemy were withdrawing and thus the drop was cancelled.

The date for the crossing of the Elbe was originally scheduled for 1 May, but this was brought forward to 29 April due to the increasing problems of large numbers of German refugees fleeing westwards into Lübeck to escape Russian forces advancing from the east.

By the evening of the 29th, the first two phases had been completed successfully, the third being carried out the following day. Along with 15th Infantry Brigade, 3rd Parachute Brigade crossed the Elbe the same day before heading eastwards to an area beyond Boizenberg where it linked up with American forces. The rest of 6th Airborne Division followed, taking over the eastern sector of the bridgehead as planned.

On the evening of 30 April, Major General Matthew Ridgway appeared at James Hill's headquarters. His orders for 6th Airborne Division, mounted in road transport with a squadron of The Royal Scots Greys in support, were to advance with the utmost haste to the town of Wismar on the Baltic coast; at all costs, it was to arrive there before the Russians.

The Division set off the following morning. 5th Parachute Brigade had been allotted the task of leading the advance but James Hill was determined that it would be his brigade that reached Wismar first. Thus the advance developed into a race with the two parachute brigades advancing at top speed along separate routes in a headlong dash to Gadebusch which lay some 15 miles to the south of Wismar. From there on it was a single route and so whichever brigade reached Gadebusch first would be the first to reach Wismar. At times, both brigades were hampered by crowds of refugees on the roads; on occasions, they drove past formations of fully armed enemy troops lining the roads as the Royal Scots Greys' tanks, with B Company of 1st Canadian Parachute Battalion aboard, thundered past. There were the occasional pockets of resistance, but these were silenced by some well-placed shellfire from the tanks.

In the event, 3rd Parachute Brigade was successful and 1st Canadian Parachute Battalion was the first to enter Wismar at 0900 hours on 2 May, having completed the 58-mile-long dash in twenty-five hours. As it did so, however, it encountered an enemy roadblock with troops dug in around it. These were soon cleared by B Company who dismounted and overran the German positions while the Royal Scots Greys proceeded to shoot their way through the roadblock.

The rest of 3rd Parachute Brigade arrived by midday. At 1600 hours that afternoon, the leading Russian troops of the Seventieth Army's III Guards Tank Corps were encountered when C Company of 1st Canadian Parachute Battalion, which was covering the eastern side of the town, met a patrol.

That afternoon, Hill despatched Lieutenant Colonel Napier Crookenden to establish contact with the Russians. Accompanied by two Russian-speaking sergeants from 1st Canadian Parachute Battalion, Crookenden set off in a jeep and shortly afterwards met a column of Russian armour. While he was conversing with its commander, another column of tanks sped past in the direction of Wismar. Accompanied by a Russian officer, he set off in hot pursuit and succeeded in overtaking the tanks just as they reached the outskirts of the town where they found themselves facing a troop of 17-pounder anti-tank guns of 2nd Airlanding Anti-Tank Regiment RA.

Thereafter there was a confrontation between a senior Russian officer, who declared that it was his mission to take Lübeck, and Major General Bols who made his position very clear by informing the Russian that he had an airborne division and five regiments of artillery at his disposal and would not hesitate to use them if necessary. Realizing that discretion was the better part of valour, the Russian backed down.

Later that day Lieutenant Doug Charlton, the commander of the 2nd SAS Regiment troop temporarily attached to 3rd Parachute Brigade for forward reconnaissance tasks, received orders to move on to Lübeck and the Kiel Canal. Wishing to say farewell to his old Commanding Officer, he went in search of Hill, as he later recalled:

> I eventually found his jeep, parked out of sight in a bomb crater with its sole occupant sleeping soundly. I didn't have the heart to wake the old boy. I left quietly, content with my memories and the fact that despite the life-threatening wounds he had suffered at Gué Hill, in Tunisia, in November 1942, plus two others received while commanding his brigade, he had made it in one piece through to the very end. Never a man for bugles and trumpets, he was always a most unassuming and goodly knight who loved the ways of chivalry, honour, faith and generosity. He will always be remembered by those he led in 1st Parachute Battalion and 3rd Parachute Brigade as the supreme professional in war. Above all, however, he possessed the one quality that those who served under him most desired, and which make comparisons with other great wartime soldiers of the past most valid. He was a winner!

During the following weeks, 6th Airborne Division remained in its positions while relations with the Russians gradually deteriorated; at one point the latter established a roadblock 100 yards from 1st Canadian Parachute Battalion's positions and positioned a troop of tanks nearby. On 7 May, Field Marshal Montgomery arrived in Wismar to meet the commander of the Red Army's 2nd Belorussian Front, Marshal Konstantin Rokossovsky, and on the following day, the war in Europe officially ended.

Years later, James Hill summed up his memories of Operation VARSITY and the ensuing advance to the Baltic:

> I remember how happy we were, so well led by Major General Eric Bols, to be alongside the 17th US Airborne Division and to come under command of the corps commander, that great American general, Matthew Ridgway. What a sight it must have been to gladden the hearts of war-weary men and women, that great air armada of some 3,000 aircraft droning relentlessly overhead in the direction of the enemy.
>
> I recall the quite remarkable affinity and hence cooperation that existed, based on respect and real affection, not only within the units of our own division and the Royal Air Force, but also with the pilots

of the USAAF Troop Carrier Command with whom we had trained so much over the previous two years. Such was our trust in their skill, for example, that we asked them to drop 3rd Parachute Brigade, consisting of some 2,200 fighting men, in a clearing measuring 1,000 by 800 yards in a heavily wooded area held by German parachute troops. The drop took six minutes to complete and was dead on target. 5th Parachute Brigade, commanded by Brigadier Nigel Poett, enjoyed the same splendid service. I thanked God then, and still do now, for those brave American pilots.

Our division, therefore, when it emplaned on that glorious sunny morning, was full of confidence. We were very experienced, with Normandy, the Ardennes and Holland behind us. We were well disciplined and were able to take advantage of the lessons learned from our previous airborne operations. As we boarded our aircraft, everyone sensed that we were entering a battle which would mark the beginning of the end.

Some 3,000 aircraft all told – bombers, fighters, reconnaissance, troop carriers, tug aircraft and gliders, were involved in this great battle and its preliminary bombardment, all linked by radio communication. What a difference in skill, technique and planning from our original 1st Parachute Battalion drop in North Africa in October 1942! Flying in tight formation, hundreds of American C-477 Dakota aircraft carried our 1st Canadian, 7th, 8th, 9th, 12th and 13th Parachute Battalions and six parachute battalions of the 17th US Airborne Division, while the British and American gliderborne regiments and divisional troops rode into battle in 1,300 gliders.

The price was paid and the sacrifice made: a total of 1,078 men of the 6th Airborne Division had been carried off the field, either dead or wounded, by the time the sun set on that lovely March day. The total airborne casualties, British, Canadian and American, amounted to some 2,500 killed and wounded, and some 500 missing, many of the latter returning in due course to fight another day. German casualties were estimated at 1,000 killed and 4,000 taken prisoner.

Thirty-seven days later, on 1 May 1945, having fought our way on foot across some 275 miles of Germany, forcing crossings both of the River Weser and Elbe, and keeping pace with the armoured division on our flanks, the 6th Airborne Division captured Wismar on the Baltic and we were the first British troops to link up with the Russians. The war in Europe was at an end.

The latter half of May witnessed 3rd Parachute Brigade, along with the rest of 6th Airborne Division, returning to England and its base in Bulford. On 31 May, James Hill, accompanied by Major General Eic Bols and many other members of Divisional Headquarters, bade farewell to the officers and men of 1st Canadian Parachute Battalion, which had established such a great reputation as an airborne unit second to none. During operations in Normandy, the Ardennes and North-West Europe, the Battalion had suffered 126 killed, 294 wounded and eighty-four captured. The gallant Canadians held a very special place in James Hill's affections and this was reflected by his insistence on shaking the hand of every member of the Battalion as, on 31 May, it boarded the train at Bulford station at the start of its long voyage home.

Two weeks later the Battalion sailed for Canada aboard the *Isle de France*, arriving in Halifax on 21 June. By this time, the tide of war in the Pacific had turned in favour of the Allies and the decision was taken not to deploy the Battalion as part of the Canadian forces in that theatre. Consequently, on 30 September 1945, 1st Canadian Parachute Battalion was officially disbanded and passed into history.

Chapter 16

It was not until many years later that full details of the reasons for the swift despatch of 6th Airborne Division to Wismar were revealed.

In 1944, when the war in Europe appeared to be approaching its end, it became apparent that measures would have to be taken to avoid any accidental clashes between Allied and Russian forces as the two began to converge. A plan was drawn up in which clear rules of engagement and lines of demarcation were laid down with the latter, running from Lübeck to northern Switzerland, later being approved at the Yalta Conference in February 1945.

On 28 April 1945, however, the Allies received firm intelligence that the Russians were planning to contravene the Yalta Agreement and invade Denmark with the aim of securing for themselves an ice-free harbour and an outlet to the North Sea; in turn, this would require them to take and hold Kiel and Schleswig-Holstein in order to provide road and rail access for the maintenance of their fleet. The Allies also learned that the Russians had given their III Guards Tank Corps the task of driving a corridor through Kiel and Flensburg.

Such flagrant disregard of the Yalta Agreement was not permissible and so the decision was taken to block the Russians, but in such a way as to avoid open conflict with them.

The initial Allied response was the immediate despatch of a strong Royal Navy flotilla comprising the cruisers HMS *Birmingham* and *Dido*, accompanied by four Z-class destroyers, to Copenhagen where they were to act as a deterrent against any attempt by the Russians to invade from the sea. At the same time, two squadrons of RAF Typhoon fighter-bombers were put on stand-by to fly to Copenhagen and land on an airfield near the Danish capital, their arrival to coincide with that of the flotilla. Thereafter Headquarters 1st Parachute Brigade, commanded by Brigadier Gerald Lathbury, and a company would be landed, ostensibly to supervise the surrender of German troops in Denmark, but also to act as a deterrent to any Russian invasion.

Thus it was on the night of 30 April/1 May that Major General Eric Bols received orders to punch a 50-mile-long narrow corridor through an area still strongly defended by German troops, and the following day launched his two parachute brigades in a frantic race against time to the Baltic with orders to halt the Russian advance there.

Events moved swiftly thereafter. On 2 May there were reports of Russian paratroops dropping south of Copenhagen. The following day, the announcement of the death of Adolf Hitler was broadcast in Denmark, along with the news that Admiral Karl Dönitz, the German naval commander-in-chief based at Flensburg, had been nominated as his successor.

On 4 May, the Royal Navy flotilla entered Copenhagen harbour, followed by the first squadron of RAF Typhoons which landed on the airfield near the capital. At 1800 hours that evening, representatives of Admiral Dönitz met Field Marshal Sir Bernard Montgomery at Lüneburg Heath for the formal signing of the ceasefire and surrender document to become effective at 0800 hours on 5 May for all German forces in North-West Europe, the Low Countries and Scandinavia. In the event, however, SS and other units disregarded the surrender and continued to fight.

On 6 May a company from 5th Parachute Brigade landed from Lübeck and secured the airport at Copenhagen pending the arrival of Headquarters 1st Parachute Brigade and its defence platoon the following day.

It was without doubt, however, the 50-mile headlong dash to Wismar through enemy-held territory by 3rd Parachute Brigade that saved the day for Denmark and Schleswig-Holstein, by stopping the Russians in their tracks at Wismar. A few days later, the Russians' intentions became all too clear when on 9 May, following a two-day-long aerial bombardment, they launched a seaborne invasion of the Danish island of Bornholm. After a short battle, the 12,000-strong German garrison surrendered and the island remained occupied by the Russians until 5 April 1946 when their forces withdrew. Having failed to secure Denmark, the Russians established their long-sought ice-free harbour at Königsberg (later renamed Kaliningrad). In 1995, following the break-up of the Soviet Union, they were forced to leave the Baltic States but retained Kaliningrad and its 6,000 square miles of hinterland. To this day, this strategically important city and port still remains part of Russia, evidence of the fate that would otherwise have befallen Denmark.

James Hill received a second bar to his DSO in June 1945, the citation stating:

His brigade finished triumphantly by reaching the Baltic at 1400 hours on 2 May, after advancing 58 miles in one day. Brigadier Hill's courage and dash in action are almost legendary. His skilful and inspiring leadership have been largely responsible for the great successes achieved by his brigade.

In addition to his DSO with two bars, and his MC, Hill's highly distinguished wartime service had already been recognized by the awards of the French Chevalier de la Légion d'Honneur, the American Silver Star and the Norwegian King Haakon VII Cross of Liberty. Sadly, however, there had been no recognition of his role in saving Denmark from Soviet occupation.

In May 2005, Major Tony Hibbert, who had served during the war in 1st Parachute Battalion and later as Brigade Major of 1st Parachute Brigade at Arnhem, visited Copenhagen for the 60th anniversary of the liberation of Denmark and was introduced to Her Majesty Queen Margrethe II. He took the opportunity of drawing her attention to the role that James Hill had played in preventing the Soviet invasion of Denmark, later giving an account of his conversation with her:

Having been introduced to the Queen, I raised the subject of the events of the last days of World War II. She confirmed that there was great concern that the Russians intended to occupy Denmark contrary to the terms of the Yalta Agreement. She did not know, however, about the role played by James Hill's 3rd Parachute Brigade in stopping the Russians at Wismar.

The person credited with the liberation of Denmark was of course Brigadier Gerald Lathbury who landed at Copenhagen on 7 May 1945 with a small headquarters element of 1st Parachute Brigade and his defence platoon. They fought a stubborn action for fourteen days, fending off hordes of beautiful Danish girls anxious to show their gratitude, and then flew back to Britain; for that Lathbury was awarded the Danish Order of The Elephant, the first and only time the order had been awarded to a foreigner.

I informed the Queen that the individual who had actually stopped the Russians at Wismar was James Hill who, with his brigade, had held them there until the ceasefire was signed, whereupon they were permitted to continue their advance to Lübeck and the boundary specified in the Yalta Agreement. I suggested she might like to make some gesture of recognition, as James was still alive, and she asked me to send the information to her military attaché, which I did. Unknown to me, however, the Russians had just completed the construction of a gas and oil pipeline as far as Wismar to supply the needs of both Germany and Denmark, and sadly it was thus considered that the timing was not right for an award to James that might upset the Russians.

Ironically, not long after 3rd Parachute Brigade's return to England and Bulford, James Hill found himself posted to Denmark as Military Governor of Copenhagen and Commander 1st Parachute Brigade. Thus, at the beginning of June 1945, he bade farewell to 3rd Parachute Brigade and the men whom he had commanded so brilliantly for the last two years, during which they had seen much heavy and bitter fighting.

His time in Denmark, however, was brief as was his tenure of command of 1st Parachute Brigade. Following its successful advance to the Baltic, 6th Airborne Division was assigned a role in South-East Asia and Hill was offered command of it. After due consideration, however, he declined the offer. The dropping of the two atomic bombs on Japan in early August, however, hastened the end of the war in the Far East and thus all thoughts of despatching the Division to that part of the world were abandoned.

Hitherto, it had been decided that 1st Airborne Division would be deployed to the Middle East as part of the Imperial Strategic Reserve. With hostilities now at an end, however, it was considered no longer necessary to retain two airborne divisions in the British Army's order of battle and thus the decision was taken that 6th Airborne Division would be retained and 1st Airborne Division disbanded. Thereafter a major reorganization of Airborne Forces took place with 5th Parachute Brigade, which was despatched to the Far East, being replaced by 2nd Parachute Brigade. 1st Parachute Brigade, along with 1st Airlanding Brigade, was to be disbanded and Hill was given the task of putting this into effect.

In July 1945, he returned to civilian life; by this time he recently had become a father as Denys had given birth to their daughter Gillian on 16 February. It was not long, however, before he was back in uniform as, shortly after leaving the Army, he was summoned by Field Marshal Viscount Montgomery, Chief of the Imperial General Staff and Colonel Commandant of The Parachute Regiment, who invited him to raise a Territorial Army parachute brigade. Consequently in 1947, 4th Parachute Brigade TA (later redesignated 44th Parachute Brigade TA) was formed as part of 16th Airborne Division TA. Hill commanded the Brigade for the following two years before retiring from military duty in 1949 for the final time; in the meantime, he had also been appointed Honorary Colonel of the 5th Battalion The Royal Hampshire Regiment TA, which during the war had formed 14th Parachute Battalion.

Field Marshal Montgomery also invited Hill to place the Parachute Regimental Association (PRA) – formed on 15 February 1945 for all those who had served in Airborne Forces – on a firm footing. Hill accepted this task and served as Chairman for the three years from 1945 to 1948, establishing a network of branches covering the entire country and appointing the first PRA Secretary, Major George Seale, in May 1946. He also served for thirty years (1946–1976) as a trustee of the Airborne Forces Security Fund, established in 1942 to provide welfare support for serving and former members of Airborne Forces and their dependants who fall on hard times, serving as Chairman during the period 1971 to 1976.

On leaving the Army, Hill rejoined his family's company, the coal distributor J.R. Wood, which was subsequently taken over by the Powell Duffryn Group, and began a long and distinguished career in business. During the three years 1948–1951 he was a director of Associated Coal & Wharf, and for some six years thereafter was based in Canada where he was President of Powell Duffryn Group, Canada from 1952 to 1958, subsequently being appointed President of the Saccor Group of companies. In 1961, Powell Duffryn disposed of its Canadian interests and Hill returned to Britain where he was appointed Chairman and Managing Director of Cory Brothers, one of Powell Duffryn's main subsidiaries. His responsibilities were extensive as Cory Brothers was an industrial holding company with offices at home and abroad, whose interests included: shipping services that included chartering, as well as the sale and purchase of small vessels; oil and chemical storage with installations at Purfleet, Barry and Ipswich, as well as overseas in Australia and South Africa; and a large group of companies in France involved in coal and oil, as well as patent fuel manufacture in Paris, Rouen, Bordeaux, Nantes and Le Havre.

During this period he was also appointed a director of Sandars & Company Ltd, another family firm, remaining on the board for fifteen years from 1958 to 1973. In 1970, he was appointed Vice-Chairman of Powell Duffryn, while also holding the post of Chairman of three of its subsidiaries: Hamworthy Engineering, Andrews Weatherfoil and Powell Duffryn Oil & Chemical Storage. In 1973, he was appointed Chairman of Pauls & Whites of Ipswich, a post he held until 1976 when he retired at the age of 65. Four years earlier he had been appointed a director of Lloyds

Bank, and during the period 1979–1981 was a member of the Lloyds Bank (UK) Management Committee Ltd.

Throughout his civilian career, James Hill always maintained strong links with The Parachute Regiment and Airborne Forces, serving for a period of thirty years (1946–76) as an influential member of the Regimental Council of The Parachute Regiment. In 1974 he was appointed Chairman of the Airborne Assault Normandy Trust, which was formed in 1978 to provide a memorial in France to preserve the history of 6th Airborne Division's operations in Normandy, thereafter holding the posts of President and Vice-Patron.

On his retirement in 1976, Hill and Denys settled in the village of Long Sutton, near Crondall in Hampshire. In 1983, however, they separated and three years later, in 1986, were divorced after forty-nine years of marriage. In 1986 he married Joan Patricia Haywood whom he had met by chance three years earlier when Hill, a devout Christian, was attending an Easter festival run by the Omega order. A divorcee with two children, she was working in a homeopathic medical practice as a relaxation therapist specializing in the use of classical music, yoga and tai chi techniques.

Hill and his wife settled in Chichester from where he continued to maintain contact with The Parachute Regimental Association and the 1st Canadian Parachute Battalion Association, regularly travelling to Canada to take part in reunions with the veterans, to whom he always referred as 'my Canadians'. June of each year also saw him attending the pilgrimages to the battlefields of Normandy, taking part in the annual commemorations of 6th Airborne Division's part in the campaign and of those of its members who fell there. He was present on 4 June 2000 when the Pegasus Memorial Museum, located beside Pegasus Bridge at Benouville, was inaugurated by His Royal Highness The Prince of Wales, Colonel-in-Chief of The Parachute Regiment. That same year saw him honoured once more by France, which made him an Officer of the Légion d'Honneur.

Such was the esteem in which Hill was held that in 2002 a full-size bronze statue was commissioned by the Airborne Assault Normandy Trust, the cost being met by a long-standing major benefactor of The Parachute Regiment and Airborne Forces, Alan Curtis. Sculpted by Vivien Mallock, it depicted him in battledress and beret, holding the hallmark thumbstick that he carried at all times. On 5 June 2004, at a ceremony attended by thousands of veterans together with himself and Joan, the statue was unveiled by the Prince of Wales at the Le Mesnil crossroads, the centre of 3rd Parachute Brigade's defensive position sixty years before and close to where Hill's headquarters had been located. Many tributes to him were paid that day, including one by the Colonel Commandant of The Parachute Regiment at the time, General Sir Mike Jackson, who explained to those present the crucial importance of 3rd Parachute Brigade's task of seizing and holding the south-eastern flank of 6th Airborne Division's area:

> We are now on that piece of historic ground. This was the critical task. If this high ground was not held, then the entire left flank of the Allied invasion would have been jeopardized. In the face of considerable odds, 3rd Parachute Brigade's success was an outstanding achievement. At the heart of this feat lay the bravery, personal leadership and the military skill of Brigadier Hill. It is fitting, therefore, that members and patrons of both the Airborne community and the local community here have combined together to pay a tribute to this remarkable man, one of the most decorated soldiers of the war and whose leadership, courage and humanity remain an inspiration to the serving soldiers of Airborne Forces and, indeed, to the British Army today.

Turning to Hill who was seated nearby, General Jackson completed his tribute by saying, 'James, you are a legend, sir.'

The following year, due to the threat of damage by local vandals, the statue was moved from the Le Mesnil crossroads to a new location at the Pegasus Memorial Museum, where it now stands.

On 16 March 2006, at the age of 95, Brigadier James Hill DSO** MC died peacefully in a nursing home at East Wittering. So passed a great and much-revered warrior of the British Army's airborne forces. There were many tributes from those who had served alongside him and under his command. The most fitting, however, was that given by Lieutenant General Sir Michael Gray, a former Colonel Commandant of The Parachute Regiment and a friend of long standing, who gave the address at the memorial service held in Chichester Cathedral on 5 April 2006 and attended by a congregation of 500 including veterans of 3rd Parachute Brigade, as well as serving and retired senior officers of The Parachute Regiment:

> Although only 33 years old in 1944, he was the oldest man in his brigade; he was known to them all and he dearly loved his soldiers. He trained them exceptionally hard and his battle discipline was fierce because he wanted them to survive. He was an exceptional leader and all who served with him trusted his judgement, especially

in battle. He was in my view the founding father of The Parachute Regiment; for sixty-five years his personal standards, methods of training and style of leadership influenced the creation of an ethos that has held the reputation of British, and dare I say Canadian, airborne forces at centre stage right up to the present time. I would not deny that many multi-starred warriors and others have played a significant part in that ethos, but none so closely or for so long. He has a red beret wrapped round his heart.

Select Bibliography

PUBLICATIONS

By Air to Battle, The Official Account of the British 1st and 6th Airborne Divisions (HMSO, 1945)

Chatterton, Brig George, *The Wings of Pegasus* (Macdonald & Co., 1962)

Crookenden, Napier, *Drop Zone Normandy* (Purnell Book Services, 1976)

——, *Airborne at War* (Ian Allan, 1978)

——, *9th Bn The Parachute Regt: Normandy 1944, The First Six Days* (privately published)

Darling, Lt Col K.T., *The 12th Yorkshire Parachute Battalion in Germany: 24 March–16 May 1945* (privately published)

Gale, Richard, *With the 6th Airborne Division in Normandy* (Sampson Low, 1948)

Harclerode, Peter, *"Go To It!" The Illustrated History of the 6th Airborne Division* (Bloomsbury, 1990)

——, *PARA! Fifty Years of The Parachute Regiment* (Arms & Armour Press, 1992)

——, *Wings of War: Airborne Warfare 1918–1945* (Weidenfeld & Nicholson, 2005)

Jefferson, Alan, *Assault on the Guns of Merville* (John Murray, 1987)

McKee, Alexander, *The Race for the Rhine* (Macmillan, 1974)

Montgomery, Field Marshal The Viscount, *The Memoirs of Field Marshal Montgomery* (Collins, 1958)

Otway, Lt Col T.B.H., *Official Account of Airborne Forces 1939–1945* (Imperial War Museum, 1990)

Quis Separabit, the Journal of The Royal Ulster Rifles, vol. XI, No. 11, November 1944 & vol. XII, No. 1, May 1945

Saunders, Hilary St George, *The Red Beret* (Michael Joseph, 1950)

Slim, Major John, *With the 12th Bn The Parachute Regiment in Normandy* (privately published)

Tugwell, Maurice, *Airborne to Battle* (William Kimber, 1971)

Willes, John A., *Out of the Clouds: The History of The 1st Canadian Parachute Battalion* (privately published)
Wilmot, Chester, *The Struggle for Europe* (Collins, 1952)

SOURCES

6th Airborne Division – Report on Operations in Normandy 6th June–27th August 1944
6th Airborne Armoured Reconnaissance Regiment War Diary
8th Parachute Battalion War Diary June 1944–February 1945
9th Parachute Battalion War Diary January–February 1945
12th Battalion The Devonshire Regiment War Diary
BAOR Battlefield Tour, Operation VARSITY, Directing Staff Edition
Engineer Operations of 6th Airborne Division
History of the 8th Parachute Battalion in Normandy
History of 591 (Antrim) Airborne Squadron RE
Oxfordshire & Buckinghamshire Light Infantry War Chronicle, vol. 4, 1944–1945
'Red Devils – A Parachute Field Ambulance in Normandy: An Account by Members of 224 Parachute Field Ambulance RAMC'

Index

209

213